Pete Carril coached basketball at Princeton for 29 seasons (1967-1996). Upon his retirement from college coaching, he was inducted into the National Collegiate Hall of Fame and the Naismith Memorial Hall of Fame. Nicknamed "The Little Professor" by some of his Princeton players, Pete Carril emphasized a strong work ethic, the importance of team-versus-self orientation and personal humility. His mantra was to compete hard every day, play to win, but always win with integrity. His Princeton teams became known for their intelligent play and routinely achieved levels of success far beyond their individual athletic skills.

Pete Carril was also a character. He was intense and demanding, but also funny and entertaining. As former Princeton star and NBA Co-Rookie of the Year Geoff Petrie stated, "Pete Carril was a unique force of nature. He could create his own weather on a basketball court." He was known for being brutally honest with his players. His style was tough love for all. Despite this, more than 30 former Princeton players came together in 2022 to write short chapters about their memories of times with a man who coached them 26-55 years ago.

COACH is the collection of these stories. While every chapter is unique, the commentaries illustrate that Pete Carril was a *teacher* committed to making his players better and making his teams better, but also a *teacher* committed to preparing his players for life after Princeton.

COACH is the untold story of a coaching legend and the lasting impact he had on his players.

Barnes Hauptfuhrer

COACH

THE PLAYERS' BOOK

Compiled and Edited by
Barnes Hauptfuhrer and Friends

Copyright © 2022 Barnes Hauptfuhrer

All rights reserved.

No part of this book may be reproduced or used in any manner without written permission of the copyright owner except for the use of quotations in a book review.

Cover and interior layout by Blue Pen

ISBN: 979-8-9864867-3-4 (hardcover)
ISBN: 979-8-9864867-4-1 (paperback)
ISBN: 979-8-9864867-5-8 (ebook)

For the Princeton Basketball Players Who Ran Coach Carril's Gauntlet
and
For Anyone Interested in Valuing and Encouraging Teamwork and Unity to Achieve Success in Team Sports, Business, Politics, or Academic Governance

CONTENTS

PREFACE .... *ix*
INTRODUCTION *1*

The Players' Chapters

CHAPTER 1: Chris Thomforde '69 5
CHAPTER 2: Geoff Petrie '70 11
CHAPTER 3: John Hummer '70 23
CHAPTER 4: Bill Sickler '71 31
CHAPTER 5: Brian Taylor '73 41
CHAPTER 6: Jimmy Sullivan '73 47
CHAPTER 7: Roger Gordon '73 55
CHAPTER 8: John Berger '74 57
CHAPTER 9: Andy Rimol '74 61
CHAPTER 10: Tim van Blommesteyn '75 65
CHAPTER 11: Armond Hill '76 73
CHAPTER 12: Mickey Steuerer '76 77
CHAPTER 13: Barnes Hauptfuhrer '76 83
CHAPTER 14: Frank Sowinski '78 91
CHAPTER 15: Bill Omeltchenko '78 97
CHAPTER 16: John Rogers '80 119
CHAPTER 17: Steve Mills '81 123
CHAPTER 18: Marty Mannion '81 127

CHAPTER 19: Craig Robinson '83 133
CHAPTER 20: Kevin Mullin '84 137
CHAPTER 21: Howard Levy '85 143
CHAPTER 22: Jeff Pagano '85 151
CHAPTER 23: Joe Scott '87 155
CHAPTER 24: Kit Mueller '91 159
CHAPTER 25: Matt Henshon '91 167
CHAPTER 26: Sean Jackson '92 171
CHAPTER 27: Sydney Johnson '97 177
CHAPTER 28: Steve Goodrich '98 181
CHAPTER 29: Mitch Henderson '98 189
CHAPTER 30: Brian Earl '99 197
CHAPTER 31: Gabe Lewullis '99 201

Other Perspectives of Coach Pete Carril and Princeton Basketball

CHAPTER 32: Marvin Bressler 207
CHAPTER 33: Gary Walters '67 213
CHAPTER 34: Jason Garrett '89 217
CHAPTER 35: Selected Managers
              (Calvin Roberts '74 and Chris Palermo '84) 227
CHAPTER 36: Selected Sportswriters' and Authors' Tributes
              to Coach Upon His Passing 239
CHAPTER 37: *Sports Illustrated* 283

Appendix 1: Coach Carril's Record at Princeton 297
Appendix 2: Selected Highlight Wins, Heartbreaking Losses 299

Acknowledgments 349
About the Editor 361

PREFACE[1]

Sometime in the fall of 2021 I got a call from my friend and former Princeton basketball teammate, Peter Molloy, giving me an update on the health of former Princeton basketball coach, Pete Carril. The report was bleak and Peter (aka Mugs) was concerned that Coach was in rapid decline. Scroll forward to July 2022 and Coach is 92, and his health appears to have stabilized. Having said this, all of us understand that no one ever beats Father Time. We can delay him through care and medicine, but no one beats him. He is the unbeatable foe. All of us who knew Coach understood that his time was coming.

After the call, I retreated to my garage office. I am not ashamed to say that I teared up. At the same time, I was swept away by a powerful feeling—a feeling that I had not sufficiently said thank you to a man who had done so much for me. This led me in two directions. First, it led me to write a book called *Teamball*, published in August 2022. It profiles several great leaders of teams that achieved extraordinary success. Coach Carril is one of those leaders because he instilled a great passion in me (and many others) regarding the value of teamwork. Lesson No.1 in Coach's philosophy was always to place *team* before *self*. This simple notion

---

[1] Written by Barnes Hauptfuhrer in July 2022, approximately one month before Coach Pete Carril died.

is what made my Princeton basketball team successful, and it is what made most of Coach Carril's 29 Princeton basketball teams successful as well.

Second, Mugs' call indirectly caused me to conduct an experiment, which led to this book—a book in which my role was not to be the author, but to be the initial idea guy, book organizer, and all-around pain-in-the-ass emailer to multiple players.

My experiment began with a conversation with longtime friend and former teammate, Frank Sowinski, who currently serves as the chair of the Princeton Varsity Club and someone who launched in 2008, and still guides, a wonderful mentoring program for both men's and women's basketball players at Princeton. That program uses a very appropriate tagline—Teammates are Forever.

I also talked with current Princeton basketball head coach Mitch Henderson. This led to a three-way Zoom call among Mitch, Frank, and me. The conclusions of that call were two-fold:

1. We agreed that even though there were already two books published about Coach, there was an untold story about him that ought to be told.
2. We further agreed that this untold story might best emerge from short chapters of authentic memories of times with Coach primarily written by his former players.

I became the lucky person who took on the task of contacting players to see if they would write about a guy who often yelled at them unmercifully some 26 to 55 years ago. To my great joy, the experiment worked. Many members of the Princeton basketball family loved the idea. Shortly thereafter, multiple former Princeton basketball players began to write short chapters. Admittedly, my contact list was a bit random, but my goal was clear—secure approximately 30 chapters reflecting a cross-section of players who interacted with Coach during his 29 years at Princeton.

My instructions to all were the same:

1. Whether you write is totally up to you. Only write a chapter if you feel like it.
2. But if you write, you *must be authentic*. I told each person, "You can write whatever you want. Your words can reflect good, bad, or ugly memories. Just *be honest*."
3. I emphasized that my goal was not to pay some tribute to Coach in his old age and that I would not cherry-pick players or content to achieve such a goal. I guess, like Coach, I demanded *the real deal*.
4. I instructed everyone to speak from his heart and from his head.
5. And I concluded by saying, "You must keep your writing short—no more than five pages or 2,000 words" (Note: One logical exception was granted to Geoff Petrie given his two lives with Coach—one as a player at Princeton and one as president of basketball operations for the Sacramento Kings, where he hired Coach to serve as an assistant after his Princeton coaching days were over.)

The bottom line is the Princeton basketball family responded robustly and we have a book of more than 30 chapters. Most of the chapters were written by former players but, importantly, other perspectives on Coach are included, such as that of longtime Princeton sociology professor Marvin Bressler, former Princeton athletic director Gary Walters, two managers, two legendary sportswriters/authors and two local sportswriters. Last, but certainly not least, I got an unexpected and unsolicited chapter from former Dallas Cowboys head coach Jason Garrett. I did not know about his relationship with Coach when I embarked on this experiment.

Connecting with older and younger players was rewarding for me. Reading their individual chapters was great fun too. Each chapter is unique. Having said this, some front-of-the-book takeaways must be mentioned:

1. All the players and managers "get it." Coach Carril was tough on his players. He made many players better through his methods, but he broke some players along his journey. Coach sought perfection, and in doing so, he stirred emotions. Hell, from time to time, all of us felt unfairly picked on by Coach as we individually sought to navigate his gauntlet. Some of us quickly got over those negative feelings and others did not.
2. All of the players understood that Coach was into brutal honesty. He demanded that individual players understand their strengths and weaknesses. He also made sure that we all knew the strengths and weaknesses of our teammates.
3. Coach was driven to:
   A. Improve his players' skills;
   B. Maximize teamwork;
   C. Maximize his teams' chances of winning games; and
   D. Always win with integrity.
4. Coach's philosophy developed the young men who played for him. He demanded hard work, honesty, humility, and other core values. He prepared us for the inevitable ups and downs of life after Princeton. Above all things, he was *our teacher* and a damn good one. You will see this theme repeated in the chapters that follow.

Coach never sought to win a popularity contest. Coach did not care how one might rank him on some political correctness scale. Coach was the son of a father who worked in a steel mill. He was the son of a mother who walked away from her family when Coach was just six years old. He understood tough times and he was committed to developing his players' backbones so that they could persevere through any tough times ahead.

It can be fairly stated that Coach knew a lot about the game of basketball. Great at X's and O's. Great at offensive schemes: he was the coach best known for the "backdoor play." Great defensively: his teams regularly ranked among the nation's leaders in fewest points allowed. Certainly, these things drove his induction into the National Collegiate Hall of Fame and the Naismith Memorial Hall of Fame.

But X's and O's did not prompt more than 30 players and managers to write emotional chapters about Coach more than 25 years after he retired from Princeton. I believe these chapters emanated from some combination of respect, a need to say thank you and perhaps even love.

Why did I take on the work associated with developing this book? Absolutely, I wanted to honor my *teacher*. At the same time, however, I felt that a "players' book" about Coach Carril might offer valuable lessons to the broader Princeton community of students, alumni, teachers, coaches, administrators, the Board of Trustees and to others beyond the Princeton community who might choose to read it. Fundamentally, I believe the value of Coach's lessons is not limited to the hardwood.

As a case in point, Professor Marvin Bressler, the aforementioned and renowned former Chair of the Sociology Department at Princeton, was fascinated by Pete Carril. Why was this towering intellect so smitten with Coach? Was it a love of basketball? I do not think so. Instead, I think Marvin's relationship with Coach had a lot to do with his interest in human behavior. I think Marvin was intrigued by questions such as:

1. How did Coach instill teamwork into a group of young men with diverse backgrounds?
2. Why did Coach's teams consistently perform above expectations and the skill levels of the players?

3. How did this little, cigar-smoking, beer-drinking, pizza-loving Spanish-American command the respect of his players when he regularly yelled at them and cussed them out?
4. What was Coach Carril's motivational secret sauce?

I believe Marvin's time with Coach was similar to a scientist's time in a laboratory. He understood that Coach was different. He also understood that Coach was special and he wanted to absorb any and every bit of learning he could garner from him.

The chapters that follow provide individual perspectives on Pete Carril. Collectively, I think they also fairly paint a picture of the man we all called Coach. Like any human being, Coach had strengths and weaknesses. He can be praised for many things and he can be criticized for others—after all, he was tough, in-your-face, annoying and abrasive at times. But when you take a step back to study the whole of this portrait, I think you will find an individual who cared deeply about the development of his players. From my perspective, I keep coming back to three conclusions.

1. Coach could easily be characterized as a mean-spirited drill sergeant. But, if you could cut through the yelling, cursing, and personal insults, you found a teacher who consistently preached the following values day after day:

Honesty	Resilience	Humility
Accountability	Adaptability	Servanthood
Loyalty	Courage	Thankfulness

2. Coach's teaching philosophy resulted in unique levels of team chemistry, unity, and performance.
3. Coach's lessons were of significant value to many players throughout their adult lives.

What a legacy to leave behind. Thank you, Coach.

INTRODUCTION

Most of the chapters in this book were written during the final eight months of Coach Carril's life. He got to read some of the chapters, but not all. Sadly, Father Time reared his head on August 15, 2022 and Coach Carril died. He had a heckuva run.

His obituary noted:

> Pete Carril grew up on the South Side of Bethlehem, Pa., where his father worked in the steel mills. The Bethlehem Boys Club helped the young Carril stay on track as he became a promising basketball player at Liberty High School, from which he graduated in 1948. He attended nearby Lafayette College and graduated in 1952 with a B.A. in Spanish. It was at Lafayette where he began his lifelong basketball friendship with the late Butch van Breda Kolff, who was the Lafayette coach at the time.
>
> Carril went on to coach at Easton Area High School for three years while earning his M.A. degree in Educational Administration from Lehigh University. From 1958 to 1966 he coached at Reading High School, where he regularly enjoyed winning seasons and trips to the state finals. He then moved up to college coaching and

went back to Lehigh for one season (1966-67), where he immediately turned around the program. In 1967 van Breda Kolff, as he was leaving Princeton to coach the Los Angeles Lakers, recommended his protégé Carril for the role of head coach. Carril accepted the job and began building a basketball program that would amass numerous accomplishments and earn him many honors. He spent 29 years at Princeton, racking up 514 wins. His teams won 13 Ivy League titles, one NIT championship (1975) and made 11 NCAA tournament appearances. Carril made a name for himself by perfecting the Princeton offense and relying on his famous "backdoor play." After Princeton, Carril was an assistant coach with the Sacramento Kings, from 1996 to 2006. He was inducted into the Naismith Memorial Hall of Fame in 1997.

In the words of Jerry Price, senior communications advisor/historian for Princeton athletics, Carril was "a very simple man, and the more the world around him grew complex, the simpler he became. Make shots. Guard your guy. Be honest with people. And above all, work hard. No shortcuts."

Shortly after Coach died, Geoff Petrie contacted me and asked me to include the following personal farewell message in this book.

Farewell to Coach

In the time that has elapsed since I wrote my chapter about our beloved Coach, Pete Carril has moved on to his next dimension. He was 92 years young. Coach meant so much to so many and especially to my life. When I played for him some 55 years ago he was a true force of nature who could create his own weather on a basketball court. He was a coach, teacher, mentor, friend, consigliere and kindred spirit during our years together. In his second act, as an NBA assistant, he loved teaching and working with the players. I will miss him terribly, but he was a lifetime gift to me and to so many who crossed his path. Coach lived with a fire in his belly and love in his heart. It does not get any better than that.

I think Geoff's sentiments reflect the views of many of Coach's Princeton players but every player had his unique experience with Coach. Let the stories begin . . .

Barnes Hauptfuhrer

CHAPTER 1

Chris Thomforde (Princeton, Class of 1969)

Giving Thanks for Coach Carril

First, a story about a story. I once heard that a famous rabbi was asked by one his students why was it that G-d created human beings. Yes, human beings are capable of great and wonderful achievements and sympathies of all kinds, but they can also be dreadful creatures: fearful, mean, violent, dull, foolish. The rabbi responded by saying that G-d created human beings because G-d loves stories! And so, the sacred scriptures of Judaism and Christianity are full of stories, stories telling of the greatness of the human spirit, as well as awful stories relating the abject failures of human beings to be faithful or loving or hopeful.

Now to Coach Carril. Coach Carril was the generator of stories. He loved to tell stories about his own life or the lives of his former players. And he was the subject of all kinds of stories. I had heard stories about Coach Carril even before I first met him in the spring of 1967. I had heard stories about Coach Carril told by Boston Celtic legends Red Auerbach and John Havlicek when I met them one day for lunch in Taichung, Taiwan, where I was teaching at the time. I have heard stories about Coach Carril all over the United States. People walk up to me and the conversation goes something like this.

"You are really tall…You must have played basketball!"

"Yes," I say. "At Princeton."

Then comes a familiar rejoinder. "Wow, did you play for Pete Carril? Let me tell you about Pete!"

What follows is often true, at least as far as I know. But not always! One person, a total stranger, came up to my wife Kathy and me while we were traveling and told us that he was once cut from his school's basketball team by Coach Carril because every time this person got the ball he shot it! No surprise there for me that this person was cut from the team! But this man seemed quite proud, almost honored, to have had this encounter with Coach Carril.

This book is full of stories about Coach Carril. When his players gather, we love to tell stories about him. And he loved to tell stories about us. Here are two of mine that, I believe, say something about his approach to basketball and his approach to life in general.

I played on Coach Carril's first two teams at Princeton, the 1967-68 team and the 1968-69 team. Both teams were highly successful, and many highly accomplished teammates played on these teams, which gained national recognition. In addition, I believe these teams were something like a bridge from the wonderful successes of the Bill Bradley/Coach Butch van Breda Kolff (hereafter VBK) era to what would become the decades of success under the tutelage of Coach Carril. My teammates and I were accustomed to the intensity of VBK and the high standards of play and expectations for success on the court which Bradley had set as part of the Princeton men's basketball tradition. But we were not ready, I think, for the fierce intensity of Coach Carril's approach to the game. In practice and in games, every pass was scrutinized, every shot evaluated, every movement analyzed with an almost exhausting critique. In addition, behind our physical playing of the game, Coach Carril saw the unfolding of our character. As one of his players once said, practices and games were like morality plays, revealing the strengths and weaknesses of our moral character. Failure to play well, according to Coach Carril, might be a physical-mechanical problem or a lack of understanding of how we were to play well, but it could also be a moral problem that had been revealed by our way of playing. So, for example, poor shooting ability might have to do with how one placed his hand on the ball, but it could also be a sign that a player was morally deficient, dishonest, or disrespectful of one's parents.

With this in mind, picture our team in the locker room at halftime during a game against Harvard. I cannot remember all of the details, but it was probably in February of 1968. We had been playing poorly, as I remember it. Our play was sluggish and not as smart, crisp, and fluid as the game of basketball is meant to be played. When Coach Carril came into the locker room, he was clearly upset with us. He turned to me, his eyes full of fire, his hair disheveled, his arms waving, and said, "How can you believe in G-d and play like that!"

The problem with my play in that game was not just lack of intensity or ability. The problem with my play was not physical or mental. It was the moral gap between the faith in G-d that I professed and its manifestation in how I lived my life, and in this particular case, the way I played the game that night.

Another story. Coach Carril and I had stayed in close personal contact throughout my life, long after I graduated from Princeton in 1969. He remained an important person in my life, a friend, and a mentor. As life unfolded for me, I had the privilege of serving as president of Moravian University and Theological Seminary from 2006 until I retired in 2013. This was an especially rich time in my life because Moravian is situated in Bethlehem, Pa., which is the hometown of Coach Carril and a short distance from Princeton where Coach Carril was living at the time. It was hard to go almost anywhere in Bethlehem and not run into one of his friends, an elementary schoolmate, or a college classmate. Stories about the Coach and his pre-Princeton days abounded! A more complete picture of the life of Coach Carril began to emerge as I learned about his escapades on Valentine's Day, his championship feats as an athlete at Liberty High School, early romantic adventures, and the hard years growing up in the soot and the shadows of the Bethlehem Steel Works. Kathy and I would invite Coach Carril to Moravian from time to time for lunch with some of his friends.

On one such occasion, Kathy and I gathered in a small dining room on the Moravian campus with Coach Carril, Bill Werpehowski (one of Coach's best friends growing up in Bethlehem), and Marvin Bressler (one of Coach Carril's best friends and a retired distinguished professor of sociology from Princeton). All kinds of stories were told that day over lunch by and about the Coach. A wide range of issues were discussed from the current state of professional basketball to national politics, to the future of higher education, to the ups and downs of the lives of our families. At one point, Bressler asked Coach what he might do differently if he had to do it all over again.

Without much hesitation, Coach Carril responded, "I would be more compassionate!" At which point all of us in the room gasped. "Compassionate!" Not that the Coach's answer was intended to evoke laughter. Not at all. But *compassionate* was not the word any of us would have chosen to describe Coach Carril's approach to us, his players. In fact, professor Bressler looked over at me and quickly called to mind the names of players for whom Coach had shown very little compassion. Coach Carril let all of this reaction play out, and then he went on to tell us that he had been calling up some of his former players and apologizing to them for his harshness and asking their forgiveness and understanding. A forthright, strong, and courageous thing to do!

Thanks be to G-d for stories, especially those by and about Coach Carril. Such stories, I believe, shed light upon the many different facets of that greater story of how we humans seek to live well, to live with courage, with love, in spite of our daily experiences of disappointment and heartbreak. In the case of Pete Carril, I like to think of the stories about his life and the stories he tells about our lives as his players as being something like common grace.

What do I mean by this? I think grace has to do with the giftedness of living, what life offers up to us all to make each new day possible and full. Common grace has to do with those everyday events, those life experiences which are accessible to everyone, but which manifest what is good and precious about life. No order of priests, no sanctioned rituals, are required for us to experience or to understand the marvelous quality about life which common grace bestows. These are not experiences reserved for a select few, the chosen ones. They are life moments available to all, and the experience of them are like epiphanies into the depths of what it might mean to live fully, encouragements to make the effort to live well, with all the courage and joy one can muster. The hopeful rising of the sun each morning and the repose of the night sky full of stars, the reassuring embrace of a friend in the midst of heartbreak, falling in love, the laughter of little children, a good meal shared with others—these are all common moments, experiences of a common grace.

And let me add, playing basketball for Coach Carril and then having him for a friend throughout one's lifetime—this too is an experience of common grace. A common, everyday experience, available to many if not all, but gracious too. Life-giving, whereby what is everyday—like playing basketball—also becomes profoundly rich in meaning and importance. Learning about life from his stories showed us how to play well, celebrated hard work, admonished us to value our teammates, challenged us to live in such a way that our espoused values were transparent in our actions. These are Carril moments of common grace. All of those everyday moments we have shared together as his players and friends and which we tell stories about—enduring those exhausting practices in Jadwin, sharing one of those long bus rides through the winter's night after a good win, drinking a beer together at Uncle Joe's, cooking a good chorizo sausage from the South Side of Bethlehem in his kitchen at the Carril home on Murray Place—these are moments of common grace whereby life became real and full.

Thanks be to G-d for stories, for the grace of common things. For Coach Carril!

CHAPTER 2

Geoff Petrie '70

It was the spring of 1967 when word began to spread across the Princeton campus that Coach VBK was leaving the Tigers to coach the Los Angeles Lakers in the NBA. I had been recruited by VBK and was somewhat shocked by the news along with some of my other freshman teammates. Shortly thereafter, it was announced that he would be replaced by Pete Carril from Lehigh University. Little did I know at the time that this barrel-chested, cigar-smoking, beer-drinking, pizza-loving force of nature would begin for me a lifetime adventure in basketball and life for which I would forever feel fortunate and grateful.

Over the next 50-plus years, Pete would take on the role of coach, teacher, protagonist, friend, and advisor. My first encounter with Coach Carril was during the annual Cane Spree game against the incoming freshman class of basketball players whom we defeated in Dillon Gym. Coach, cigar in hand, was there and made some introductory comments. It was the first but certainly not the last time I heard his oral greeting: "Yo."

Our recruiting class was highly rated, with John Hummer, Mike Mardy, John Arbogast, and me, just to name a few. Along with the returning varsity players, Joe Heiser, Chris Thomforde, John Haarlow, and David Lawyer, expectations were high. We were all about to enter Pete Carril's basketball crucible. It was not to be a comfortable environment for everyone and that's O.K., but for those of us who persevered, it would provide lifetime experiences, associations, and a gutty understanding of competing. There would be jubilant victories and soul-crushing defeats.

"Am I tough enough, am I rough enough, am I rich enough, I'm not too blind to see..."
—The Rolling Stones

The 1967-68 Season

One thing that became immediately apparent about Coach Pete Carril's life philosophies was that there was life and there was basketball, but there was no life without basketball. The practices were long, grueling, and at times filled with blistering assessments of our individual play. I also began to learn the how, why, and when of going backdoor in Pete's offense. Going backdoor, of course, would become the seminal feature of what would become known as the Princeton offense. We would also be occasionally reminded that going backdoor in basketball was not a sexual experience. Practices and games would be their own morality plays that exposed your competitive character, or lack thereof. I soon learned that if you grew up in a three-car garage, your toughness was questionable. Drinking water during practice was a sign of weakness. Rebounding was inversely proportional to how far you lived from the railroad tracks. In 1967, Coach encapsulated what Pat Riley would express many years later as head coach of the Los Angeles Lakers for most of the 1980s—"There were two states in basketball, Winning and Misery."

I was in the early stages of trying to understand one of Coach's core beliefs: you can't separate the man from the game. Pete immediately saw that my future in the game was as a guard. Having been primarily a forward in high school, this meant my game had to change and my skill level had to expand. So many things to learn. The crossover dribble, inside hand change, left-handed, right-handed, do not turn your back on the defense. I had to have a long shot, a mid-range game, and various ways to finish at the basket. A hard cut in some situations was better than a pick. I was in love with the spin dribble, which at times caused too many offensive fouls and brought Pete's ire down full force. There was, however, one common trait Pete and I shared—an unadulterated love of basketball.

The season itself was a mixture of high expectations and conflict. We were co-favorites along with Columbia to win the Ivy League. Columbia had Jim McMillian, Dave Newmark, Heyward Dotson, and they were formidable players. Our early games had mixed results. A mediocre showing in the Far West Classic along with some uneven performances back in Dillon Gym, which had Pete standing on the sidelines as described by Bill Sickler, a freshman at the time, screaming "Where is all the firepower, where is it?"

In truth, our team never developed the chemistry it needed to reach its full potential. Many of the seniors, with the exception of Joe Heiser, chafed at Pete's demanding pursuit of perfection and, being a sophomore, I was still trying to figure it all out. In spite of all this, we stayed tied with Columbia until we lost a home game on February 24, 1968 to a mediocre Dartmouth team. This meant we had to defeat Columbia in our final home game of the season to tie them for the Ivy League title. On March 2, 1968 we were able to beat the Lions 68-57 to end the season in a tie for the Ivy title. Forced into a playoff game on March 5, 1968 at Fordham University, we were blown out by McMillian and Company. In horse racing, we would have been described as "never a factor." The season ended on a very raw note for everyone. Feelings were strained, and the future for me felt unsettled.

"Joy to the world!"

—Three Dog Night

The 1968-69 Season

The summer of 1968 quickly came and went. I spent most of it on the playgrounds of suburban Philadelphia working on many of the things Pete had emphasized to me regarding how to improve my skill level. One thing we both agreed on was that I was a gym rat with a tendency to like the street game a little too much at times. Back at Princeton in September, we began scrimmaging down in Jadwin. Being reunited with my other junior teammates was refreshing. John Hummer, an incredible talent, Arbo, Dominic, Jabo. Chris Thomforde and Tom Chestnut were returning seniors. Bill Sickler would prove to be an invaluable addition to our team as a sophomore guard/forward.

Armed with a better understanding of the demands and expectations that would be placed on us by Pete and Artie Hyland, we all approached the new season with a refreshed spirit. I was feeling much more comfortable in the backcourt. Playing with two passing bigs like Chris and Johnny was a blessing too. Princeton in those days always played a big-time schedule outside of the Ivy League. UCLA, North Carolina, Michigan, Indiana, Duke, Davidson, Maryland, and Villanova were on the list at some point during my time at Princeton.

There were some wins and tough losses. Pete's passion was always on display and it proved to be terrific preparation for the Ivy League season. The confrontation with Columbia was again the major obstacle to overcome in the race to the title. My relationship with Coach Carril had grown, but at times my game got a little too wild for his taste. During a game at the Holiday Festival in New York, I came down on a fast break against North Carolina and launched a running hook shot from the foul line, a miss. Chris Thomforde was open on the wing for a possible layup. Well, most of Pete's diatribe during halftime centered on me being the wildest man from the wildest country on the planet for not passing Chris the ball. He was right, of course, and we have had a few laughs about that exchange over the years. It was not so funny at the time, however.

Fast forward to the Ivy League and, as expected, Princeton and Columbia were the class of the Ivy. Both of us were undefeated with a showdown game coming at Jadwin. The specter of McMillian and Dotson loomed large heading into the contest. Pete had a tendency to cast them as some type of superheroes—fast, athletic, and skillful. In front of a full house at Jadwin, we routed the mighty Lions by 20 points. A demon exorcised, or so it felt for the time being. This was a watershed game for the team and me.

The elusive chemistry that teams must have to be better than the sum of their parts had arrived. We were cruising through the Ivy League. Our offense was fluid and our defense could be stifling at times. I began sitting with Pete during some of the long bus rides after away games. We talked about the games, life, and the future. I wanted to be a professional player and I was beginning to believe that Pete might think it was possible too.

The season rolled along and we remained undefeated in the Ivy League. The final test would be our second game against Columbia in New York. A win, and we would go on to become the first team in Ivy history to go undefeated in league play and secure the title. Prior to the crucial Columbia game, Tom Chestnut, one of our starting forwards, flunked out of school and was ineligible. Tom could be a difference-maker at times, so his loss further complicated the upcoming challenge. The sound of *Jimmy Mack* was blaring and rocking in the Columbia gym. We played a disciplined and tenacious game leading most of the way, but it still took four clutch free throws by Bill Sickler to ice the win in the last few seconds. Even though it had been said that Pete could find a dark cloud in every silver lining, I never saw him that happy during my three seasons at Princeton.

We went on to lose to St. John's in the first round of the NCAA tournament. Unfortunately, we just did not play well, losing 72-63. Shortly thereafter, there was one of the all-time post-season team parties at the boathouse on Lake Carnegie. The beer and the Old Grandad were flowing and the music was groovin', the Stones, Temps, Beatles, CSNY, and so on, guys and gals dancing. The Yo Man, ubiquitous cigar in hand was the master of ceremonies. It was the best of times.

"Sometimes the hard times won't leave me alone…"
—John Denver

The 1969-70 Season

The summer of 1969 began with my getting a construction job with a local Princeton company. Coach had helped me get approved by the union. Ironically, the project was digging out the foundation for the addition to Firestone Library. I was put in charge of a jack hammer to get some of the rock out. So, for six weeks I hammered away and made my greatest contribution to Firestone during my four years at Princeton. Pete and I grew closer. We would get together on weekends, maybe go to the gym; or go tubing on the Delaware River.

Bill Bradley had returned from Oxford and started playing for the Knicks. He was doing his six-week Army reserve commitment at nearby Fort Dix. Pete and I started going over to work out with Bill once a week or so in the evenings. Pete would run the workouts. Shooting drills, dribbling drills, conditioning drills, and full court one-on-one games. Needless to say, Bill and I were exhausted but grateful for the time and opportunity. It was during these workouts that I started to feel that if I could hold my own against Bill, my dream of playing in the NBA might be within reach.

The rest of the summer came and went. September rolled around and my teammates and I were excited about the prospect of building on the success of our championship season. John H, Bill Sickler, Arbo, and Dominic were all returning. We had a sophomore point guard named Reggie Bird who would turn out to be one of the most tenacious defenders I have ever played with on any level. Al Dufty was a promising sophomore forward as well. We had lost Chris Thomforde's ability and spirit to graduation, so Hums was going to have to play center. I felt my transformation to the guard position was nearly complete.

Coach was already worried about the ongoing challenge from Columbia along with the rise of Penn. Little did we know at the time, but the 1969-70 Tiger season would never be allowed to happen as we all envisioned it. Pre-season practice began uneventfully. The three-hour practices, endless "and 2's" as Coach would call them. Pete's "one more time" when working on a particular play could last an hour. One day in early November, after practice and then dinner at Cottage Club, I was playing pool and reached over to take a ball out of one of the pockets. Suddenly, I had an excruciating pain in my lower back. I could not straighten up. I was barely able to make it back to my dorm room. Treatment in the training room over the next few days was ineffective. Eventually, I ended up in a Philadelphia hospital in traction for the better part of two weeks.

I was angry and feeling cheated. Pete was feeling angry and deserted by the basketball gods. The season was about to start with no chance for me to be able to play. Worst of all, there was an upcoming game against Penn in Philadelphia. We lost to Penn 85-62. The traction had been only partially successful, so I started seeing an old school chiropractor out of desperation. I was finally able to start some running in early December, although I had to wear a corset-type brace. You could hardly breathe wearing that thing. Finally, I was cleared to play with the corset against Navy.

We won the Navy game at their place. A week later, we were off to Los Angeles to play in the Bruin Classic at Pauley Pavilion. We beat Indiana 82-76 in a wire-to-wire victory. What came next was one of the greatest basketball games ever played by a Princeton team that ended in a loss. We were to play UCLA in the championship game. UCLA was in the middle of winning their seven consecutive NCAA titles. They had not lost at Pauley in a thousand years. Wicks, Rowe, Patterson, Vallely, Bibby. Coach started off our practice the day before with these instructions.

Number 1: We were not going after any offensive rebounds because we were not going to get them anyway. Just get back on defense. This effectively stifled UCLA's running game, which was potent. The matchups were Bird on Bibby, Sickler on Vallely, Johnny H on Wicks, Bob Ryder on Rowe, and I had Steve Patterson, the center. We were supposed to be cannon fodder for the Bruins, but on game day we led the mighty Bruins for most of it. Sidney Wicks made a baseline jumper over the outstretched arms of Johnny Hummer with less than three seconds to go to win the game. UCLA: 76 Princeton: 75. I was named MVP of the tournament amid chants from the crowd of "We want Sidney," but it was the most bittersweet moment of my Princeton career.

The rest of the season was disappointing. Another loss to Penn in early January at home pretty much eliminated us from the Ivy League race. Things had become somewhat combative with Pete again as he would lament that the team he had was not the team he wanted. I was a fan of the Knicks with Bradley playing for them. His teammate Earl Monroe, known as Black Jesus around Philly, was another favorite. Monroe and Walt Frazier, the Knicks' other guard, were known for their sartorial splendor, in addition to being terrific players. They would often wear fur coats. Not to be outdone, I went out and bought a faux fur coat. Coach came into the locker room at Jadwin where I was changing before a game. Cigar in hand, flicking a few ashes on the floor, he looked at me and said, "Where did you get that f##kin' thing?" Definitely not impressed.

The next several months of the season were frustrating. We ended up 16-9 overall with five losses in the Ivy League. I think we were all glad when it was over. The excitement and anticipation that prevailed coming into 1969-70 were never realized. Pete and I ended the year with feelings of mutual disappointment.

Spring came and so did the NBA draft. I was picked eighth by Portland, Jim McMillian 13th by the Lakers, and John Hummer 15th by Buffalo. Three Ivy League players taken in what is now called the lottery. The class of 1970 was Pete Carril's on ramp to a 29-year Princeton career. The wins would begin to pile up, and the legend would grow. For me, despite some of the ups and downs in our relationship, it was still transformative. Marvin Bressler, my junior and senior adviser in the sociology department, would become one of Coach's closest friends over those next 26 years. When Marvin passed away, Pete tossed a basketball into his burial plot. He called him "the best assistant coach I ever had." My ongoing opportunity in basketball was in large part due to The Yo Man's life force.

"You've got a friend in me."

—Randy Newman

The NBA Years: Sacramento Kings

I kept in touch with Pete over his remaining 26 years at Princeton. The frayed edges of my senior year quickly abated. My playing career in the NBA ended in 1978 due to recurrent knee injuries. Even though we were separated by time and distance, I would try and make it to any Princeton games on the West Coast. Whenever we did get together, it was always like yesterday. The Blazers initially hired me to do color for radio broadcasts of games, but by 1990, Paul Allen had put me in charge of the basketball operations. Pete came out for some summer league games and a couple of days of fall camp at one point. It was during this time that I told Pete that if he ever had any interest in the NBA and I was still running a team, I wanted first dibs.

Fast forward to 1996, when Pete won his penultimate game as coach at Princeton against UCLA, the defending national champion in the NCAA tournament, 43-41 on a backdoor cut. I was now in charge of the Sacramento Kings, a languishing franchise which I had joined for the 1994-95 season. The Kings had not won 30 or more games for eight consecutive seasons prior to 1994-95. In 1994-95, the team won 39 games and missed the playoffs by one game. In 1995-96, the team won 39 games again and made the playoffs for the first time in 10 years. I invited Pete out to our playoff games against Seattle. He met Gary St. Jean, our head coach at the time, and was excited about the NBA playoffs. Pete agreed to join our coaching staff, and by mid-summer he was hired as an assistant coach.

Technically, I was Pete's boss. In reality, we were kindred spirits. He would live with my wife, Anne Marie, and me periodically when he was between apartments. He affectionately nicknamed her "Crusher" for her vivacious, full-frontal personality. There was no smoking allowed so he planted the remaining part of his cigars in various planters outside on the patio for retrieval the next morning. Once after returning to the house after a game and late dinner, Anne Marie saw Pete taking a leak on the side of the house.

She said, "Coach, what are you doing?"

"Every good coach pisses in the parking lot," Pete said.

It became clear to me that the flowing waters of time had smoothed over some of his rougher edges. He took to the elder statesman role in stride while suppressing his head coaching instincts as much as possible. He soon became known as Coachie to players, staff, and media alike. He went back to his teaching roots as an assistant. Working with individual players on their games rejuvenated him. Occasionally, however, Pete would report that you cannot carve rotten wood.

In the summer of 1998, we replaced Gary St. Jean with Rick Adelman, a future Hall of Fame coach, with whom I had worked in Portland during an incredible run of three consecutive conference finals appearances and two NBA finals trips. Rick always had a great feel for free-flowing offense. Pete's offensive philosophy would prove to be a good fit with a newly rebuilt Kings roster. The team had two star passing bigs in Vlade Divac and Chris Webber, creative point guard play in Jason Williams, and a great young shooter in Peja Stojakovic. Rick began to integrate aspects of the Princeton offense into his overall offensive system. Low-post play, corner, some high-post splits were included. The Kings' style of play became one of the most exciting and entertaining in the NBA. *Sports Illustrated* ran a cover story calling the Kings "The Greatest Show On the Court: Basketball The Way It Oughta Be." Sacramento arrived on the world's basketball map.

A run of eight consecutive Kings playoff appearances would begin, culminating in the 2001-02 season with a league best 61-21 record. Webber, Vlade, Bibby, Peja, Hedo Turkoglu, Bobby J, Doug Christie, and Scott Pollard were denied a possible NBA championship after suffering a Game Seven overtime loss at home to the Lakers. It was a crushing defeat for an incredible team. Rick, Pete, John Wetzel, Elston Turner, and T.R. Dunn had coached their hearts out too.

Pete and I had many "Dinner with Andre" moments over these years. There were the days of tennis in my backyard and vodka tonics afterward in the hot Sacramento weather. Pete frolicking in the swimming pool with our favorite golden retriever, Romeo. Paella-cooking contests. A two-week vacation trip to Spain where he would use his fluent Spanish to full effect.

In 2000, Pete was found collapsed on the third floor of our offices in Arco arena. It occurred after a Saturday practice, so there was no one on the office floor. Our trainer, Pete Youngman, happened to go up there to get something and found Pete, who was suffering from the beginnings of a serious heart attack. I was driving to practice when I got the call. Coach was in the emergency room at Sutter hospital. I quickly arrived at the hospital and was greeted by one of our team doctors. I almost fell to the floor when he told me he was not sure Pete would make it. Fortunately, the Basketball Gods were smiling. He was stabilized and taken to Mercy Hospital, where a brilliant heart surgeon, Dr. James Longoria, performed a quadruple bypass operation the next day. Pete's bypass served him well for the next 22 years.

2011 came and Pete said goodbye to me and the Kings to return to Princeton. His legacy was complete. Basketball Hall of Fame, Joe Lapchick Award, Carril Court at Princeton, all the Ivy championships, and influencer on the best teams in Sacramento Kings history.

The Yo Man!, now in the winter of his years, and I certainly in the late fall of my own, had traveled the same trail but on slightly different paths. We both were able to experience the intoxicating feeling of competing at the highest levels the game had to offer. The highest mountain did elude us in the end. In the beginning, I was just a kid with dreams and some talent. A lot of them came true. The eventual success I had as a player and executive were due in large part to my lifelong association with Coach Carril. I consider it an overall blessing that I was coached by him, befriended by him, and advised by him. I am sure that a piece of him travels on with all the people and players who experienced his unique life force. The Yo Man!

CHAPTER 3

John Hummer '70

The Princeton basketball tradition, and what I call the Princeton basketball family, began under Coach VBK, with the great teams of 1965-67. The 1965 team, sometimes referred to as Bradley's team, went to the Final Four. Also, earlier that year, they put on an incredible show at the ECAC Holiday Festival in the "Old Garden." As a senior in high school, I remember listening to that tournament's Princeton-Michigan game on the radio, as my brother Ed was a sophomore on that team and later captained the 1967 team. Michigan's star player was Cazzie Russell and, in a twist of fate, Cazzie and Bill Bradley would become Knick teammates and go on to win an NBA title together.

Later that season, the 1965 team won the Ivy League, beat Penn State in the NCAA qualifying round, then defeated North Carolina State and Providence in the East Regional on their way to the Final Four in Portland. The country became aware that the Princeton team that won the Ivy League was now one of the best in the country.

The 1967 team was equally good, perhaps even better. It won the Ivy title and went on to the East Regional as well, beating West Virginia but then losing to North Carolina in overtime.

Princeton basketball had come of age, a fact not lost upon others, even those 3,000 miles away. The owner of the Los Angeles Lakers, Jack Kent Cooke, made an offer to Coach VBK to come coach for them. It was an offer VBK could not refuse.

For those of us who had either played for VBK or were recruited by him, we were left in a state of suspended animation until the next coach was hired. VBK was a great coach with a larger-than-life personality. He would be very hard to replace. We heard rumors of many famous applicants for the job, but as players, we were kept in the dark. We had no idea what to expect.

And so it was in the spring of my freshman year, in 1967, that Princeton hired a relatively unknown, young coach from Lehigh University, Peter J. Carril. And over the next 29 years, Pete would become the winningest coach in Ivy League history and a college basketball legend.

At the time, Princeton was an all-male school. Dillon Gym was our home court, right in the middle of campus. Unlike today, freshmen could not play varsity. Our freshman team was coached by a wonderful man, Eddie Donovan. VBK had recruited Chris Thomforde, Johnny Haarlow, and the wonderful Joe Heiser—we called him Nitro-Joe—with whom I had the great pleasure of playing. He also recruited the incomparable Geoff Petrie, so VBK left Coach Carril with quite a bit of talent. Artie Hyland, our assistant coach, also played a huge role in our success and occasionally provided a buffer during hard times between Pete and some of the players. I mention these coaches because they are an integral part of the Princeton basketball family. It continues today in the very capable hands of Mitch Henderson.

In Coach Carril's first year at Princeton, we shared the Ivy title with Columbia, whose star was my nemesis and archrival, the great Jim McMillian. He later starred for the Los Angeles Lakers. We lost to Columbia that year in an infamous play-off game at St. John's, but the following year—1969—we came back with a vengeance to go

14-0 in the Ivy League, the first Ivy team in history ever to go undefeated in the league. It was only Pete's third year as a college coach. One year at Lehigh and now two at Princeton—by any measure, an inexperienced, young college coach who was quickly successful. Our 1969 team did something remarkable, but it was uneasy for many of us, especially for those of us who had been recruited by and played for Coach VBK. For those who had played for VBK, the transition to Pete was very difficult.

It must have been 10 years ago when we had a large gathering of ex-players back at the university to honor Pete in some fashion, possibly the commemoration of the Carril Court. The one thing I remember as I walked among the tables was that each table was full of players of different teams and different eras, all laughing and telling stories—stories about Pete. I listened in on a few and came away with one conclusion: the stories were all different, but upon reflection, they were all the same. They were stories of a very demanding coach, a young coach in my case, who pushed us in many ways and at many times past what we believed was our capability. He pushed us physically, mentally, and emotionally, sometimes far in excess of what normal 19- or 20-year-olds could handle. Most of us came out of our three years with Pete for the better. Most, but not all.

Coach Carril had a real sense for the game. He understood matchups extremely well. I was amazed how he knew exactly who could guard whom and who could not. In December of 1969, we lost to UCLA 76-75 in Pauley Pavilion. Geoff was hurt, had a terrible back, and could not guard anyone. Pete's decision to have him guard the Bruins' center, Steve Patterson, was a stroke of genius. Patterson was not the most mobile player on the court, so Geoff could save his considerable skills for offense—which he did by the way, finishing with more than 25 points. But the stories are much more personal than X's and O's, and they run the gamut from the lighthearted to the heavy, to expressions of genuine caring, even love—even if that caring and love were hard to decipher at the time. I am reminded of the advice of the Danish philosopher Kierkegaard who said: "Life can only be understood backwards, but it must be lived forwards." I think this applies to my time at Princeton. I doubt I am alone.

Pete Carril was diminutive in stature, but his effect on the game was huge. He was quite precise in his language about the game, and his language to many of his players was precise, direct and oftentimes graphic. Sometimes his words carried the weight of sledgehammers. His compliments were few. Coach Carril pushed us sometimes far beyond what we were capable of, not physically, although we all remember the grueling "and 2's" at the end of practice.

Pete had a way of saying things that end up embedded in your memory. In some ways, he was a sportswriter's dream because he spoke directly with not a hint of artifice. Early in the 1968 season, we were about to play Rutgers. Their coach had made the comment, picked up by the *Trentonian*, that Princeton had "an All-Pro frontline." He was referring to Chris Thomforde, Geoff Petrie, and me. As we were warming up, Pete brought the newspaper to practice.

Laughing sarcastically, he said, "All-Pro frontline, huh? Ha! More like All-Prophylactic frontline."

To this day, Geoff and I still laugh about this every time we get together. A few years later, both of us were picked in the first round of the 1970 NBA draft, so the Rutgers coach was not that far off the mark.

If you were looking for compliments, Coach Carril was definitely not your source of solace. In Supreme Court Justice William O. Douglas' autobiography, *Go East, Young Man*, he recounted a hike he took in an arid, craggy area up in the mountains, where he came upon a bright red rose sticking out between two rocks. He mused how much it meant to him and how the scarcity of this rose added value to such land. A compliment from Pete was a rare rose among the rocks.

In December 1968, we played in the ECAC Holiday Festival. Yes, the same Holiday Festival that the 1965 team had made famous against Michigan four years earlier, when Bradley ran up 41 points in a game that has become part of the lore of Madison Square Garden. This time we were in the "New Garden," which had quickly become the mecca for all of college basketball. As we took the floor, our whole team felt a sense of history. Our opponent was UCLA, the current NCAA champion. Their center was Lew Alcindor, now known as Kareem Abdul-Jabbar. I would guard him and he would guard me. There is not much more a college player could ask for, playing in the Garden against the best team in the country and the best player in the country. It just does not get any better than that!

UCLA prevailed, 83-67. It was pretty close, but down the stretch they were a bit too much for us. I had a good game, scored 28 off Alcindor (full disclosure, he got 40 off me), but we brought our shoes with us. After the game, sitting on the locker room floor, I was emotionally and physically drained, tears streaming down my face. In those moments, you never quite know where the tears come from or why, but you are just overrun by the emotion. Pete walked over, kicked the bottom of my sneakers, and said, "Johnny, you were a joy to watch tonight." He then turned and walked out. That was it. And I think that was the only compliment he ever gave me in the three years I played for him. Maybe Justice Douglas was correct. Scarcity does add value, as here I am some 54 years later, remembering the exact place, the exact time, and Pete's exact words.

After my senior year, I was in Jadwin working out with a promising freshman who had enrolled at Princeton. As for all the players who had played for Pete, once your senior year was over, the relationship really changed, all for the good. Mine was no exception. But this poor guy was about to enter the gauntlet, already enduring some of Pete's barbs, as he metaphorically had come from a family with a three-car garage, one of Pete's favorite observations. I was working out with him, trying to show him a few moves. Pete was watching, cigar in hand, sending a few zingers his way, all alluding to his perceived lack of toughness, the whole three-car-garage thing.

I stopped, looked at Pete. "You know, one day this guy is going to just haul off and hit you right in the mouth," I said.

"I know, Johnny," Pete replied. "But it won't hurt."

It reminded me of a similar exchange after practice one day, guarding my very close friend, Gerry Couzens, who we lost way too early in life to a heart attack. Gerry had a jump shot that he held way, way over his head.

I told Coach, "I just can't quite get at it."

"Yeah," Coach said. "But do you want to, Johnny?"

Classic Pete Carril.

My senior year, at practice in Jadwin, a junior teammate came in about 10 minutes late. He quickly jumped in the lay-up lines, clearly a bit embarrassed, hoping all would pass. Not so.

Pete stopped practice, looked at everyone, and said, "You know what he just told you? He just told you he does not love his teammates."

Pretty brutal stuff for a 19- or 20-year-old to hear.

One last story, and it's a doozy and quite personal to me. In December of 1969, we were playing Maryland in Jadwin. They had a fairly good player named Will Hetzel against whom I had played in high school. But that is not the story. A friend of mine had fixed me up with a Maryland cheerleader for a date after the game. I am half-laughing because, as I mentioned earlier, Princeton was an all-male school at the time, and I bet I had about five dates my entire time at the university. Late in the game, we were winning but I was not exactly setting the world on fire. In a moment of sheer, bone-headed stupidity during a timeout, I winked at my blind date, who just happened to be cheering right behind our bench. What happened the next day, I will never forget.

Walking down the little path from Cottage Club to practice, I ran into my dear friend Hardy Menees, who had played on our freshman team and knew Coach Carril pretty well. He stopped me on the path behind Cottage.

"Hey, you better be ready to play today," he said.

I was a bit puzzled, did not quite get it, and continued down to Jadwin, albeit with some trepidation. We started practice. Pete was just silent, but I could just tell there was something bad about to come down the pike. Pete called us all over to the stands for a chat, which was something he often did the day following a game to review how we individually played. And then it happened.

Suddenly, he looked at the entire team, and said, "And my captain, my g-ddamn captain, is winking at some f##king cheerleader during a time out, when I'm trying to talk to him." He then looked right at me, his voice slightly cracking, and said, "Johnny, you can do whatever you want, but don't break my heart."

Pete was in his fourth year as a college coach, and I was 20 years old at the time. Mind you, I had lost my own father at the age of 15. I am reminded of the Kierkegaard quote. As much as this devastated me at the time—and it did—I am trying to understand this event looking backwards. Pete really did care for me, cared for me genuinely, and I know he cared for others. Not every player, but most. He really did, yet there were moments that were really tough, almost too tough.

About six or seven years ago, I went back to Princeton to catch a game at Jadwin. I got hold of Pete and we watched the game together, sitting courtside, which is always a real treat. Even in retirement, Pete was still quite the draw. So many people wanted to shake his hand and say hello. After the game, we went to Conte's for some beer and pizza. In truth, I journeyed to Princeton that evening not to see the game but really just to see Pete and tell him what he had meant to me and what he had done for me.

As we sat at Conte's over a few beers, he said, "You know, Johnny, when I had you and Geoff, I wasn't a very good coach. You know how I know that? Because later, I won a lot more games with less talent."

As I boarded the last train out of Princeton that night, I flipped back one of those large seatbacks as I had done countless times before. I kicked my legs up on the seat, leaned back, and looked out the window into the darkness as the train headed north to New York City. I think Pete Carril had just given me my second compliment ever. Kierkegaard was right. Life must be lived going forward. I am 74 now as I write this, and Pete is 91. We both have grey hair. As I have written this, I have tried to understand many things. Pete obviously had a huge impact on me and even perhaps changed the arc of my life all for the better. Yet, after all this, there still is a good chance I would wink at that cheerleader.

CHAPTER 4

Bill Sickler '71
The Man I Barely Saw — Ode to a Great Teacher,
Mentor, and Friend

There's Charisma, and Then There Is *Charisma*

The first time I met Coach I really did not see him. I was not highly recruited out of high school but had attended summer camps with the then-current Princeton coach, Butch VBK. With his foghorn voice, large personality, and track record of winning basketball, VBK had big, bold charisma. I wanted to play at Princeton for VBK and was beyond excited that he was in the lobby of our high school in the fall of 1966.

I barely saw the shorter, balding man next to VBK. VBK introduced him as the coach at Lehigh, and said that he was "showing him the recruiting ropes." Coach did not utter a word during the whole conversation I had with VBK. Coach could see that I was starstruck and had eyes only for Princeton. At the end, he looked at me, smiled, and just said, "If you don't get into Princeton, maybe you could come to Lehigh." That was our entire conversation.

There are different kinds of charisma. Some are big and bold, like VBK's; others, like Coach's, come from a unique, uncompromising character. He was honest with straightforward beliefs and did not believe in sugarcoating or spinning. He knew I wanted Princeton and did not bother with a recruiting pitch. Coach was authentic—truly one of a kind.

Here, Take This Paycheck To My Wife

Coach was uncompromisingly honest in his evaluation of his players. It was not fun for a player to hear that he had no vision, was not fast, was always palming the ball, etc., but Coach was always honest in his criticisms. By correcting failings and working around shortcomings, Coach believed that we would become better players and a better team. But during practice these criticisms could be very loud with profanity used for emphasis.

When my girlfriend (now wife), Gail, would come down for weekends, she asked me if she could sit in the Jadwin stands and study while we practiced. I naively said yes. The first time Coach saw Gail in the stands he approached her, gave her his paycheck, and told her to take it three blocks home to his wife, Dilly, whom Gail had never met. The next time he saw her in the stands during practice, Coach came up with some other excuse to send Gail home to Dilly. We got the hint. Coach wanted to be unrestrained with his players, and maybe yell at his players, without family and friends around to hear.

You're As Tough As He Is, Billy

While Coach was outspoken in criticizing his players in practice, he was loud and loyal in supporting them during games. We played Army at West Point my sophomore year. Army was coached by Bob Knight, known by his sobriquet, The General. Knight's teams were tough, well-disciplined, and relentless on defense. He beat many teams which had better talent than his did.

The game was close in the second half and I was guarding an Army senior known for his toughness. As he was dribbling the ball across half court, I heard Coach yelling, "You are as tough as he is, Billy. You are just as tough as he is."

I do not recall how many points that Army senior scored off me that night, but I do know that he had to claw and scratch for each one. We beat Army that night. I would have walked through a wall for Coach and will never forget the spirit he instilled in me.

Cleanliness Is Next To Godliness
(or how to clean up efficiently after summer camp)

Long Island Lutheran was a basketball power on Long Island and the high school attended by Chris Thomforde, a Princeton teammate. Each summer, Long Island Lutheran held a six-week basketball camp for high school players. During my Princeton years, I worked there as a junior counselor. The camp would have college coaches come spend a couple of days and teach the high school players. And that is how Coach came to be there on this particular day.

The summers on Long Island could be brutally hot, and after playing all day the protocol was to take a quick shower on the pool deck and jump in the pool. There was an older gentleman who was the lifeguard and in charge of enforcing the rules. I got to the pool deck and saw Coach standing there in his Princeton basketball shorts holding something behind his back. He was watching the lifeguard like a hawk and as soon as the lifeguard ran off to discipline some high school rule-breaker, Coach ran to the side of the pool with the previously hidden soap, proceeded to lather himself completely from head to foot and then dove into the pool leaving a soapy wake behind him. On returning to the pool deck, Coach must have seen my surprised expression. Looking toward the now returning lifeguard, Coach said, "Well, that guy doesn't like it, but the chlorine dissolves all the soap."

Innovative as always, Coach had found a more efficient way to clean up after basketball camp.

But He's Our Ref

It always seemed that we played strong, non-league teams on their home courts, necessitating long bus trips. Coach loved discussion and had strong opinions, but he also was a good listener. During my sophomore and junior years, Coach often engaged with one of the players, Dom Michel, on these bus trips. Dom often had opinions different from Coach's, but like Coach, he was a good listener and was tolerant of different views.

Davidson College was a top-10 power and we played them at their place both my sophomore and junior years. The first year we got beaten pretty badly. Both referees were from Davidson's conference, and they defined the term "homer." John Hummer got called for a foul on a play when the Davidson player broke John's nose. Coach was livid and insisted that the next year one of the refs had to come from our conference.

The next year we lost again, this time in overtime. Coach was livid again but for a different reason. On the bus ride home, Coach and Dom got into a lively debate regarding referee ethics. The Davidson ref again skewed his calls in Davidson's favor. But our ref called the game straight up, favoring neither team. Coach felt that our ref should have skewed his calls in our favor to compensate for the Davidson ref favoring Davidson. Dom's position was that it would be wrong for our ref to knowingly call the game in our favor even if he realized what the Davidson ref was doing. A lively back and forth ensued, with the debate expanding into a more general discussion of ethics.

Coach was emotionally wrung out after that second loss to

Davidson. But he never lost his cool with Dom. He listened to Dom's comments and made several good arguments backing his position. Dom did likewise. I always got the feeling that, with Coach, it was never a one-way street. Coach learned from his players.

Crushers and Non-crushers

Coach generally divided the girlfriends/wives into two categories: crushers and non-crushers. Crushers were women who interfered with their men doing "man" activities, whether it be playing pick-up ball on weekends, going out with the guys, or whatever. There was no worse condemnation of a woman than when Coach would say, "She's a crusher." Non-crushers were women who did not restrict their men and did not exhibit any of the behaviors that crushers did.

I do not think my wife, Gail, ever came close to being put in the crusher category. The same cannot be said of Geoff Petrie's wife, Annie. Years ago, when Coach was sitting on a sofa in Geoff and Annie's home in Sacramento watching a game on TV, Annie came home after working a full, hard day.

Coach looked up at Annie, and said, "Hey doll, ya got any of that good water?" He expected Annie to wait on him and bring a glass of water.

Without missing a beat, Annie said, "You've got legs. Get your own damn glass of water."

On that occasion, Annie may have strayed perilously close to the "crusher abyss." Fortunately, she developed a warm relationship with Coach and remained far away from the abyss.

Expectations Dashed; Relationships Broken

Before accepting the Princeton job, Coach had had only one year of being a college head coach. He was succeeding VBK, a legendary college coach. And VBK's last team not only had won the Ivy League, but also had been ranked in the top 10. And Coach was inheriting Geoff Petrie and John Hummer, two of VBK's prized recruits. Expectations for Coach's first team were high.

The team lost to Dartmouth at home and wound up tied for the Ivy title. The team lost badly to Columbia in the one-game playoff. It was not a terrible year, but given the initial high expectations, somewhat of a disappointment.

Coach's second year, my sophomore year, Princeton not only won the Ivy League but for the first time a team—our team—had gone undefeated in the league. It was a great year. That spring, Coach partied with us at the eating clubs and was as happy as I have ever seen him. Some pressure was off his back. What was even better was that Geoff and Johnny, his two best players, were coming back for their senior years. Expectations were sky high again for his next team.

Unfortunately for that team, everything that could go wrong did go wrong. Losing Chris Thomforde to graduation meant that John Hummer, a forward, had to play out of position, at center, although he did so valiantly. We lost early to Penn and Columbia and were never in the Ivy League race. But the most disheartening development was the break in the relationship between Coach and Geoff Petrie.

Before the season even started, Geoff badly wrenched his back playing pool at his eating club. Weeks of traction and visits to doctors and other medical professionals did not seem to help the problem. None of them seemed to be able to diagnose what was wrong. Efforts to cure the problem were like playing darts blindfolded. Geoff missed some of our early games and, most critically, the first games with Penn and Columbia. When he finally did return his back was visibly out of alignment and he was out of shape from being out so long. He played some good games, but he was not the same player.

Geoff had had a great junior season. He had come back with the expectation that the team would do well and that he would improve his position on the radar of every NBA coach and general manager. Due to a freak injury, those expectations were now disappearing. He was frustrated and angry.

Coach had expectations that this team would be even better than his previous one. But as the season progressed and those expectations were dashed, he too became frustrated and angry. He did not fully understand why one of his best players could not perform the way he used to and why he had become so sullen. While it was not the only reason for the team's poor performance, the deteriorating relationship between Geoff and Coach became the focal point of a disappointing season.

I had formed strong bonds with both Coach and Geoff during the previous season. Coach had believed in me, given me a chance to play and had become a trusted teacher. Geoff, as an older player, had taken me under his wing even though I was not close to his zip code as a player. It depressed me to see two people whom I admired and cared for deeply barely speaking to each other.

The story has a happy ending. Several weeks after the season ended, Geoff called me and said that we were going over to Coach's that evening. When we got there, it was apparent that they had hashed it out and were friends again. At various later times I have asked each of them how they had patched up the seemingly irreparable rift. Neither has given me an adequate answer, but it really does not matter. What does matter is that each of these great people was big enough to acknowledge his part in the breakup and to reach across the rift to the other. In later years, Geoff brought Coach to the Sacramento Kings as an assistant coach. They became the best of friends, and after Coach left Sacramento talked on the phone frequently and saw each other whenever they could. I feel really good about that.

This Is For You Peter J. Kaminski

Coach did a great job of being our friend during the off-season and then becoming an authority figure once the season began. He would drink beer with us at the eating clubs or at his house. But once the season began, he would say, "One cannot fly with the owl at night and expect to soar with the eagle during the day." There would be no more beer drinking at the clubs. He wanted us to observe training rules (sort of).

During my time on campus there was an article in *The Daily Princetonian* on Peter J. Kaminski, the president of the student chapter of the Students for a Democratic Society (SDS). In the article Kaminski criticized the student body for being apathetic and more interested in sitting around drinking beer and listening to *Light My Fire* by The Doors than in taking an active role in politics.

Peter Kaminski's politics and Coach's were very different. I can recall going to the Coach's house one spring night and he was feeling no pain. With a beer in one hand and a cigar in the other, he kept playing *Light My Fire* over and over on his record player. Each time the song started anew, Coach would raise his beer can and yell, "This is for you, Peter J. Kaminski."

That Is Utterly . . . Unincomprehensible

When inspired, Coach could reshape the English language. During my junior year the starting guard opposite Geoff Petrie was Reggie Bird, a sophomore. Reggie was one of the toughest players I ever played with or against. He was a beast on defense—very difficult to drive around.

But Reggie had this bad habit of reaching in with his hands too much and getting called for ticky-tack fouls. During the first few games that year he tended to pick up his third foul before halftime and had to be taken out of the game. In practices before our next game, against Navy, Coach spent considerable time with Reggie counseling him not to reach as much. Reggie played well in the first-half against Navy. He ran the offense smoothly and played tough, intimidating defense. And the best news—with less than a minute to go in the first-half, Reggie only had one foul!

And then it happened. Reggie reached in and was called for the ticky-tack foul. Coach fumed, then decided to sub Reggie out of the game. For the first time that season, Coach was determined to get Reggie to halftime with fewer than three fouls. But in the time it took to get his sub up and reporting into the game, Reggie committed another reaching foul, this one even worse than the previous one.

Coach was usually pretty analytical during halftime. He would talk about what we had to do better in the second half to win. But not this time. He stalked around the locker room where we were seated, seemingly with his hair on fire. Finally, he confronted Reggie.

"Reggie—what were you—how could you—that was completely—utterly—unincomprehensible!"

Another player might have been scarred for life, but Reggie came from Boston and had the hide of a rhino. We won the game with Reggie playing well, so all was forgiven (sort of). And the bonus—Coach had coined a new word for the English language.

Take Two Shots of Cognac and Call Me in the Morning

Coach not only taught basketball but was concerned with the health and mental well-being of his players. He had a number of remedies which were on the unorthodox side. The only way I can describe his cure for cold and flu is to say it was very much like a sweat lodge. You swallowed this warm drink (do not remember exactly what it was), plus two shots of cognac. Then you bundled up in warm sweat clothes, turned the thermostat up as high as possible, and spent the night sweating (no chanting involved). Amazingly, not only did I use this remedy, but it worked!

During my senior year, right before the handful of days that we would have off during the Christmas holidays, I was not shooting the ball well and told Coach that I wanted to stay at Princeton an extra day to work on it. Coach said that was not a good idea. Then he went to Gail then my girlfriend (now my wife) and told her to take me out and get me drunk (and take some other unprintable actions). This remedy also worked. I came back after the break and was shooting much better. Coach knew that I had been too tense and that the best cure was some relaxation.

In the fall of 1966 when I ran down to my high school lobby and met the man I barely saw that day, little did I know that he would become such a great teacher, mentor, and friend to me—not to mention cleanliness innovator, English language contributor, and medical shaman. When we were back at Princeton for the 50th reunion of our undefeated Ivy championship team, one of the highlights for me was going to be able to see the current team practice. However, I never made the practice. Coach had misplaced his phone, so I took him first to the Jadwin office restroom, then to the Princetonian Diner, and finally back to his apartment where we found it. Initially, I was disappointed to miss the practice. But then I realized that I had just spent an hour and a half with a man who was one of the most important, positive influencers in my life. I was blessed to have had that opportunity, just as I was blessed back in 1966 to have met the man I barely saw.

CHAPTER 5

Brian Taylor '73

People thought I left Princeton University after my junior year due to some unhappiness I had with Coach Carril. That could not be farther from the truth.

While I did make some negative remarks about my challenges at the University, I never once suggested that I had problems with Coach Carril, whom I admired and respected from the first time I met him.

Fifty-plus years later, I do not remember exactly when and how I met Coach. I do remember how my high school teammates would always comment when Coach would come to see us play. They would say, "Columbo is in the house." *Columbo* was a TV detective show in the late 1960s and early 1970s. To some people, Coach Carril's size and looks reminded them of the actor Peter Falk who played the title character. My teammates would ask me, "BT, is he here to recruit you to be on his show?"

After Coach Carril made a few visits to my hometown of Perth Amboy, N.J., and met my family, I knew that my mother adored him. He distinguished himself with my mom by not offering her flowers and chocolates like many other recruiters. Instead, Coach offered her a beer, and they became beer-drinking buddies.

What Coach offered me was the honest truth about how I needed to improve my game in order to be a complete player. I liked that about Coach. His radical transparency and honesty were refreshing. During my junior and senior years at Perth Amboy High School, I became a big fan of Princeton's teams. I especially loved watching John Hummer and Geoff Petrie. I admired the way Coach had those teams playing together. I was already a fan of Bill Bradley and Coach VBK. I wanted to be a part of the Princeton basketball family. I have vivid memories of the day Coach called me and told me I was accepted—I still get chills thinking about that moment. It changed my life.

During my freshman and sophomore years at Princeton, my teammates and I spent many days hanging out at Coach's house enjoying burgers and the trimmings. I enjoyed being in Coach's company, but once we were on the court it was all business.

I still remember the times Coach verbally ripped me apart. His voice would get a little higher and everything would stop. In one practice, I had thrown another turnover from the top of the key attempting to dump it down low to Bill Kapler or to the high post to Andy Rimol. Coach would snatch the ball and yell while demonstrating what he wanted. "Brian, when are you going to learn you have to fake one to make one?" He would snatch the ball from me and show me how to make a low fake, the defender would move his hands down low, and he would make an easy pass over the defender's hands or shoulders.

Even though Coach Carril was extremely intense and would frequently be critical of my game, I loved playing for him. I knew he was a winner as a Little All-American player at Lafayette, and he had an excellent coaching record. I admired his intensity and dedication to making his players better. Despite Coach's critiques of me, he instilled in me a confidence and a fierce determination to be a successful basketball player and a successful man.

Beginning as a freshman, I bought into his Love & Win approach.

During the 1970-71 season, when our varsity team was struggling to win, he was able to keep us from getting down on ourselves. We were a young group with four sophomores starting and our schedule had us playing the top teams in the country, including Duke, Kentucky, and Davidson. Even though we were losing too many games that year, Coach had us playing a good brand of basketball. As we matured, we turned those losses into big victories. My junior year, Coach designed game plans that enabled us to beat North Carolina, Villanova, Penn, and Michigan. At our best, during the 1971-72 season, we were ranked as high as 13th in the nation.

After my junior year, I received an offer from the New York Nets of the American Basketball Association to forgo my senior year and turn professional. For me and my family (who lived in the projects in Perth Amboy), the offer was too attractive to pass up. It was a difficult decision that I knew was not going to be popular with many Princeton fans.

During this tough time, Coach was a positive influence. Although he was not happy about my deciding to leave, he never expressed any negativity towards me. He made only positive comments to the press.

"When Brian was here," Coach would later recall, "he was a perfect gentleman, not the wise guy some people thought. Losing him hurt, but Brian had no obligation to play four years for me. He had an obligation to his family."

Despite Coach's understanding and public support, I felt awkward coming back to Princeton to watch my former Tigers play. For about two years, I watched them only on television. When there was a break in my schedule in my third year with the Nets, I went to see the Tigers play at Jadwin. I was afraid of staying to see Coach. I overcame my jitters and waited to say hello to Coach. He was happy to see me, even though they had just suffered a tough loss against Penn. If anyone has witnessed Coach after a loss, they would understand his intensity and his total dedication to the game of basketball and the importance of winning. We worked so hard for ourselves and for Coach not only to play well but also to play to win. When you do not win, you should be in agony like he was after each loss.

After a few years of estrangement, I began following the Tigers more closely and loved coming back to reunions so I could play in the alumni basketball games. Coach always emphasized the importance of teamwork, which continued long after the playing days were over. Because of Coach Carril's love of teamwork and camaraderie, the Friends of Princeton Basketball picnic at reunion time continues to be something I look forward to attending.

After 10 years of playing pro basketball, I decided to return to Princeton to complete my bachelor's degree—honoring a promise I had made to my mother. My fondest memories of those days were the three-on-three games we played with Coach during lunchtime in Jadwin Gym. Watching Coach shoot his long-range set shot was something I laughed at. However, he was a deadly shooter, and he was great fun to play with and against. I will never forget those wonderful days. Coach also allowed me to be a volunteer coach and play with his team. He would yell at me like I was one of his current players. At the time, I was recovering from a torn Achilles and still had a slight limp, but it did not matter to him that I was a step slower. He still had high expectations of my playing the game the right way.

Coach would shake his head and tell his players that it was a shame that they had not seen me play when I could fly. Those days remain memorable and I continue to be grateful to Coach for accepting me as part of the Princeton basketball family.

After finally graduating and returning to my home in Southern California, my relationship with Coach continued to be close. Long after Coach retired from Princeton and was a Sacramento Kings assistant, he asked me to help him coach a Chinese touring team that wanted to play in the NBA G-League. They wanted to learn the Princeton offense from the great Princeton coach Pete Carril. We trained in the Los Angeles area and had a Chinese interpreter to help us translate the instructions to the young players. After about a month of training and teaching, he told me that he had to return to Sacramento for training camp and the team was all mine to coach. He gave me the confidence to take on that assignment.

As we were preparing the team to enter the upcoming G-league season, Coach told me that the owner told him that he was removing the interpreter. Coach was confident I could do a great job, even without an interpreter. He warned me to watch the owner, who he said was a tough cookie and may have had ties to the mob.

I thanked Coach for the opportunity, but I was nervous to continue without him. I decided to take on the challenge and the results were laughable. Coach called me about two weeks later. I gave him the news that I had been canned for losing a game to a Korean team. It was only our second game, and we had won the first game. They accused me of not playing the two American players enough and in their minds my decision-making was not good enough to take the team to the next level. Coach and I had a long laugh after that experience.

I liked Coach from the first time I met him and loved him for his belief in me, his character, his humor, his seriousness, his teachings, and his heart. I love Coach Pete Carril!

CHAPTER 6

Jimmy Sullivan '73

I met Coach Carril at the Five-Star Poconos basketball camp after my junior year of high school. The camp director was a young coach by the name of Bob Knight, who tried to dismiss me from camp because I had the silly idea that I was there to play ball and not do jumping jacks at six in the morning. Little did I know that Coach Carril felt the same way I did. After bailing me out of jail, he told me that Knight would not even play in the three-on-three games with the other coaches. Shameful. When I made the Five-Star All-Star team, Coach asked me to think about Princeton—a new concept for me. I can tell you that in four years we never did jumping jacks at Princeton. And we beat Bob Knight both chances we had.

I arrived at Princeton with no clue. All I knew was that it looked better than the Army in 1969, and I was going to be a teammate of Brian Taylor. I had watched him shut out future Providence All-America Ernie DiGregorio in a high school all-star game and had heard that he had scored 84 points in a game. Brian was also all-state at quarterback in football. It turns out he was better than that. Coach would always have Reggie Bird guard Brian in practice. Reggie had to be one of the toughest defenders Brian ever played against. Very good players could not get the ball past half-court against Reggie.

Good preparation for the pros. Brian was in a league of his own. But he never acted it. A joy for Coach.

Petrie's In The House

Sophomore year took us on a road trip to Stanford. After a successful game, we were back at the hotel and the rumor went around—Geoff Petrie was in San Francisco on a road trip with the Trail Blazers, and he was in the hotel, looking for Coach.

You will pardon me if I tell you that my first thought was, "Is there going to be a fight?" The prior year from the freshmen court, we had listened to Coach ream Geoff out day after day. Nothing was ever right. He shot too much or too little, took the wrong shot, did not guard—whatever. Loud. Every day. He wants to find Coach? What kind of a brawl will this be?

You know the rest of the story. We got to see one of the great friendships in the sport. Hours of basketball talk in Coach's room (I remember Geoff's reverence for Lakers' superstar Jerry West.) This underlines what I learned later: While you are playing for him, Coach is going to take you apart every day and every way. Once you survive it and graduate, you join the special group that he calls friends.

Pete Loved Butch

During one of his coaching interludes, Coach VBK was swimming through the nightly rigors at the Jersey Shore. Coach reached out and asked Butch to come and oversee the B squad—my squad—until he could get resettled.

Everybody loved Butch, and he loved music. With assistant Bobby Dukiet in tow, every bar was a concert. Bob could play anything on the piano, and Coach and Butch had a long roster of favorite songs and a healthy appetite for cheap beer. Somehow, I ended up on a couple of those tours.

Fortunately, Butch liked the way I tried to guard my man. And he let Coach know. I was close enough to the end of the bench that my conversations with Coach that year were few. And short. After I tripped on the end line during a practice in February, Coach looked over at me on the floor and said, "You and I are going to be friends one day." Talk about picking somebody up! I always thanked Butch for that.

They Are Out To Get Me

I always had trouble with the energy that Coach put into riding the referees. When I brought it up, he would always tell me, "Sully, they are all out to screw me." And he would rant. In 1970-71, a season when Villanova would go to the NCAA finals, we had a game with the Wildcats at the Palestra in December. We were up 12 points in the second-half. Then referee Jim Hernjack called three fouls on Sickles in about four minutes. Taylor accidentally tripped a guy on a break. The ref called a flagrant, and Brian let him know what he thought. A technical, and Brian was gone. An overtime, and the Tigers were gone. Later, Coach said to me, "What do you think now, Sully?"

Sometimes you cannot argue.

A Very Few Words About Defense

Perhaps because we had so much trouble scoring, our teams were usually in the top five for defensive efficiency.

Somebody asked me, "How come you are so good on defense? What does Pete coach?"

I said, "I don't really know. We never practice defense. Coach spends all his time trying to teach us offense. All I know is, if you don't guard your man, you don't play."

Reminds me of a Carril-ism for the press: "Dartmouth had guardable players, and we guarded them."

Who Needs A Jump Shot?

I received a very Catholic upbringing where shooting a jump shot properly was like the catechism—there was only one way to do it. Start at six feet and work your way out. Thirty years after my time, I was very frustrated about a terrific Princeton guard from my backyard who had everything but a shot. How hard is it to learn a foul-line jump shot? I went to Princeton practice one day just to see how the shooting practice was going. Needless to say, for my star, not well. Bunch of push shots from three and then drives—never took a mid-range shot. I was looking for a Michael Jordan pull-up at the foul line.

I flagged down Coach Carril to vent about the no jump shot. He said, "Who needs a jump shot? Bill Bradley didn't shoot a jump shot. Neither did Larry Bird." I might argue about Bird, who could do anything, but it underlines what Coach always taught—the farther away you can shoot, the better. A push shot. That is how he made All-American at Lafayette.

It's Always The Passer's Fault

Sometimes you get a lesson on basketball; sometimes it is about life. This leads to my corollary from the 1974-75 and 1975-76 teams; no telling what a team can do if the best player would rather pass than shoot. These teams were very important. Coach had fairly good teams up until then, but Penn had won six straight Ivy championships. Despite a nice run my senior year (1972-73) when we beat Virginia, Temple, and Rutgers (at Madison Square Garden), and

Florida State (the second-ranked team in the nation at the time), we split with Penn and lost the Ivies. The 1974-75 team changed that with a (then-prestigious) NIT championship, and the 1975-76 team won the Ivy League before falling to the number two team in the nation (Rutgers) by a single point in the NCAAs. And that Tiger team was fun to watch. Later, I told Coach I never understood the offense until I watched that team. That is about when the Princeton offense started to be discussed. Coach told me they would all rather pass.

TLC From Andy's

Coach was always very tender to us at practice, especially after a loss. After Friday night games, Coach would invariably confer with Andy, owner of the famous Andy's Tavern. I gather it was famous because Billy Raftery of television fame came into Princeton with his Seton Hall team and, after beating Coach, took the whole Seton Hall team bus to Andy's. They needed a libation.

Coach would try to beat Andy at pinochle while getting advice from him on basketball. Andy must have had lots of advice because Coach would arrive at Saturday morning practice without having slept but with lots of ideas on how to improve our conditioning. I am not sure Coach ever caught on to the fact that Andy was an all-world pinochle player who was not going to lose. Locals say Coach left Andy's for Conte's because Andy had passed away. I wonder if Raftery had something to do with it.

The Professor

Coach had a friend—a professor—who came to every game and would follow him to Conte's for post-game discovery. Coach would patiently listen to his analysis. Professor would always say to me, "You'd never make it today, Sully." Coach never told me what he meant. Thirty years later, I read a biography that explained it. I was a student who you might kindly say had a "low profile." At least, that is what my senior advisor wrote. It turns out that at the height of the Vietnam War, teachers felt that they were sending you to Vietnam if they failed you. So, I passed. It only took me 30 years to figure it out.

Teacher

I would bring friends to Conte's. A couple of their wives were teachers. Boy, did Coach love to talk teaching. That was his real joy, and my friends loved to visit with him. He would pepper the teachers with questions and remember them when they returned two years later—which they loved. It reminds me of Coach's answer when my son asked him how he liked the pros. "I love to find a player who is willing to learn," he said.

I got married during senior year, and my wife Katie thought she would come to a practice and watch Coach teach. It was quite a lesson, but Katie decided not to come to any more practices. I think she was one of the few wives from whom Coach took lessons and was friends with both Coach's wife Dilly and his subsequent close friend Marion. He always asked her about our kids (we had four very quickly), and she would tease him about everything he never heard from anybody else. Some of my friends were shocked when I would tell them, "Coach kind of likes me—maybe—but he loves my wife." It is that way to this day.

Retirement

Coach took the best team he ever had and turned it over to Bill Carmody for the 1997-98 season. When I accused him of doing it for Bill's benefit and that it was a great sacrifice, he all but called me a liar. "Strictly for myself," he answered.

Sometimes you cannot argue.

Last Call

One of those educators I told you about asked Coach at Conte's one night, "What did you like best about coaching?" As I was returning from the men's room, he nodded in my direction. "I got to meet people like that," he replied. The memory still brings a lump to my throat. I hope—dare I say trust—that his other players have also learned what he thought of them.

CHAPTER 7

Roger Gordon '73

Meanwhile, as the story goes, methinks that genius Peter J. Carril suddenly installed little known sophomore, Roger Gordon, on the Princeton varsity basketball team so that the ultra-visible rising star, Brian Taylor, would have at least one Black teammate and never be asked by the press how it felt to be the only Black player on the ballclub. Of course, the price paid by Coach Carril (and others) was that Roger Gordon was not very good.

Coach made use of me in practice sessions as best he could to impersonate big guards and small forwards against the first team. Having to guard (or attempt to guard) people like Brian Taylor, Ted Manakas, Reggie Bird, and, on occasion, Al Dufty, was not much fun.

One day, during a spirited practice session in Jadwin, I saw Coach Carril coming over to me at my usual position on the bench. At that point, I tried to anticipate the problem which I would be called upon to solve—orange juice cartons too small at training meal, some Starr Transit bus being inadequate for a road trip, or maybe we needed more Coca-Colas in the locker room refrigerator?

I was correct in that it had nothing at all to do with the quality of my basketball performance. Instead, he was holding the keys to his car, because he wanted me to drive over to his home and pick up his bag of sandwiches from Mama Carril for his evening recruiting drive. Luckily, I was still in my sweatsuit because it was far too early in the practice to have me on the court for any purpose. Accordingly, I had no identification on me at the time. I drove over to Murray Place and went into the house where Mrs. Carril was ready with the goods, although to make certain she asked me if Coach wanted tuna salad or roast beef for his dinner.

Since I had no idea, I offered to call over to Coach and find out exactly what he wanted, but Mama Carril stopped me. She told me that I could get in all kinds of trouble with Coach if I had to check this with him.

I told her that it should not be a problem because I was already standing in his living room during a basketball practice session. There was no way to imagine that I could possibly be demoted or banished or dropped down to an even lower position than this. On the way back, I was briefly stopped by a borough police officer who knew that this was Coach Carril's motor vehicle and that I was not Coach. He asked me if I was the Philly guy with the Pennsylvania license. (I was.) He shook his head and let me go.

Coach later took me with him on that trip to a suburban Philadelphia high school where he watched a prospective recruit drop three balls passed to him in the first quarter… whereupon we immediately jumped back into his car to return to Princeton. He had seen enough. There was only one Pete Carril!

CHAPTER 8

John Berger '74

"What doesn't kill me makes me stronger."
—Nietzsche

The transition from a small high school to playing at Princeton was a big step. Since freshmen could not be on the varsity at the time, Princeton had a freshmen team coached by Artie Hyland. Coach Hyland was tough but not any tougher than my high school coach. Beginning sophomore year, playing under Peter J. Carril was a different story. Going back to Bill Bradley '65 and his coach, Butch VBK, Princeton basketball had a great reputation, and the Tigers played at the highest level of competition. Coach Carril was ultra-competitive and was a basketball genius with a volcanic temper. He had a vision of how basketball should be played. If you did not see what he thought you should see or do what he thought you should do, things became existential. A missed cut, a bad pass, or a perceived lack of effort were all evidence of serious character flaws. There were no small mistakes. Anything less than perfection would cause Coach to go ballistic.

At the beginning of my sophomore year, the 1971-72 season, we were scheduled to play the University of North Carolina. The Tar Heels were ranked second in the nation and were an all-star team that included two future NBA greats, Bob McAdoo and Bobby Jones. They were known for their full-court press and we were practicing how to break it. The essence of it was to have one of the forwards (me) break up to half-court, get a pass from Teddy Manakas, and then pass to Brian Taylor, who would be sprinting down the sideline. Coach Carril's philosophy was that you wanted to break the press and score quickly. Do this a couple of times and the press would come off. So, the play started…Teddy had the ball…I flashed up and got the ball from Teddy…I turned and threw the ball to Brian. The problem was I threw the ball to where a normal human being would have been. Brian was *much* faster than a normal human being and my pass was about two feet behind him. Coach came over to me and let loose a string of profanities (unprintable) and insults (unprintable). He then proceeded to tell me I had a serious character flaw and would not amount to anything in life. We reset the play and ran it many times. All my passes from then on were perfect. We went on to beat UNC two days later, 89-73. Andy Rimol, a fellow sophomore, outplayed McAdoo and was the star that night.

The berating and insults continued for my three years of varsity basketball. It took me years to realize that I was not anything special. Coach handed out abuse indiscriminately. I had been out of school for maybe 20 years, and I was watching practice with Professor Marvin Bressler. Professor Bressler was head of the sociology department at Princeton and was a world-renowned scholar. He was a huge Princeton basketball fan, loved the players, and was great friends with Coach Carril. At one point in practice, Coach was mercilessly berating one of the players. Professor Bressler leaned over and said to me, "You know, Johnny, we should come up with an All-Abused Team." To which I replied that I would certainly make it. The Professor looked at me and said, "You would not even make Honorable Mention."

After Princeton, I played in Europe for three years. I met my wife while living in Switzerland, came back to the US, and started a career in business. We have three fabulous daughters (two are Princeton alumnae), five wonderful grandchildren, and one more on the way. A few years ago I was at an event at Princeton with my wife. Coach was there and we were talking. Coach turned to my wife while gesturing with his thumb towards me and said to her, "He turned out a lot better than I thought he would." To me, this is proof that once a Carril player, always a Carril player—abuse and all.

My three years of varsity ball had their ups and downs. We won no championships and I certainly did not garner any personal accolades. My sophomore year was the most memorable season. We had a promising start. Our beginning home schedule was Rutgers, North Carolina, Villanova, Michigan, and Stanford. We won all those games. Penn had won something like 48 Ivy League games in a row, and we ended the streak with a decisive win at Jadwin. I had worked my way into the starting lineup and had the best game of my career against Penn. We then lost a close game at Dartmouth and were blown out at the Palestra. We finished in second place with a 12-2 record. We were then the first Ivy League team to be invited to play in the NIT (when the NIT was a big time tournament) at Madison Square Garden. We opened against Bobby Knight's Indiana team on national TV—and won. We lost a close game against Niagara in the second round and what could have been an incredible season became a footnote. At 79 points per game, we still were the highest scoring team in Princeton history.

As tough as my Princeton years were, I would not trade them for anything. It has been more than 52 years since I first stepped on to the Princeton campus. Coach Carril has had more impact on me than any professor and has been the most influential person in my life after my great parents and my wife of 45 years. So many of the things he said have stayed with me. Here are some of my favorites:

"When you are winning, all your problems are small. When you are losing, all your problems are big."

Another: "Whatever you are doing at the time, make it the most important thing to you."

And, after winning the NIT in 1975, he said, "The strong take from the weak. And the smart take from the strong."

With time, I have also realized that it is rare to be around someone who is obsessed with excellence—every second of every minute of every hour of every day. In my business career, I was fortunate to start several companies. There were often trying times. But they were easy compared to being 19 years old and incurring Coach's wrath.

I am lucky to be part of the Princeton basketball family. I am fortunate to have played with great players like Brian Taylor, Ted Manakas, Reggie Bird, Andy Rimol, Armond Hill, Barnes Hauptfuhrer, and Mickey Steuerer to name a few. It has also been good to be friends with the likes of Frank Sowinski, Peter Molloy, and Jeff Pagano, players who were younger than me, but ones who also have stayed close to the Princeton basketball program. And every time a group of us gets together, sooner or later the conversation pivots to legendary stories about Coach Carril.

CHAPTER 9

Andy Rimol '74

In 1968, my high school coach, George Wilson, and Coach Carril started a basketball camp together called Camp of the Lakers, in the Pocono Mountains of Pennsylvania. I attended the first camp as a heavily recruited 6' 9" high school basketball player with a hundred or so scholarship offers. My teammates and I thought that we were very good. Indeed, the next season we were New Jersey Group One State Champs. Little did we know about Princeton basketball.

The main teachers/coaches at the camp were Butch VBK (Princeton, NBA), Coach Carril, Gary Walters (Princeton), and Art Hyland (Princeton freshman coach). Butch, Pete, Gary, and Art would play against the star players every night after the camper games. They won every game even though we were younger, bigger, and stronger! I was introduced to the "backdoor" cut, which changed my life forever and gave me a new perspective on how to play smart Princeton basketball.

After two years of Camp of the Lakers with Butch, Pete, Gary, and Art, I knew that my game was best-suited for their school. I committed to Princeton and started an amazing education about basketball and how it relates to life. We had really good teams, and I made several friends for life who have inspired me in many ways during the last 50 years or so. Our practices were intense and each one amounted to a degree in both basketball and life.

Fast forward to the summer of 1973. Camp of the Lakers was now at the Hun School in Princeton with the same cast of coaches. It was the summer before my senior year, when I would captain the team. I was experienced with Coach Carril and his style of motivation, which was very rough at times! Coach and I organized an evening pick-up game at Hun with five Rutgers/future NBA players, including Eddie Jordan and Phil Sellers—both college All-Americans. The Princeton team was Andy Rimol, John Berger, Armond Hill, Joe Vavricka, and Brian O'Neill—quite a solid team. They beat us 11-10, 11-9, and 11-9. I was thinking that we were going to be a very good team in the upcoming season, and I was not disappointed in our performance.

Suddenly, after the last game, Coach ran onto the middle of the court and screamed, "You f##king pu##ies! You f##king pu##ies! I'm not putting up with this now, and I am not putting up with this during the season. This is unacceptable!" The parents and the campers on the sidelines were in total shock. The Rutgers players were in shock. Afterwards, in the locker room as we were changing, John, Joe, and Armond told me that they were not coming back again to play that summer and that they would see me in the fall. This was one of many incidents where Coach tended to lose his mind over little things—it did not surprise me. This was another lesson in intensity, craziness, defense, and never accepting defeat.

Coach was one of the most intense and perceptive people I ever knew. He liked me because I always hustled and had to work harder than everyone else. He always told the team and me in particular that we must look at ourselves in the mirror and ask, "Have I given it all my effort to be a better athlete, or did I dog it today?" We heard that many times. I have applied that message to my personal life frequently throughout the last 50 years, and it has served me well.

Coach was fair and passionate about his beliefs, and without a doubt, the most positive influence in my life! I learned more on the court than in the Princeton classrooms. Coach stressed teamwork and unselfishness along with the technical aspects of the game—two things that I have used with my family and in business my whole life. It was tough at times, but it was a great accomplishment to have had a successful and winning career at Princeton. I am eternally grateful for the chance to be part of the Princeton basketball family.

CHAPTER 10

Tim van Blommesteyn '75

Pete Carril: Coach

Playing for Pete Carril (Coach), learning from him, and now trying to put in some perspective my three years under his tutelage (1972-75) is difficult and is not helped by age which can cloud 50-year-old memories. For me, they were three tough years—certainly some good times (1975 NIT) but offset by some really challenging periods. For many of us, I would say that is more the norm than not, but that is only my assessment and others might disagree. Looking back, however, they were the three most important years of my life.

To talk about Coach, to try to offer some insights into his basketball philosophy, his approach to the game, or the things he accomplished, is beyond my ability to put into words. John McPhee might be able to do it, but better to go to Wikipedia and The Coach's book *The Smart Take From The Strong* to learn about the man. All I offer is a simple view of one player who can recount instances that helped define how I see and what I learned from The Coach.

Looking back 47 years, I can say without equivocation that Pete Carril was the toughest SOB I ever knew. Other coaches, players, CEOs, co-workers, and all the people I have met through my life—none were as tough as Coach. He was unforgiving in his approach to basketball and expected total commitment and adherence to his philosophy of the game if you wanted to play for him. How he survived for nearly 30 years at a school that put academics ahead of sports is a testament to his persistence and what I believe to be one of his main drivers in life—teaching. What he wanted did not always sit well with a 20-year-old kid from an elite prep school, but if you loved the game and you wanted to play, there was only one path to follow—his.

Getting To Know You

Coach was a man of few words. He communicated with many facial expressions, and was often dismissive—if he liked you. If he was not a fan, if you were a reporter asking a silly question, or the New Jersey governor asking about the next game, or an alum who thought he had a right to make some inane comment, the interaction could be brutal. I learned early. I was not recruited by Coach, so he did not know me. (I was off to Davidson until I was accepted by Princeton in July after my senior year in high school.) While I knew his name, I knew nothing about him or the program. After playing in the annual fall Cane Spree basketball game as a freshman, I received a surprising invitation to visit Royce Flippin (assistant athletic director at that time, I think). Somehow, I found his office, and when I walked in, Coach was sitting there, unlit cigar in hand. After Royce introduced me, there was no small talk, no good to meet you or welcome to Princeton. Instead, he said he spoke to the soccer coach and thought it would be a good idea for me to try out for the freshman team. He did not imply that I play soccer now and basketball later; his message was just go play soccer. I did not say anything, as I was under the mistaken impression I played well in Cane Spree (evidently not), and was about to say something when this crazy little man got up and walked out without another word.

Long Live The Cigar

Coach was famous for a number of habits and traits but maybe none more so than his love of cigars. At practices, if he did not have a basketball in his hand to demonstrate something, he often had a cigar somewhere on his person—unless he was upset with something or someone and used the cigar as a projectile to make a point. At the start of the 1975-76 season, Coach surprisingly started smoking a pipe (why is a mystery), and that pipe traveled to Notre Dame—highly ranked with one of the premier college players in Adrian Dantley—for the third game of the season. We flew to South Bend on a Friday and had a walk-through practice on Saturday to go over the game plan. It was one of those days when the team and Coach were not on the same wavelength. As the practice progressed, you could see his frustration growing, and we all knew his breaking point was near. When he finally got to that point, the pipe, which he had been carrying around, was hurled at high velocity to the gym floor and pretty much disintegrated. I never knew if he was aware he had a pipe and not a cigar, but in all the time I have known him since that day, a pipe never returned.

The NIT

The fact that we were invited to the 1975 NIT after a season during which we, again, lost out to Penn for the Ivy championship was a mild surprise but provided an opportunity for seniors like me to play in a postseason tournament for the first time. While the NIT has since been diminished by the expansion of the NCAA tournament to more than 64 teams, in 1975 only 32 teams made it to the Big Dance, so the NIT included a number of high-quality teams that included most of the second-ranked teams in each power conference. According to our assistant coach at the time (Gary Walters), we were the 16th-ranked team in a field of 16 teams, so expectations were not particularly high. With no conference tournament to play in, we finished our season more than two weeks before our first NIT game. It was a challenge for Coach to keep us sharp as we worked to get ready for Game One. His solution—unleash the dogs (the freshman team).

In 1975, freshmen could not be on the varsity, so they played their own schedule. They had a great team that included Kleinert, Omeltchenko, Rizzuto, Sowinski, Starsia, and Snyder, who would all go on to have three outstanding varsity years. Coach's plan was to have the freshman team challenge us regularly over the two weeks, running us into the ground on offense and beating us up physically on defense. By the time we were set for our NIT opener against Holy Cross, I was convinced the freshmen were the better team. I had a personal battle with Bob Kleinert, who was a smart, physically strong player but who was no match for me on speed. I learned quickly that when I tried to use my speed to go by him, an arm would reach out to slow me down, or when I tried to dribble, I would get pushed around and hacked. All would have been fouls in a game. If I looked over at Coach, he would only smile and have us play on. He knew for us to be ready to play against top teams we had to be tough—and this was his way of making that point.

Be All You Can Be

Coach was always critical of my play and unsparing in his comments. What I failed to understand until late in my career was that his critiques were intended to focus my attention on ways to become the best player I could be. Not the best player—just my best. He hated to see someone who underachieved. His observations in practice were unvarnished and intense. In other settings, however, he was more circumspect. When he made comments to the media, he dialed back the intensity and could actually say something humorous.

During my sophomore year in a post-game interview, this was his impression of my play: "He can't dribble, he can't pass, and he can't shoot, and sometimes he's a pain in the ass to the other team, and sometimes he's a pain in the ass to us." Pete Carril Motivation 101.

Playing Within The System

The best player I ever played with at Princeton was Armond Hill. By the end of the 1974-75 season, it was obvious he was one of the great players in the country, but you would not know that from his statistics, which were good but not outstanding. Of course, stats do not tell the story of how he quarterbacked the team or took on challenging defensive assignments every game. Armond could have averaged 20 points and 10 rebounds a game, but by playing within the system, he was not able to achieve those high levels and instead sacrificed and made the team better. This is a primary tenet of any Carril team—team success is paramount and individual greatness (if at all) can happen only within that framework.

1997 Naismith Hall of Fame Induction

The 1997 induction ceremony should have been the just reward for a 29-year tenure at an elite, non-scholarship university in a league not known for producing Hall of Fame coaches. Coach was nationally recognized for creating the Princeton offense, for having highly-ranked defensive teams, for his quick understanding of how the three-point shot would fundamentally change the game, and for his ability to get the most from his players. Five hundred wins, many league titles, the 1975 NIT, and the admiration of coaches and players throughout the country should have given him the platform to talk to the many former inductees and stars and his former players about his success, his life in basketball, and the drive to rise above humble beginnings (and diminutive size) to become a larger-than-life figure in the game. I think it is fair to say, it was not one of his better speeches.

I can only guess why his talk was not memorable. Maybe it was because, as usual, he did not want (or seek) the limelight, and he was never a fan of media attention. Maybe it was nerves? Whatever it was, I do not remember the substance of the speech except for one point he made, and it offers an important insight into his philosophy. When he had the stage to highlight any number of his great players, his success, or his views on basketball, he mentioned George Boccanfuso, a custodian at Jadwin Gym. George was a small man, older, who came to work every day, did his job with a smile, never complained, and did it well. He worked into his 80s, cleaning what is now Carril Court at halftime. Others might look down on someone who was "just" a janitor, but to Coach, George was a superstar. In his world, respect is earned not by your position, wealth, or school affiliation, but by your character, your commitment to your job, and your honesty and integrity. He judged all his players the same way.

Lasting Vision

During reunions, Coach hosted a half-court game for former players at Jadwin. It was not highly organized—no officials or crowds—just a group of guys who showed up with sweats and sneakers and the chance for younger players to show older players how to play the game.

I returned on major reunion years, and I think it was probably my 15th when I last played in the game. In typical fashion, Coach would start by roaming the outside of the court, cigar in his mouth, and would launch multiple left-handed shots from a few steps inside the half court line. When he moved to the sideline, the game increased its pace and intensity. After he stepped away, I was running around on defense trying to track John Rogers '80 with limited success. At one point, John cut backdoor and all I could do was grab him to stop an easy layup. Clearly, this was a signal that I should not be on the court. Shortly after, I walked to the sideline for a breather expecting to see Coach critiquing and assessing his old players. Instead, he was at the other basket having set up a couple of folding chairs, working with players' kids, showing them spin moves, inside hand changes, and cross-over dribbles. No interest in us "old" players but definite focus on working with and teaching these kids the basics of the game. It was a great sight.

This is my lasting vision of Coach: doing what he loved to do for all his adult life. He was a teacher, sometimes about basketball but mostly about life. These lessons at Carril U were not immediately internalized at the time of delivery (it could take years), and they were often delivered in a brutally frank and direct way. You never had to guess what he was trying to communicate as there was never a time I remember him beating around the bush to make his point. He was always direct and honest. And for me, 50 years on from being a C student of the Little Professor, I am still working to put those lessons to use in my life while also trying to pass that wisdom on to my daughter and granddaughters—albeit in a kinder, gentler manner.

CHAPTER 11

Armond Hill '76

First, let me say that Coach Carril taught me everything I know about basketball. Period!

It started the very first time I met him. I saw this little guy with a bowtie laying down in the bleachers watching my high school game in Brooklyn. My high school coach, Ray Nash, introduced me to him after the game. The first thing he said to me after he shook my hand was that my left-hand dribble was weak, that I needed more snap on my two-handed chest pass, that I needed more spin on my shot. At the time, I thought I was an O.K. player. All the other coaches who were recruiting me told me how good I was and how I could help their programs. But in the back of my mind, I knew that Coach Carril was right. He also told me that the only thing he could offer me was a hard time (and trust me, he delivered on that promise. Ha!), but he said he could make me a better player. To an 18-year-old, growing up in Brooklyn, that was music to my ears because I wanted to be able to play against the best in the world. I walked away saying to myself that I wanted to play for that little guy.

When I finally got to Princeton, I had a blast playing on the freshman team with my teammates who are still my best friends today—Barnes Hauptfuhrer, Peter Molloy, and Mickey Steuerer.

We built a bond that could never be broken. It was one of the most important lessons I learned playing for Coach Carril. To him, basketball was all about teammates, hard work, and friendships.

During my first practice with the varsity team, Coach Carril tossed me the ball at half-court and told me that I had to see all nine people on the court—my four teammates and the five guys trying to stop me. No one ever said that to me before. That was the beginning of his teaching me how to see.

After five minutes of playing, I heard this loud, "Yo!"

Everyone stopped. He said to me, "S##t or get off the pot!"

Apparently, I had gone into my New York City dribbling act, and he was telling me, in his unique way, to go somewhere with my dribble. Attack the basket or pass the ball. Lesson duly noted!

In between classes I would run down to Jadwin Gym and watch film with him. I would load the large reel-to-reel projector to begin my lessons on how to see the court. He would stop the film periodically and ask me, "Where should the ball be?" I would point to the screen, and he would let out a resounding "No!" He would point and say "Over there!" After a couple of months of these visits, I started to point to the correct player, and he would give me a little smirk with a stogie in his mouth and nod his head. I knew I was making progress seeing the whole court.

I remember on one of my film visits he asked me what the easiest shot in basketball was. I thought I was being wise and said a free throw. He said no. It is a layup. If you are playing to win, we are going to get a wide open "Sunday afternoon shot" or a layup. He explained that a Sunday afternoon shot is a shot you get on your driveway with no one guarding you. Even though I did not grow up with a driveway, I understood the picture he was trying to paint for me. Basically, he was saying that we were going to move the ball around until we got the shot we wanted. The value of his legendary backdoor layups also became very clear to me. While opponents were thinking we were stalling the ball, he was teaching us how to get the shot we wanted in order to win. He was the master of teaching execution. It seemed as if we would work on one play for an hour in practice. But after that hour, we knew every which way a team would try to stop us. The games became easier than practice.

Fast forward to the NIT, where he told me before the Providence game that sometimes you beat a guy with your body and sometimes you beat a guy with your brains. Tonight, you are going to have to beat him with both. Talk about motivation. I can go on with the lessons he taught me as a player, but it was when I had the opportunity to coach with him that I learned about the genius of Coach.

It started with my first meeting as a coach. He went to the chalkboard to start drawing up a play, and I pulled out my pen and pad. He looked at me and said, "What the hell are you doing?"

"Coach," I said. "I'm writing down what we're going to work on."

He looked at me with a puzzled look. "We don't write anything down here. Everything we work on is in your head!"

Coaches around the country would call and ask if we had pamphlets on our offense. It was easy for us to say no because it was true, but they were always invited to come watch practice. He would answer any questions they might have.

During one of our meetings, Coach asked me again, "What is the easiest shot in basketball?"

"You asked me this question before when I was a player, and you said a layup."

He looked at me with another smile on his face. "No, it's a three-pointer!"

"Why?"

"Because they give you three points, stupid!"

We both broke out in laughter, but the point was well-taken. We were going to move the ball around until we got a three-point shot. His teams consistently led the nation in three-point shooting. He was 25 years ahead of his time. Today, because of analytics, all the NBA teams, colleges and high school teams are shooting threes and layups. We were getting threes and backdoor layups with precision. How many coaches have an offense that is named after them? Pure genius!

I can go on for days about my time spent with Coach. He taught me things on and off the court that I still use today. Every time I spoke with him, I learned something new. Not long before he died, I had occasion to visit with Coach and my teammates (Mickey, Peter, and Barnes). I told them that I looked upon Coach as the ultimate teacher. The greatest compliment I ever received from Coach was that I can "see!"

In closing, I would like to thank two of his friends he introduced me to at Princeton: Tony (Red) Trani and professor Marvin Bressler. Both became invaluable to my growth as a person and as a student. Red taught me about life off campus, and professor Bressler taught me about being a seeker of learning. Coach Carril, forever the teacher, knew what I needed off the court. Thanks, Coach. You taught me well!

CHAPTER 12

Mickey Steuerer '76

I attended Archbishop Molloy High School in Queens, New York and played for Coach Jack Curran. Molloy had recently produced several all-city players. It was not uncommon to see esteemed college coaches such as Frank McGuire, Dean Smith, and Al McGuire at school. I was recruited by a handful of schools, but I was also aware of the Princeton basketball program and thought it might be a good fit for me. Coach Curran reached out to Coach Carril and arranged for me to attend a Princeton game. Princeton had just come off its long exam break and was playing Fordham. When I walked into Jadwin and saw Coach, I thought to myself, "He sure doesn't look like the college coaches I've seen at school." He had on a short-sleeve shirt with a bowtie, and he looked like he was long overdue for a haircut. The team seemed a little off from the long exam break and lost the game. I was very impressed with their straight up man-to-man defense, how well they moved the ball on offense, and how unselfish they were as a team. Coach Curran and I went down to the locker room. Coach was so upset with the loss, he looked like he had just received word of a death in his family. He thanked me for coming down, said he would be in touch, and walked away. Not exactly a recruiting hard sell.

After weighing my options, I decided to attend Princeton. Freshmen were not eligible to play varsity, and that year I had minimal interaction with Coach.

Everything changed the following year. Practices were intense and any sort of slip-up could easily set him off. Some of the upperclassmen called him a psycho. But after a few weeks of practice, I developed a better understanding of his style of coaching. He was a stickler for effort and precision. He would not tolerate mistakes caused by lack of concentration. Passes had to be thrown to the right spot at exactly the right time, every time—no exceptions. To him, it meant more than that. If players were not living up to their full potential, he took it personally. Each team seemed to have a player or two who increasingly frustrated Coach because he felt like he was not getting through to them, and thus he felt he was failing them. Armond Hill was by far the most talented player on our team. Coach was on him constantly for not always playing with his maximum intensity. Many would say he was being overly harsh, but the truth was the players he rode the hardest were the ones he cared about the most.

We came back to practice on Christmas evening one year. We had a mediocre practice, and Coach sat down to give us one of his infamous player evaluations. He would go down the bench and tell each player what they needed to work on. When he reached Armond, he ripped into him again for his lack of intensity. When Armond did not respond, he went right up to him, stuck his chin in his face, and said, "Go ahead and hit me. It would be worth it just to get a reaction out of you."

That is when Peter Molloy leaned over to me on the bench and whispered, "He better not come down and ask me that because I'll pop him."

Coach could only accept what he believed was a player's expression of his full potential. Armond went on to become the Ivy

League Player of the Year, a first-round NBA draft pick, and a very successful pro.

Coach's mantra was that hard work, intelligence, and courage could overcome a lack of physical talent. During this era, other coaches would boast about how hard their teams worked and how they would practice five to six hours a day. Coach believed that if a team practiced with maximum focus and effort, the practice should not last longer than two to two-and-a-half hours. Anything longer, he would say, would lead you to experience the "law of diminishing returns."

Coach was all business on the floor, but he also had a great sense of humor. One time at practice, someone got badly beaten on defense. He immediately started into his rendition of Linda Ronstadt's *Blue Bayou.* Junior year, we played in a Christmas tournament at South Carolina. Their coach was the aforementioned Frank McGuire. The other visiting teams in the tournament were Duke and LSU. The organizers held a dinner the night before the tournament began, and each coach was asked to give a short speech. The Duke and LSU coaches each spoke of how honored they were to be invited by Coach McGuire, raining one accolade after another on him, and saying he was the main reason they had accepted the invitation. When it was Coach Carril's turn to speak, he took a puff on his cigar, and said, "It was great to get the invite from Coach McGuire, but the main reason we came down was for the $10,000 guarantee."

As mentioned, Coach firmly believed that hard work and effort could overcome lack of talent. He would say that it takes the same amount of time to do something correctly as it does to do it incorrectly, so why not do it the right way every time? Coach had grown up in a working-class environment. He was a little rough around the edges, and it seemed somewhat odd that Princeton had hired him to coach basketball. I believe he knew players at Princeton for the most part would be disciplined and intelligent. He felt that if he could instill a certain toughness and work ethic along with these attributes, they could be successful. It was meeting this challenge with many of his players that caused him so much stress and long nights at Andy's Tavern. His interaction with players was not always pretty, but it is unbelievable how many players he got through to and who improved dramatically.

A few years after graduation, I returned to Princeton to work for Coach as one of his assistants. What I soon came to realize was that Coach was the exact same person behind the curtain. I already knew he was obsessed with improving and tinkering with things to try to make his players and team better. In my role as an assistant coach, I could see more clearly what really drove the man. He cared so much for his players and knew that players whom he motivated to practice and work hard, to be courageous and to play intelligently, would carry these traits for the rest of their lives. This is what mattered to him. I think back to the first time I saw him and think that his unconventional dress was intentional. Maybe he was trying to send a message to the other coaches, who dressed impeccably, had manicured fingers and all sorts of jewelry, that none of that mattered to him. He once said to me that wealth might be the biggest obstacle to success in basketball.

Coach and I have remained friends over all these years. I enjoy nothing more than meeting up with Coach, drinking a few beers, and listening to his take on life. You never know what you are going to get, but some of his stories are classic. I liked the one where he was a senior in college, majoring in economics. He slacked off his last semester and was enjoying himself. In one class his final exam required him to explain, in detail, the difference between a recession and a depression. His answer was: "A recession is when your best friend loses his job. A depression is when you lose your job." He got an "F" in the class, but he stood by the accuracy of his answer.

His humorous stories were balanced by more serious words of wisdom. He said that most people think they have many friends, but in reality, you are extremely lucky if you have one true friend in your entire life. In that regard, I consider myself extremely lucky.

Not every player was a big fan of Coach's style and intensity. However, as I look back, it is remarkable how many players he significantly influenced as both players and people. These men often went on to become successful in whatever they pursued. One could argue their success was in part due to the ethics and principles instilled in them by Coach. I was so fortunate to cross paths with Coach and will never be able to thank him enough for the impact he has had on my life.

CHAPTER 13

Barnes Hauptfuhrer '76

I suspect that most college basketball players were the stars of their high school teams. I was not. Arguably, I was not among the four best starters on my team.

Certainly, the vast majority of college players were also recruited players. I was not. Coach Carril never saw me play a high school game. I learned later that Princeton's freshman coach at the time, Artie Hyland, had seen me play. He told Coach, "Barnes will never play at Princeton."

Well, Artie's scouting report did not quite pan out, as I was a starter for all three years of my varsity eligibility. So, how did this happen? Pete Carril.

Coach made me a better player. More importantly, he prepared me for life. He was a great teacher of core values, such as work ethic, team over self, and the importance of personal humility. I consider him to be the most impactful teacher I had at Princeton. Memories of times with Coach are many. Those noted below still make me laugh.

Coach Carril was a quick study of a player's strengths and weaknesses. Early in my freshman season, he sized me up right away—some potential, but too skinny. I needed to get stronger and tougher. Coach knew that I was a private school kid from an upper-middle class family. As I came to learn, Coach was not a fan of kids who went to private schools. To him, those kids grew up in "three-car-garage" families and would be too soft in crunch time. I had no chance unless I could prove that I was an exception to this rule.

Before earning a starting spot as a sophomore, I had had a decent year playing on the freshman team. More importantly, Coach had seen me go beyond program requirements by lifting weights, running stadium steps, and showing up at Jadwin Gym most every day pre-season and post-season. He came to see me as a hard worker. Personally, I think everyone on the team worked hard, but I was not complaining that Coach put this label on me.

Sophomore season was a tough one. I was excited to play, but my weight was increasingly a problem as the season went on. I dropped from 212 to 188 pounds—not so good when you are 6'8". I had to have my practice time limited to sustain my weight. I was eating like crazy, but nothing would keep my weight up. High metabolism and high intensity created the problem. Coach, who was not exactly a conventional guy, recommended that I drink four beers every night to solve the problem. Was he serious? Yes. Did I comply? Yes. Was I able to maintain my weight and stay on the court? Yes. Coach's physical therapy program worked! Somewhat amazingly, my grades improved too!

Life with Coach was not easy. I think he cursed me out at least once in every practice. He demanded intensity, personal improvement, and teamwork. He insisted on players honestly understanding their individual strengths and weaknesses, as well as those of their teammates. Coach's hard edge was always fine with me for two reasons. First, when I made mistakes, I was inwardly yelling at myself just as hard as, if not harder than, Coach. Second, I always knew that the yelling meant that Coach cared. His style was tough love personified.

Coach deeply cared about his players. Interestingly, he rarely called me by my name; he just referred to me as "40" or "F##ing 40" or "40, you are so f##ing stupid." I did not find this problematic; rather, I found it amusing. To this day, I usually address former teammate Frank Sowinski as "25." I view the number calling as a term of endearment.

Sophomore season (1973-74) was disappointing from a win/loss perspective with the team going 16-10. My teammates and I got lots of endearment that year.

Junior year (1974-75) was more interesting. As juniors, Armond Hill, Mickey Steuerer, and I were now more experienced and confident starters. We won our first two games and headed to South Bend, Ind., to take on highly ranked Notre Dame and the country's leading scorer, Adrian Dantley. We led at halftime but wilted under Notre Dame's full-court press in the second half. The game was memorable for me for three reasons. First, Mickey's defense on Adrian Dantley was phenomenal; I think it was Dantley's season low. Second, I shot 11-11 from the field (a nice looking but misleading statistic on a score sheet). Third, and far more important, I knew that I was invisible when the pressure was on. Coach never missed such things. After the game, I recall sitting on the floor of the Notre Dame locker room leaning against one of the metal lockers. Coach stormed in and started screaming at me. He grabbed a Notre Dame football helmet, drop kicked it at me, smashing the locker a few inches above my head. The helmet then landed in my lap. To this day, my score-book achievement is just a reminder that I simply did not get the job done that night.

Junior year really got interesting when we had an away game at Virginia, triggering a run of 13 straight wins, including the NIT championship. This game was most noteworthy for an incident in which Coach Carril got ejected after he dashed across the court and charged one of the referees following an outrageous foul call. Every hot Spanish vein in his neck was on fire. It cost us five technical fouls, but not the game. With no assistant coach in attendance, Coach nominated my savvy teammate Peter Molloy (the only Princeton player/coach in history) to coach us to victory. Now that was fun.

Coach's wicked sense of humor was on full display well before game time that day when a classic southern belle Cavalier fan (maybe 40 years old) saw us boarding our team bus. She sauntered over to Coach and said in her best southern drawl, "Bless your heart, Coach. Our Cavaliers are just going to whoop your boys today."

Expecting Coach to respond, all she got was the silent glare of a guy who resembled some deranged psychopath. Frightened, she started to back away. Then Coach gave her a loud Tiger-like growl. The lady rushed away in shock, leaving our team in hysterics. Funny how Coach sometimes relaxed the team. Perhaps my memory is off, but as I recall, we jumped out to a huge lead in that game and never looked back.

Later that year, we were in a practice session before playing South Carolina in the NIT. We were posting up Armond down low. I had the ball on the wing looking for him. He was covered, so I went up for the jump shot. Before I released it, Armond suddenly got open and I tried, pathetically, to switch from a shot to a pass. The ball wandered aimlessly between Armond and the rim. Coach halted practice and walked over to me, standing about two inches away with his face and cigar at the level of my navel.

He calmly asked, "What was that?"

I offered no excuse. He just looked up at me.

"Don't do it again." He then pressed his cigar butt against my uniform burning a hole in my practice jersey. Guards Steuerer and Molloy thought it was hysterical and were rolling in laughter. I wanted to crush the little bastard who just looked up at me with his trademark, s##t-eating grin on his face. Once again, Coach had relaxed the team. Led by Armond's surreal performance, we romped to an 18-point halftime lead over highly favored South Carolina the next day.

My senior year (1975-76), we had a big, televised home game

against St. John's with both teams ranked in the top 15. Coach was due for a pre-game interview with CBS broadcaster Don Criqui. Alarmed by Coach's absence seconds before airtime, Criqui bolted into our locker room and asked, "Where is Coach?"

A second later, you heard the flush of a toilet. The stall door opened, and Coach waddled out in his boxers.

With pants still crinkled around his ankles, he told Criqui, "I'm here. Do you want to do the interview now?"

You cannot make up stuff like this. Coach was his own guy, capable of going ballistic with unparalleled fury or he could bring the house down in laughter. In this instance, his antics had us all laughing. We played loose again and won in overtime.

A final story from my senior year entertained the team, again at my expense. Grace Kelly (of Hollywood and Princess of Monaco fame) was a client of my lawyer father and had become a friend of my mother. Late my senior year, my mother called to tell me that she was bringing Princess Grace to our home game against Harvard that evening. I remember hoping that Coach would not hear about this because absolutely nothing good (for me) could come from it.

The game itself was an easy 20-point victory, but late in the game, I uncharacteristically missed three foul shots. In the locker room following the game, I was feeling pretty good. After all, it was an easy win, and I did not think anyone noticed Princess Grace's attendance. Wrong. Coach did.

Coach bolted into the locker room. "40, g-ddamn it, if you weren't so worried about f##ing kings and f##ing queens and f##ing princesses, you'd make those f##ing foul shots."

He then stormed out of the locker room, slamming the door behind him. Of course, my teammates were all laughing while I was left defenseless—again.

Another story from senior year involved our final regular season game, an away game against Columbia where we played poorly. I got knocked unconscious in the first half and was taken to the locker room for stitches under my left eye. While lying on the trainer's table, I heard Coach go off on teammate Frank Sowinski.

"Look at you, 25," he yelled. "You make me sick, you f##ing coward. When Barnes got knocked down, your face turned whiter than an albino."

Now that was seriously funny, particularly considering that Frank was injured and in street clothes. Who cares? Coach always saw things that others did not.

The stories of Coach above are just the tip of the iceberg of many funny stories during my years at Princeton. Certainly, life with Coach was not all fun and games. It was hard work. But Coach's constant pushing prepared me for life after Princeton. His focus on every little detail was invaluable to my subsequent career. His insistence on humility was never forgotten by me. He prepared me for life's inevitable ups and downs. Getting back up off the canvas after some setback in business was never a problem following my days with Coach.

When I think of Coach today, I think of a plaque on one of his office walls. The plaque displayed the famous "man in the arena" passage from Theodore Roosevelt, lauding those who bleed and sweat and work tirelessly, even in loss or failure, over those who never sufficiently commit themselves to know victory or defeat at all. Coach lived in the arena. And he motivated me (and many others) to live in it too. For this, and so much more, I humbly say: Thank you, Coach.

Addendum (written after Coach died): Over the past 45 years, I have often been asked the following questions:

1. Was Coach Carril tougher than Bobby Knight or Mike Krzyzewski?
2. Was Coach more foul-mouthed than those two coaches?

I have no answer to these questions because I did not play for those other coaches. What I can say is that the best way to visualize Coach may be to recall the following characters from the movies.

1. **From Hoosiers** – Picture coach, Norman Dale, played by Gene Hackman. To some, Coach was a bit rough around the edges, but in reality, he was a teacher, who constantly stressed fundamentals. Because of this, his teams consistently "punched above their weight-class."
2. **From Indiana Jones and the Temple of Doom** – Picture the intensity and evil smile of Mola Ram clawing the heart out of the chest of a hapless Indian peasant. Coach was always after our hearts with equal intensity.
3. **From One Flew Over the Cuckoo's Nest** – Picture asylum patient McMurphy, played by Jack Nicholson, teaching "Chief" how to play basketball. Like Nicholson, Coach traveled his own unique road. He was one of a kind, and he could make all of us laugh whenever he wanted.

My percentage weightings may be off a bit, but I think Coach was maybe 70% Norman Dale, 15% Mola Ram, and 15% McMurphy. How lucky were my teammates and I to have such a character to coach and teach us?

CHAPTER 14

Frank Sowinski '78

I cannot tell you how many times I have used these three five-word phrases in my life.

The first was from my mom: "Do the best you can."

The second was from my dad: "You can count on me."

The third was from Pete Carril: "You're right, but you're wrong."

I have used these three phrases often in my life, and I have used them to provide perspective and context in many personal, work, and athletic situations.

While I have spoken about the first two phrases before, I would like to talk about the third phrase and how the words of Pete Carril have affected much of my life. While doing the best you possibly can and being an individual who can be counted on is fundamental to being a trusted and reliable person, the third phrase is about doing the things necessary to be successful given the situation at any time.

This lesson was impressed upon me and my teammates every day for the four years that we played in Jadwin Gymnasium. Freshmen could not play varsity back in the day, but we had a very good freshman team that defeated highly-ranked junior college teams, and we acted as the practice squad running the plays of the upcoming opponent when the varsity won the NIT in 1975.

The following fall I had the chance to try out for the varsity, and I became a starter on the 1975-76 undefeated Ivy championship team. The fall preseason was all about learning the nuances of Princeton basketball. While I thought I was a pretty good team player who had a very solid freshman season under my belt, I quickly learned that I had a long way to go under the watchful eye of Pete Carril. In fact, my teammates can attest that I was not called by my name by Coach for over a month during the preseason, but was simply called some variation of my number, which was 25.

In fact, during one practice about two weeks before the season opener, I made a steal and was about to break out into the open court when I was clearly tripped from behind.

Rather than acknowledging a good defensive play, Coach ran up to me, yelling, "What good are you, two-five, when you're on the floor? How can I ever play you?"

I could not believe it, but I just turned back to practice because I knew there was no point in arguing with Coach.

About a week later, nearly the same thing happened. I made a steal, but was pushed down as I was about to break free. This time I jumped up and stared at Carril. He walked over and, calling me by my name for the first time in a month, said, "Frankie, I saw you got tripped there, and I saw you got tripped last week, but you were feeling sorry for yourself so I yelled at you any way." (Yes, other than my grandmothers, he is the only person who called me Frankie).

That was one of many examples of what it was like to play for Coach Carril. The essence of "you're right, but you're wrong" was not about running the play that was run in practice or even running the play that was outlined during the last time out. The key was to run the play that best fit the situation based on what the opponent was doing. The lesson learned and the continual message was: Yes, you did what we talked about, but you did not do what it takes to maximize the probability of success.

That is what Princeton basketball was all about. It was about taking advantage of what the opposing team gave you. It was about having five teammates who all understood what it took to win, and winning was the ultimate measure of success. A simple nod of the head or a raised eyebrow meant your teammate saw the same opportunity as you did. It also did not hurt that we had a number of players who could hit an open jump shot that resulted from seeing the situation, consistently evaluating our options and executing on our opportunities.

This was one of the primary reasons that the Princeton basketball team under Pete Carril could compete with some of the top basketball schools in the country while maintaining the academic standards of one of the great universities in the world. Teams hated playing against us. We were not flashy, but we knew how to win. We knew that we would never be the best team in college basketball nor would we ever be the smartest people in a class of Princetonians, but we learned how to compete and give our best. It has been extremely gratifying to see the lessons learned on the basketball court at Princeton pay dividends throughout players' lives.

I was very fortunate to have teammates who understood what it took to win. Coach Carril required them to give their best and they could always be counted on—both while we played at Princeton and in our lives since graduation.

People like Armond Hill, Barnes Hauptfuhrer, Mickey Steuerer, and Peter Molloy all taught us what it meant to be a Princeton basketball player. My classmates including Billy Omeltchenko, Bob Kleinert, Rich Rizzuto, Doug Snyder, and Rich Starsia all remain very good friends to this day.

Getting over Coach Carril's standard for performance was very challenging, and, perhaps, what helped us become closer as players and friends. Not everyone appreciated Coach's approach and several very good athletes found that they could not play for him. However, I have found that those who were tested every day in Jadwin Gym were well-prepared for the challenges life brings after graduation. At a minimum, we all knew how to give our best while getting yelled at under pressure and we understood how to perform while being criticized.

Of course, Coach relaxed once the season was over. I can still remember that he came to Doug Snyder's and my room after our loss in the Palestra to Kentucky in the NCAA tournament. Kentucky won the national tournament in 1978. While enjoying a beer or two, he continually played *Isn't She Lovely*, a song from Stevie Wonder's album *Songs From the Key of Life*, which had been purchased by our roommate early that week. This was back in the day of vinyl records and turntables, and I know that the record was never the same after that evening.

There was no team banquet or official recognition of individual achievements during my days as a player, but we had an annual picnic in the spring with terrific food, karaoke, and more than a little beer. It was great fun. We celebrated the past year and valued the contributions of everyone involved with the team. The party consisted of the players, the coaches, and friends who made the season special. I was fortunate to have success as a player at Princeton, but I learned of the awards and honors I received either through *The Daily Princetonian* or from the material in the letter-size envelope given to me by Phil Langan, our sports information director, at the end of the year. While individual honors were certainly nice, Coach continually emphasized that the overall results achieved by the team were what really mattered.

I have used the phrase "you're right, but you're wrong" many times with my kids, as well as in business situations. I have often said that while we might be executing on our strategic plan, the question is whether the proposed action will be successful in today's marketplace. In other situations I have asked whether our human resource development strategy was the best way to maximize team performance. The message was to keep your eyes open, to listen, and to modify your approach based on what it would take to win.

I have had many opportunities to pass these lessons on to the next generation as the coach of my kid's travel soccer and AAU basketball teams.

While at the core the implemented action plan might be consistent with the guiding principles of the business or team, ultimately it is about winning and satisfying the needs of those who count on you while staying true to yourself and what is important.

Playing for Coach was tough. Everyone had to deal with the intense scrutiny of the "little Spaniard." For those who learned the lessons taught on the floor in Jadwin, however, I have continued to hear many stories about how we were well-prepared to face the challenges and adversity that eventually come later in life. These are lessons that were learned not only by my teammates but also are common themes whenever players from the Pete Carril era get together.

At this point in my life, I think I will stick to my three phrases. I will always do the best that I can. I will aspire to be someone who can be counted on. And I will be sensitive to a situation where you can be right about the game plan but wrong about maximizing your chances of winning.

I have many people to thank for those lessons, and Coach is one of them.

CHAPTER 15

Bill Omeltchenko '78

Winning Breeds Friendship

Coach used this phrase as an inspiration to work hard and play to win. Practices focused on achieving perfection in every drill, all the time. He would say "the pass is off" even if it was six inches too high, too low, or to the side. It had to be received squarely in the chest since it would give your teammate an easier setup to shoot or make a play.

The offense was predicated on taking what the defense gave you. If the flow to the right side was denied, then everyone knew what to do when we had to go the other way.

Foul-shooting contests after practice would reward the shooter with two points for a swish, one point for a make, and zero for a miss. The idea of making the foul shot was not enough to win. The perfect foul shot was the goal.

Scrimmages were extremely competitive and difficult because everyone knew what the other was going to do. Execution was critical in these scrimmages and often was more difficult to achieve than playing in a game against an opponent who could not defend every move.

When you had 12 people working hard every day, giving maximum effort, and driving each other to perfection, the result was mutual respect and appreciation of the sacrifice involved. Talent was not always the difference-maker. The ability to make those around you better certainly was.

With this as a backdrop, the members of the sophomore class who were together through our senior year developed a bond that could not be broken. We won the Ivy League title and the automatic NCAA bid that came with it during our sophomore and junior years. Frank Sowinski, Rich Starsia, Rich Rizzuto, Bob Kleinert, Doug Snyder, and I shared in the victories and success of those two years. Our senior year was very unfortunate in that we ended 17-9, with eight losses by a total of 21 points. Unlucky circumstances, bad bounces, short by inches from victory all dealt us some bad hands.

Coach would often pull me aside and want to know why we were not at each other's throats with each loss. I told him it was his fault. The bond was based on our trust that each of us did our very best in every practice and in every game. The friendship that was established when we walked on campus as 18-year-old freshmen endures today, as we have made that same effort to stay close with each other even as our families have grown and relationships evolved. When we get together a few times a year, it is not a reunion but rather a part of who we are and how we are defined.

Paying It Forward

I am not sure if Coach actually used this phrase, but it certainly resonates with the basketball program. He would make sure that the upperclassmen took the rookies under their wings, provided guidance, taught them nuances of playing on the team, and made sure they were managing the transition from high school to college. Barnes Hauptfuhrer, Bob Slaughter, Mickey Steuerer, Peter Molloy, and Armond Hill were our mentors and have continued to be our friends ever since. They were all leaders with different ways of exhibiting that trait. I found it astounding that they would always look to teach and guide us in ways that made us better players and more importantly better people—although I doubt that they looked at it that way at that time.

We tried to do the same with those who came after us—Bobby Roma, Johnny Lewis, Johnny Rogers, Steve Mills, Dave Blatt, Roger Schmidt, Jon Dunlay, Timmy Olah, Tony Trani, and others. The shared experience as basketball players at Princeton can all be traced to Coach and the program he ran.

Hanging Out with Coach

There were certain rules during the season that we all observed. Coach would not come to the bars that we frequented, and we would not go to Andy's Tavern, his place of choice. Since the drinking age was 18 at the time, it was normal to have an occasional beer. But once the season was over Coach would join us at some of our events and would basically take over the song selection.

His listening tastes reflected his practices. Repetition made for perfection. So, we listened to Stevie Wonder's *Isn't She Lovely* and Al Stewart's *Year of the Cat* for hours on end. No other songs were allowed.

Recruiting the Parents

Coach had come to one of my high school games and still wanted me to come to Princeton. He made arrangements to come to my house for dinner. My mother was part Spanish, and I was born in Madrid, so there was a connection with Coach's Spanish heritage.

My mom wanted to impress Coach as well, so she made her

signature dish—paella. Coach had three helpings during dinner, which is extraordinary for a man of his size. When it came time for a dessert of flan and berries, Coach asked for a fourth helping of paella.

Needless to say, he won my parents over. I had no choice but to come to Princeton!

Coach Carril as a high school senior at Liberty High School in Bethlehem, Pa. Coach is number 17; his coach, Joe (Pickles) Preletz, is immediately to Coach's left.

Coach in his Lafayette uniform

Coach with Butch van Breda Kolff, bowtie, beer, and coffee

Coach's first Princeton team (1967-68); captain, Joe Heiser (Nitro Joe) front and center

Coach with Chris Thomforde. (Coach "inherited" Chris from Butch van Breda Kolff's outstanding 1966-67 team; Chris was a Second Team All-American that year and appeared on the cover of *Sports Illustrated* on Feb. 27, 1967).

Coach, in 1968, with future pros John Hummer and Geoff Petrie, who were dubbed part of "Princeton's All-Pro frontline" by a local newspaper. Coach brought the article to practice, shook it, queried, "All-Pro… All-Pro?" Then, he stated, "More like All-Prophylactic." (He never missed an opportunity for a direct frontal assault.)

Geoff Petrie driving past Columbia star, Heyward Dotson. Princeton, Columbia, and Penn were each top-10 teams nationally between 1968 and 1972. It was an extraordinary time for Ivy League basketball. In 1968-69, despite such stiff intra-league competition, Princeton became the first team to go undefeated in Ivy League play.

The Players' Book

Coach coaching...

Pete Carril Quotes:

- Coaching is preparation.
- A coach's job is to put his team where it can function effectively and win.
- Coaches win practices, players win games.
- I believe the objective of coaching is winning with integrity.

Coach pleading his case

Coach pleading his case… a little more forcefully

Coach in a foul mood...

Pete Carril Quotes:
- The quality of the pass leads directly to the quality of the shot.
- Get the kids to understand that they shouldn't worry about who makes the shot, only whether or not the shot is made.
- A player's ability to rebound is inversely proportional to the distance between where he was born and the nearest railroad tracks.

Coach in front of Jadwin Gym

The Players' Book

Coach with Georgie Buc. Coach never forgot the contributions of Jadwin custodian George Boccanfuso, and he made sure that his players never forgot them either.

Coach in Madison Square Garden after capturing the 1975 NIT championship

Co-captains (Armond Hill and Mickey Steuerer) holding the NIT trophy aloft

Coach lights up his trademark cigar

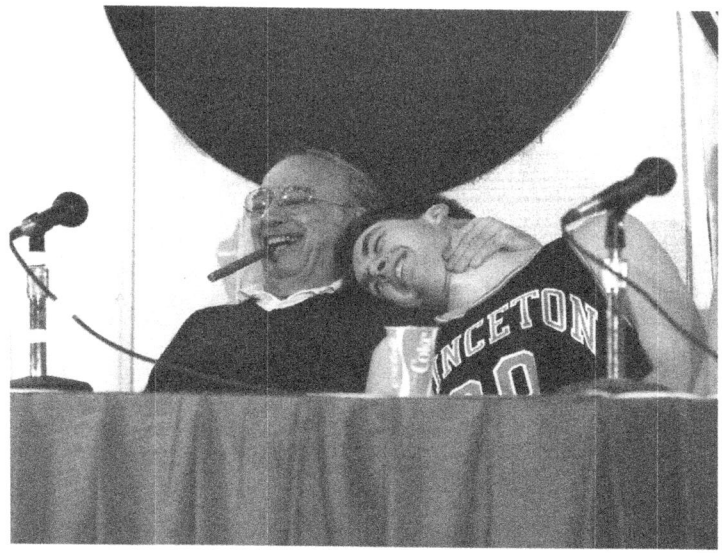

Coach with Kit Mueller… and his cigar

Coach during the 1996 NCAA game versus UCLA—his final win

The happy camper post game with CBS' Andrea Joyce

Chris Thomforde with Coach and Coach's longtime friend, Bill Werpehowski

The 50-year reunion of the first team to go undefeated in Ivy League play (Princeton 1968-69)

Geoff Petrie and Bill Sickler with Coach in his final year

John Hummer, John Arbogast, and Dom Michel with Coach in his final year

Pete Carril Quotes:
- The sterner the discipline, the greater the devotion.
- If you yell at a kid and he gets mad at you, you've lost him. If you yell at a kid and he gets mad at himself, then you have something.
- Once practice starts, we work hard, and that's the best conditioning there is. Everything counts. Every little thing counts. Run hard, play hard, go after the ball hard, guard hard. If you play soft (what I call signing a 'non-aggression pact' with your teammates), you won't ever get into shape.

Barnes Hauptfuhrer, Armond Hill, Peter Molloy, and Mickey Steuerer with Coach Carril (1976)

Same cast of characters in 2021 with Coach

Pete Carril Quote:
- Everybody makes such a big deal today about team play because there's such a scarcity of it. Greed is a reason. You have to understand the influence of greed. A player has to be selfish in the pursuit of the development of his skills, but he cannot be selfish when it comes time to blend them in with what's good for his team.

On Sept. 30, 2022, more than 90 former players and managers gathered in Jadwin Gym to celebrate the life and legacy of Coach Pete Carril.

Pete Carril Quotes:
- The two ingredients to success in basketball are playing hard and playing intelligently.
- The strength of my Princeton teams has always been attitude, intelligence, and discipline.
- I don't recruit players who are nasty to their parents. I look for players who realize the world doesn't revolve around them.
- In a team sport like basketball, every time you help somebody else, you help yourself.
- If you think you are working hard, you can work harder. If you think you are doing enough, there is more that you can do. No one really ever exhausts his full potential.
- Winning takes character. Workers get the most out of themselves. When a body has limited talent, it must master all its resources of character to overcome adversity.

CHAPTER 16

John Rogers '80

Coach Carril changed my life.

I remember calling Coach ahead of my first official visit to Princeton. Instead of calling the athletic department, I was advised to dial Andy's Tavern, and Coach promptly came to the phone. Calling the local bar to reach him was unusual but fitting as a first introduction to the man who would have such a big impact on all of us.

I have vivid memories of my first visit to campus. Assistant Coach Bob Dukiet picked up my father and me at the airport and brought us straight to Jadwin Gym to meet my host Bob Slaughter '78, who was a junior on that year's Princeton team. I can remember walking around that day and falling in love with the campus, particularly Jadwin.

My father was orphaned at 12 and later became one of the original Tuskegee Airmen, flying more than a hundred missions during World War II. Coach took to him pretty quickly, starting at dinner that night, as they both had a penchant for communicating directly and honestly. Coach also appreciated that my dad did not have a three-car garage. In fact, he had no garage at all! Coach did not gravitate to those who grew up overly privileged, "the type with multiple car garages," as he explained. That night I had no conception of

Coach's temperament, nor did I have any idea that he would become the best teacher that I would ever have (by far). All I knew at the time was that he was a unique personality with an extraordinary basketball mind.

After an intense freshman year playing under a great coach, Tony Relvas, I desperately wanted to make the team my sophomore year. I was very fortunate to do so and be named the 15th man on the 15-man team. Coach Carril once told me I was "legally blind and that nobody wanted to play with me because I could not see." He made it very clear that he only kept me around because I worked so hard. Fast forward to the end of my junior year. After being the last man on the bench, I finally had the opportunity to play, and I started in the last three games of the season. After the game, local sportswriters asked why I had not played more. Coach responded, "If Johnny Rogers could pass or dribble a little bit, he could have been playing a long time ago." While his comments rarely let up and were certainly not easy to absorb at the time, his direct and unapologetic honesty played a major role in shaping me to be the person I am today.

It took a couple of years to start to fully realize the enormous, positive impact that Coach had on me. In particular, he instilled two distinct lessons that completely transformed the way I thought about teamwork and leadership.

The first lesson is to have a team-first mentality. This is a true staple of Princeton basketball, and something that Coach continually emphasized. This approach had a huge influence on how I operate in and view collaborative environments. As an only child, I had been accustomed to prioritizing myself and my own success. Coach taught us to put our teammates first and do everything possible to make their lives easier. It was truly a transformative experience for me, and one that sparked a new level of joy in playing.

I am reminded of the importance of teamwork every day at Ariel Investments, the firm that I founded in 1983, where it is a core value of our culture. Embracing this concept also led to me meeting my co-CEO, Mellody Hobson '91. Following graduation, I brought my love of prioritizing teammates back with me to Chicago, where I joined a number of teams through boards and other volunteer opportunities. One of the teams I joined was the Princeton Schools Committee, where I worked hard to assist alumni interviewers to ensure that all prospective students from Chicago were interviewed. As part of this effort, I started a program to encourage prospective minority students to consider Princeton. One year, we held a dinner at the Chicago Yacht Club to celebrate admitted students and, in some cases, guide them toward black and orange. One of these students was Mellody. Richard Missner '65 had overheard her mentioning to another prospective student that she was only in attendance out of courtesy to me and for the free meal. Apparently, she had already decided to attend Harvard.

After hearing this, Richard managed to switch seats to sit beside Mellody, a couple seats down from Kit Mueller '91, and help her at least start thinking about Princeton. Now that we had neutralized Mellody, we had to find a way to sway her toward Princeton. Richard realized that Bill Bradley '65, one of Richard's classmates, was passing through town, and Bill was selflessly willing to spend some time with Mellody over breakfast. Of course, Bill was the perfect person to close the deal and convinced her to come to Princeton. By volunteering to help the Schools Committee team, I was afforded the opportunity to meet Mellody, my future MVP at Ariel. To me, this was proof that all things come back to Princeton basketball and the core value of teamwork that Coach had instilled in us.

The second of the vital lessons Coach taught us was the value of precision. As we all know, he obsessed over making sure that every pass was right on target and that the angle of every cut was exact. This no-plays-off-mentality gave us an edge and continues to be an advantage as we exercise discipline and encourage one another at Ariel to do things the right way, no matter the environment in which we find ourselves. In an inherently volatile industry, it is important to keep your wits about you and live through the inevitable, dramatic ups and downs of the stock market. Because Coach pounded home these values so forcefully, we began to internalize them in a meaningful way.

Some of my best memories with Coach have come over the last 40 or so years after graduating. I have been fortunate to spend time with him at Reunions, as well as at some games and practices. For a time, I was also his unofficial chauffeur when he would come to Chicago for periodic recruiting visits. Other than the fear of getting us lost somewhere in suburban Chicago, I truly treasured those one-one-one car rides. I even found myself noting the garage size outside recruits' homes!

Years ago, in honor of Coach and his importance in my life, I named my primary conference room at Ariel the Pete Carril Room. I filled it with all things Princeton, including multiple photos of him, all reinforcing the core Ariel values he inspired—teamwork and precision. I host most of my meetings in this special room and could not have been prouder when President-elect Barack Obama used the Pete Carril Room as his interim transition office for three days in November 2008 while forming his administration. The room serves as a reminder of how fortunate I am to be part of the Princeton basketball family.

Special thanks to Ariel summer intern, Tosan Evbuomwan '23 for his help on this chapter.

CHAPTER 17

Steve Mills '81

Lessons Learned Between the Lines

When I was 17, I took my official visit to Princeton. Most of my interactions up to that point had been with coach Bob Dukiet. He was the prototypical college basketball recruiter. I would see him at basketball camps and many of my high school games. He was very different from Coach Carril. He was tall and a very cool dude. I was immediately comfortable with him and could tell that he was a good player during his time.

After touring the campus with coach Dukiet it was time to go to Jadwin Gym to meet with Coach Carril. When I walked into Jadwin, I was awestruck by its sheer size and the number of seats. I just stood there and envisioned playing in front of 7,000 people for an important game. It also made me think of Brian Taylor and Armond Hill because they were both part of my recruiting process. My father was raised in New Jersey, and he and my uncles could talk all day about the Taylor brothers from Perth Amboy, N.J. Growing up in Long Island I was fortunate enough to watch Brian when he played for the Nets. Armond Hill was playing for the Atlanta Hawks, and he invited me to a game at Madison Square

Garden. Over dinner he told me how great the basketball was at Princeton but also warned me of the academic rigors, especially writing a senior thesis.

As I sat in Coach Carril's office, he turned on his infamous film projector and we watched Brian Taylor dart all over the court and score with ease. Coach told me that this is how he envisioned me playing. In hindsight that was very funny because I never was able to get the team to play at that pace.

After the film session Coach took me down to the court. We discussed the other players he was recruiting as part of my class. It was exciting to hear him talk about Dave Blatt, Marty Mannion, and Randy Melville. At some point just the two of us walked out to center court. He looked at me and said, "Stevie, if you choose to come to Princeton, you have a chance to be a very good player. What I need you to do is look at the four lines surrounding the court—the baselines and the sidelines."

He described this area as the Great Revealer of Character. He said in life you can usually fool people into thinking that you are something that you really are not. He said that in one's day-to-day existence, it is quite easy to be phony. He stressed that between these four lines your true character is revealed, especially to your teammates, to your coaches, and even sometimes to the fans. If you are selfish, if you are not tough enough, if you take shortcuts, we all see it and know it.

He told me if I came to Princeton, I would be given the opportunity to confront my weaknesses. He asked me to think of it as looking in the mirror and having two choices. Either accept your flaws or acknowledge them and commit to doing everything in your power to confront them and develop a corrective game plan.

After a few moments of complete silence, he took a puff of his cigar and said those would be my choices to make. But he said if I were the kind of person who chose the first option and accepted my flaws, playing for him and attending Princeton would not be my best choice.

I ultimately chose Princeton because my parents raised me to value academics as much as basketball. I also believed in myself as a player and looked forward to proving that I was up to his challenge. It was also obvious to me that we were going to win a lot of games, play nationally-ranked teams, and if I were good enough to play in the NBA, I would be able to prove it at Jadwin.

Over the years, this message resonated with me very deeply and is why I feel that playing basketball at Princeton for Coach Carril changed the trajectory of my life. His brutally honest nature, his demand for attention to detail, and his commitment to bringing out your best are things that will never be forgotten. These principles have impacted and guided me through every aspect of my personal life and career.

In an odd way, my life has been profoundly shaped by two men that share a place in the Naismith Basketball Hall of Fame: Coach Carril and NBA Commissioner David Stern. In 1984, David offered me my first job at the NBA, just three months after he had become commissioner. He said that he was intrigued by me, because as a basketball player, I made one of the most complex decisions a young man could make: I chose to play at Princeton with very rigorous academic demands. As an alumnus of Rutgers University, he also knew that I chose to play for a coach who held me and my teammates to an even higher standard.

To the casual observer, Coach and the Commissioner could not have been more different as people. I fortunately had a front row seat to see that their demand for critical thinking, hard work, and attention to detail are the threads that weave them together in my mind and in my heart. I do not think that I would have been able to succeed in the demanding world of David Stern's NBA, where I worked for 16 years becoming senior vice-present of basketball and player development before taking on new roles and challenges for the Madison Square Garden organization, Magic Johnson Enterprises, and ultimately becoming general manager and president of the NBA's New York Knicks, had it not been for the lessons I learned in Jadwin Gym under the eye of Coach Carril.

It all comes back to the lessons you learn between the lines. Thank you, Coach.

CHAPTER 18

Marty Mannion '81

Much like a character from Dante's *Inferno*, I had an interesting start to my basketball experience at Princeton. "You can't dribble, you can't guard anyone, and you're legally blind." ("Abandon hope all ye who enter here.") So began my recruiting trip to become a Princeton basketball player.

As I sat in Coach Carril's office, I listened as one of the top coaches in all of college basketball reviewed my skills. It was not exactly the assessment I was hoping for as I had just completed a season leading all New York City Catholic School players in scoring. As I would later come to learn, that was not one of the accomplishments that made you a great player. Coach Carril had just issued his first challenge. Growing up in a fifth-floor tenement in the Bronx with a single mother, I had often heard I could not accomplish certain things, and this was just another challenge being issued by someone I wanted to impress. It was the perfect thing for me to hear (and, in hindsight, largely accurate).

Let me start by saying that my basketball career was not what I (or anyone who has ever played) had hoped for. I entered Princeton with six other recruits (we were the last class to be required to play freshman basketball). Looking back, we had some success but always seemed to find a way to become not quite the dominant team that we had all hoped. We had talent with Steve Mills, Randy Melville, and Dave Blatt all becoming All-Ivy players during their careers. Freshman year we started 9-1 only to lose the next seven games by a combined 10 points. Sophomore year was the transition year from the great teams of Frank Sowinski and Billy Omeltchenko, and the team struggled (with Penn making an appearance in the Final Four). Junior year we tied for the league title only to lose a playoff game by one to Penn. Finally, senior year, we again tied for the title with Penn and then won the playoff game to qualify for the NCAA tournament. However, we always had a bit of a feeling that we had not lived up to the standard of prior Princeton classes. "We used to beat Notre Dame, Villanova, St. John's, and now we can't beat St. Mary's School for the Blind!" was a common refrain we would hear during practice.

Playing for Coach Carril was part psychology and part sociology seminar. He was incredibly good at recruiting players who had something to prove and wanted to play at the highest level. Then began the long process of molding us into a team, with lessons that later served me well in life.

My first lesson was the level of preparation required to succeed. We never went into a game not knowing what to expect the other team would do and how to combat it. After two days of practice, we knew their tendencies and how to counteract them. And to react improperly during a game was as close to a mortal sin as one could imagine. We were playing Louisville our junior year (the Cardinals subsequently won the national championship), and Coach had warned us of their propensity to run a play off of the opening tap. He basically told us to not worry about winning the tap, but to make sure we got back and set our defense. Unfortunately, we did not listen, and they ran a play and dunked the ball two seconds into the game. Timeout. After questioning whether anyone on the court for us had ever scored above 10 on an IQ test, he went and sat up in the stands. We came into halftime with a lead, largely because we were so prepared for their offense that they had a hard time scoring after that play.

The second lesson was that you may succeed if you work hard, but you will not succeed if you do not. I have found in my professional career this is often the hardest thing for people to accept. Working hard does not guarantee success, but slacking off guarantees failure. You can work around talent deficiencies; you cannot work around effort deficiencies. Often, Coach tied effort to background. Princeton in the 1970s was very different from Princeton today, and athletes from less affluent backgrounds often had a harder time fitting into the school. Coach would often use this fact as a rallying cry for his players who, for the most part, came from lower- and middle-income families. You knew you or one of your teammates were in trouble if he accused you of having a "three-car garage" or the words "day," "prep," or "academy" were in your high school's name. In Coach's world, he wanted players who *had* to win, not who wanted to win. And while over my career I have come to believe that where you come from economically is not the single driving force to success, it does focus your effort. There are numerous athletes from successful families who have this drive and there are athletes from poor backgrounds who do not, but the image of the athlete who has a certain drive to improve because he/she has limited options is what Coach was looking for.

Third lesson from playing for Coach is that there a difference between being a teammate and being a coach. In my career, I would run into many successful Princeton players, and we were always happy to see each other and catch up. There is a brotherhood there that you can attribute directly to the way Coach handled the team. It was always us against the opponent. It was often us against Coach. (As professor Marvin Bressler once said, "He says you are no good because he wants for you to prove him wrong.") But it was never teammate versus teammate. I remember one practice where the second team (which I had the pleasure of being on for my career) was playing defense for over an hour because the offense was not being run to Coach's specifications. A few times one of my teammates did not box out his player, and his player essentially outjumped me for the ball (which was not hard to do). I finally decided to tell my teammate I was tired of him not doing his job (I may have used more colorful language), and to my surprise I found myself sitting on the bench. Coach later told me it was not my job to embarrass my teammate; it was his job to coach him. It was O.K. for me to have high expectations for all my teammates, but it was not my job to be critical in front of my teammates.

The fourth lesson from my career is the need for feedback. No one ever thought that they did not know exactly what Coach was thinking. I remember my sophomore year we were at Columbia and losing by double digits at halftime. Coach decided to shake things up and started John Rogers and me in the backcourt. We led a spirited comeback (got the score to within one, only to still lose the game). John and I had acquitted ourselves decently, but a loss is a loss. Coach walked into the locker room and said, "Two of the worst players I have ever had just acted like they could play tonight." Not exactly what John or I was hoping for, which gets me to another life lesson: feedback is critical. You need to know where you stand, and Coach was great at that. He sometimes stepped over the line and made the attacks too personal (Dave Blatt suffered unfairly during his four years) or unfixable (I remember Mark Valderas being told he was slow because his feet were too big—kind of hard to address).

However, if you look at all the great success stories out there, there is always a question of whether someone stepped over the line. Was Steve Jobs too tough? Was Michael Jordan too competitive? Sometimes when you are driving to do the impossible, you end up crossing the line. I just always tried to be aware of when the line was approaching. And many times, Coach was deadly accurate on what you had to fix.

There was one amazing thing I did observe with Coach's feedback. He was incredibly tough and exacting with his players, but you never felt like you were not going to win if you performed to his standards. I had a good friend who played for Bobby Knight and we were telling competing stories one night. Someone observed how it must have been hard to play for Coach Knight and Coach Carril. His response was spot on: "We won, and he always made us believe we could win." Sounds funny when I think about some of the trials and challenges Coach laid in front of us, but you always knew he believed he could mold us into a unit that could compete and win against anybody.

I look back at my business career and realize that playing for Coach made me tougher, more prepared, and more willing to accept feedback to improve. He was a true innovator in the game of basketball, but he was old school when it came to motivating his players. Most players today would be challenged to respond to Coach's tactics, but I know I can thank him for preparing me for the challenges that I faced throughout my career. No one was tougher, but no one wanted me to succeed more.

CHAPTER 19

Craig Robinson '83

Upon being asked to participate in this project, I immediately thought about all of the funny and tough things Coach Carril said to his players over the years. No one was immune to his acerbic tongue and his biting wit. He truly motivated by character assassination. I could offer some examples here, but these stories have been chronicled and many will probably be retold in this tome.

The stories I would like to share are about a side of Coach that many people did not get to see. In his own way, he could be thoughtful and inspiring. I remember a time when I went to see him in Sacramento where he was an assistant coach for the Kings. I expected to find him in his office, drawing up sets, or puffing a cigar while waxing poetic on how NBA players "couldn't see." When I got to the gym, I saw a group of about six players huddled near the scorer's table laughing while listening to the familiar voice of Pete Carril. They called him Coachie, a name for which I tried to uncover the reason. It seems that endearing moniker was given to him by a player, maybe Hedo Turkoglu. Coach introduced me to the Kings players as one of his former players, and I immediately became the focus of their attention. The players wanted to hear about what Coach was like, what his practices were like, and how good our teams were.

None of them asked me to share the biting criticisms that they had heard about because they had not heard about them. I was astounded by their care for and attention to him in every interaction. I saw a different side to his ability to relate to players.

We rarely saw that side of Coach. I say rarely because there were few people who could bring out the best in Pete Carril, especially when his players were around. One of them was my dad, Fraser Robinson. My dad was a hard-working family man who respected coaches, raised his children with loving discipline, and taught them to be workers. He provided us with a modest apartment, three square meals a day, and focused on education despite not being a college graduate himself. My dad did all this while being disabled. He had been diagnosed with MS and went to work every day at the Chicago Water Department on crutches, dragging legs that had long ago betrayed him.

When Coach came to our modest apartment for a home visit, he and my dad hit it off. Coach talked to him more than he talked to me. He seemed eerily connected to my dad's upbringing. Looking back, I think they both felt they were cut from the same cloth—hard-working, disciplined, and from the wrong side of the tracks. (Although if Coach had known my dad was really Fraser Robinson III, he never would have walked through the door.) They bonded over the fact that I was not "that good" and needed to be pushed to get better. Coach made a huge impression on my dad, which made a huge impression on me. That is because my dad was my hero. I worshipped everything about him. He was my first coach, my fairest critic, my mentor, and I loved him very much. When Coach came to my house and spent time with him, making him the focal point of my recruitment, I thought that was the best thing anyone had ever done for my dad. That made me think, this guy cannot be that bad.

Once I got to Princeton, Coach's admiration for my dad did not spare me from his sharp tongue. I was subjected to the same treatment as everyone else. My most oft-used nickname was Grandfather

Time. Teammate Neil Christel was Father Time. He used to point out my physical deficiencies on a daily basis by stopping practice and making me do push-ups and arm circles on the spot. Once, when our team was in Chicago's O'Hare Airport standing at the departure gate with players from the University of Illinois headed to Hawaii for a tournament, he compared my less-than-stellar athletic figure to my good friend from Chicago (Eddie Johnson), who played for the Illini and was quite athletic-looking. Coach said something like, "You sure don't look like most of the players from the South Side of Chicago."

I cannot remember many parents being allowed to watch practice. Coach found out my dad was coming to campus, which he did once a year. He invited him to come watch practice. That raised a red flag in my mind, as I thought nothing good can come from that. As it turns out, my dad being at practice was the best thing that could happen to the team. We had never seen Coach so docile, outwardly. I say outwardly because my teammate, Gordon Enderle, reminded me that Coach managed to say to him quietly, "Are you going to guard that guy?" ("That guy" was Marty Mannion, who was cut up due to a fight he had been in the night before, and Gordon was taking it easy on him. Another story).

"Am I going to have to yell at you when Craig's dad is here?" Coach asked.

Not many people know that side of Coach. I sometimes wonder if Coach even knew that side of himself. While I got my share of Coach's ire, I was also the beneficiary of the time he was willing to work with me individually to get better. I found myself working harder to please him just as I did with my dad. Most of us worked to keep his wrath aimed at someone else. I found myself craving any small inkling of a compliment. Once you got one, you held on to it like a drowning man holds onto a life preserver. But deep down, I could not be too upset with the things he said to me, because I knew Coach respected me—because he respected my dad.

CHAPTER 20

Kevin Mullin '84

At a New Jersey high school state tournament game my senior year (1980), future Hall of Fame coach Pete Carril came to scout me. In his mind, I was a so-so player competing in a lousy league. I might be more interested in playing tennis at Princeton than basketball anyway. So, I was a very marginal prospect in his mind.

I know he was not expecting to see much because, when he was scouting me, he laid down sideways on the bleachers while still managing to smoke his cigar. But when I finished the first half with 26 points, he sat up. At halftime, our locker room was buzzing with excitement. In the second-half, my teammates made an effort to get me the ball. When the final horn sounded, I had poured in a career-high 50 points and moved up on Carril's list of recruiting prospects.

When I first met Coach in the basketball office, he did something unexpected. He changed my name from "Kevin" to "Moon." *Moon Mullin* was his favorite syndicated comic strip, which ran as a daily and Sunday feature from 1923 to 1991. Most people in my life still call me Moon, and I just turned 60!

"Coach," I said. "I want to go to school here, and I have applied for early admission."

Carril looked at my SAT scores. "Moon, with those board scores, I believe you are applying for early rejection! There is a reason I call the admissions office Heartbreak Hotel!"

"Moon, I saw you score 50 points and I still don't know if I want you," he continued. "You're too skinny to be any good, you can't dribble with your left hand, you can't pass, you can't defend, and you don't understand anything about the game." Then he added, "But you can shoot, and I can't teach that. I see something inside of you. You really want to be a player here, don't you?"

"Yes sir!"

"If you work hard," Coach said, "I believe that you have a shot at making the varsity and being a player here someday." Carril commanded my respect from day one because he was willing to take a chance on me. I was willing to work very hard to prove he was right.

During one practice at Princeton, Coach was irate over a game we had lost the previous night. At the very end of the game, the other team's forward, built like a Greek God, came barreling down the lane like LeBron James. He was going full speed ahead, and two of our defenders (I was one of them) parted like the Red Sea. The forward thunder-dunked with one hand to put us down two points with only seven seconds left. Our half-court desperation shot to tie the game clanked off the front of the rim for a tough loss. Carril was on the sideline pulling out his hair, throwing his rolled-up program into the crowd, stomping his feet, with an expression on his face as if his heart was being ripped out of his chest. He was screaming at the top of his lungs. "We had to have that charge!"

The next day in practice, instead of getting our Yo! Yo! Yo! down-the-line talk, he told us to line up underneath the basket. Coach was only 5' 6" and looked older than his years, but he had the heart of a lion. He told the first player in line to walk up to the foul line as Coach stood at half-court. He told my teammate to run at him as fast as he could and run into his chest. Coach was pushed backwards but maintained his footing. The next player at full speed, ran through Coach and he was catapulted backwards. His back, neck, and head whiplashed against the hardwood floor. He got up and yelled, "AGAIN!" He repeated this three more times. From that moment on, there was no more parting of the Red Sea by me or my teammates. For the rest of the season, we all stepped up, stepped in, and tried our best to take charges. In teaching us courage, Coach led by example.

The thing I did not do well was defend. In a summer league game, I guarded Brian Warrick, a future NBA player for the Washington Bullets. Coach told me that he got a call from a friend who saw me play. The good news was that I scored 42, but the bad news is that I guarded Warrick, who had 44.

Coach yelled at me. "Moon! That's a f##king negative-two contribution!"

My senior year, after we had won three Ivy titles, Coach talked to us in the locker room.

"After the opening weekend of our season, when we went 0-2, I couldn't even get out of bed. For you guys to come back from that type of adversity and win this thing, I'd have to say that this is the toughest and the most rewarding season that I have ever had as a coach. We were supposed to have a losing season and here we are—champions!"

After the game, while we made a big rugby pile at half-court, Carril did a belly-flop dive on top of the pile. I had never seen him that happy!

I scored 38 points in an NCAA tournament game at the Palestra in Philadelphia. After the game, Dick Vitale of ESPN's Sports Center said, "I just want to know one thing. I wonder if Lou Carnesecca called up Carril and said, 'Hey Petey, do you want to borrow Mullin?' Are you sure that wasn't Chris Mullin in that uniform? No that was Kevin. The kid was brilliant! He put on a super show, baby! One of the best individual performances I have seen all year."

Before our next tournament game against UNLV, Vitale continued,

"Hey, Petey! Why don't you call the co-ed, Brooke Shields, for some cheerleading on the sidelines? She can call her buddy, Michael Jackson, a little Thriller in the locker room. Princeton will be fired up to play!"

The next day, I headed to practice with a bounce in my step and a smile I could not hide. In our locker room in Caldwell Field House, my smile got even wider. Hanging in my locker were my practice jersey and shorts. My teammates had written Haverford College on pieces of athletic tape and covered up Princeton wherever it appeared. Coach used to say that I belonged at Haverford with the tennis crowd. My teammates congratulated me. As I stepped out onto the hardwood of Jadwin, Coach noticed my Haverford regalia and laughed, and laughed, and laughed. "Moon!" he yelled. "What are you doing?"

We had a tough loss to UNLV in the next round of the tournament. Howie Levy and Billy Ryan had great games. Billy was a major reason for my success at Princeton. We nicknamed him Bird after Larry Bird. He seemed to have eyes in the back of his head and could thread a pass to you anytime and anywhere. Billy still holds the all-time assist record at Princeton, and I was lucky to be on the receiving end of his passes.

In June 1984, I got a call from K.C. Jones, the head coach of the Boston Celtics, informing me that I had been drafted by them in the fourth round. They were the defending NBA champions with a starting five of Larry (The Legend) Bird, Kevin (The Torture Chamber) McHale, Robert (The Chief) Parish, Danny Ainge, and Dennis (DJ) Johnson. It was one of the best teams of all-time.

My first NBA pre-season game was against my beloved 76ers. We were getting dressed in the locker room. Some reporters were doing pre-game interviews. My locker was next to Quinn Buckner's. The reporter asked, "Quinn, what words of advice does a veteran player like yourself have for a rookie like Mullin before his first NBA game?"

Quinn looked at me and put his arm around my shoulder with the camera rolling. "Moon, when you get in the game and you are guarding Doc [Julius Erving], make sure you force him to his right."

"Yeah?" I said. "Why to his right?"

Quinn replied, "That way you'll be sure to make the highlight film!"

Although Red Auerbach and Coach spoke several times about the fact that I was performing at a very high level, I was the last player released from the team in favor of my roommate, Rick Carlisle. I went on to play overseas.

All of this happened because Coach saw something in my eyes. You want to work hard for a Coach like that, someone who believes in you. Thanks, Coach Carril!

—Moon

CHAPTER 21

Howard Levy '85

*"Dear Impossible Dream,
You can't run, you can't jump, you get tired.... But there's something about you I like."*

The above is not a direct quote but a fair summary of Coach's recruiting pitch to me. Coach first saw me as a ninth or 10th grader at the Pocono Mountain Basketball Camp run by coaches Bill Foster and Harry Litwak, and while I thought I was a good player, Coach saw something else. He listed the above-mentioned flaws again and again, but always closed with an optimistic note that he saw something in my character that would allow me to overcome these deficiencies. In a nod to Don Quixote and his Spanish heritage, Coach nicknamed me The Impossible Dream.

Coach arranged to visit my home in Suffern, N.Y. My father Syd, an old school NYC basketball player, was generally a stoic guy, but I could tell he was excited. He asked his buddy Les Yellin (also a friend of Coach's) what kind of beer Coach liked. At the time, I think it was Miller Lite. So Coach and my dad sat and talked and watched the 1981 NIT Final and drank some beer. I sat and listened, but it was pretty much as if I were not there. Soon afterwards, I participated in a high school all-star game attended by Coach and by Bob Weinhauer, who was the Penn coach at the time. I played just O.K., and the next day I was headed down to Princeton for my official visit. Coach analyzed the game and my performance and mentioned that Coach Weinhauer walked out of the gym before the game ended. I have no confirmation whether or not that was true (although years later, Coach Weinhauer tried to trade for me when I was playing for Phil Jackson in a minor pro league, the Continental Basketball Association).

In any event, the "you stink now but if you work hard I think you can be good" rap appealed to me, and I committed to Princeton on that visit. I could tell my dad was happy even though it meant loans and financial struggle to pay the $11,000 tuition. (Coach wrote in a letter to me, "If your dad decides to rob a bank, don't go with him.") Thus began one of the most important relationships of my life that has benefitted me in so many ways—educationally, spiritually, and practically—well beyond my four years as an undergrad at Princeton.

At Princeton I had a mostly upward, though by no means smooth, trajectory as a player. Coach would broadcast my progress to the team on a regular basis, from Impossible Dream to Improbable to Possible to Start Sucking! (Coach claimed that, when watching me in high school, another coach offered to perform oral sex on him if Coach were able to make me into a player—in six years! I do not know whether Coach cashed in on that bet, but on the day in practice when he got on his knees and yelled "Start Sucking!" to the rafters of Jadwin, I knew he was saying that I was ready to help the team win).

Playing for Coach was incredibly demanding, sometimes heartbreaking, but also important and rewarding. We believed that we were part of something special and that it was us against the world. That combination brought us together as teammates. As difficult as it was—four-hour practices were not uncommon, and character assaults were common—you knew you were not alone. If you were the object of Coach's wrath on Monday, it was likely to be one of your friends on Tuesday, and another one on Wednesday, so we would pick each other up while pointing out the absurdity of our situation, as so many of Coach's comments were perceptive, biting, highly personal, at times hurtful and, more often than not, unintentionally hilarious.

Compliments were rare and subtle ("You've got guts," "Not too bad, kid," "You can see") or not so subtle ("You're f##king the dog." "Your parents did a horrible job raising you!"). I think this comes down to Coach's world view that was more common then and almost nonexistent today. The things that Coach demanded of us—to strive for excellence, to pay attention to detail, to work as hard as you could, to be a good teammate—are what you are supposed to do, so why make a federal case about it? Today, this behavior is sadly considered extraordinary.

This became apparent to me when trying out for the Nets in 1985. Our training camp was at Princeton, and I had the benefit of Coach watching practice upstairs in Jadwin, yelling "Yoooooo!" every time I made a good play! I was struck by how easy it was. Of course, the competition was great and I was in shape, but the practices for the most part were not that hard physically (though I took a mean elbow to the face from Buck Williams during a drill) or mentally, as there was no yelling, no cursing, and no character assaults. We were commended for doing very ordinary things, and I do not think we were pushed very hard. Darryl Dawkins, who was a wonderful guy, probably never reached his potential because he was not pushed. On the rare occasions that he would run down the court, three coaches would exclaim "Way to run down the court, big fella!" (I thought to myself, that's a far cry from "He's f##king the dog!") I had some success playing against him as I knew that if I stayed on his good side, he would not try to crush me. I can only imagine how good he could have been if Coach had been able to work with him.

At Princeton, we would often hear about the previous generation of players—how great they were compared to us. Professor Bressler coined a term for that phenomenon: "retroactive sanctification." The generation before us had a lot of good players, including Billy Omeltchenko, Frank Sowinski, and Mickey Steuerer—great guys that we grew to hate because Coach made it clear that we were nothing compared to them. One time at practice, Coach said, "Mickey Steuerer could drink a case of beer and still kick your asses." On reflection as an adult, I realize that he was telling us that we needed to be at our best every day no matter what. At the time, our response was, "Well, f##k you Coach and f##k Mickey Steuerer, you want us to go drink a case of beer tonight? We'll drink a case of beer and see what happens in practice tomorrow!" During my junior and senior years, Brian Taylor and then Armond Hill came back to finish their degrees and practice with us. No retroactive sanctification there—they really were great and did kick our asses every day, whether or not we drank a case of beer the night before!

We had some good successes as a team and some great celebrations afterwards. Coach knew how hard he drove us and realized the importance of letting off a little steam, whether that meant a few cases of beer that magically appeared on the bus after a successful Ivy League road weekend or an impromptu party in Jadwin after returning from the NCAA tournament. After our 1984 NCAA tournament loss to UNLV in a hard-fought game, we somehow found a fair amount of beer in the "dry" town of Salt Lake City and had a great night celebrating a successful season. There was some extra beer, and Coach, not one to waste anything, told us to pack it up and bring it home. This is hard to believe, but several of us walked on the plane with pillowcases filled with cans of beer. The flight attendants were shocked and asked who was in charge of our group. When they told Coach what was going on, he feigned anger, saying we would be punished when we got back to Princeton. Needless to say, in Princeton we put the beers on ice and had another party.

After graduation, I played pro ball for a few years, which was a great but incredibly frustrating experience after my time at Princeton. On the positive side, I was well-prepared for the physical and mental demands—nothing we did approached the intensity of what we did at Princeton. However, with that came a level of frustration—the environment that Coach created at Princeton did not exist in the pros. The coaches cared less, did not pay as much attention in practice, and took little interest in the individual improvement of the players. As for the players, there was a lower level of commitment to winning and to team play—everyone was trying to "get theirs." Ultimately, the frustration got the best of me, and I knew it was time to move on. I note that as a coach I have always encouraged those players with opportunities to play professionally to do so for as long as possible because even though it is "not Princeton," it sure beats working.

After "retiring," I was a graduate assistant coach and law student at George Washington University. Playing for Coach was incredibly helpful in both endeavors—maybe even more so in school. The bulls##t detection instincts that Coach instilled helped me to do well and to avoid a lot of needless interactions and wasted time at school. The simplicity and logic with which Coach taught was incredibly helpful in framing arguments and in my writing. In 1990, my last year at GW, I got a call from Coach inviting me to accompany him on a trip to Israel to give a week of clinics to the Israeli Coaches Association. I quickly said yes, not knowing that this would be a trip that would change my life as, thanks to Coach, I met my wife on this trip.

A few other memories from that trip:

Coach, assisted by David Blatt and me, gave a week of talks and coaching sessions to about one hundred Israeli coaches of all levels. We had a team of good young players to help us and by the end of the week the team started to look like a Princeton team. Coach's overriding point the entire week was to "do in practice the things you do in games." After a week of two-a-day sessions with Coach, there was a final lecture given by a well-known Israeli coach to close out the event. While Coach, David and I watched this coach set things up—chairs, cones, ropes, tires—we looked at one another quizzically, wondering what would come next. We soon learned. The team we built all week was put through something I had never seen before—running around chairs, jumping over ropes, I cannot even remember what the tires were for—all while getting basketballs thrown at them and getting screamed at. The exact opposite of what we had spent a week preaching!

We went out for dinner almost every night with the three or four coaches that organized the clinic and we were soon accused of "trying to drink all the beer in the country."

Jerry Simon, a 1989 Penn graduate and a teammate of mine on the US team at the 1989 Maccabiah Games, was in Israel at the same time, trying to catch on with a professional team. He needed a place to stay for a few days. Coach invited him to sleep on the floor of our hotel room in the Tel Aviv Hilton. Jerry was stunned, to say the least, but accepted. Jerry was a terrific player, did a little bit of everything (he would have been really good at Princeton), but was not the most confident kid. In conversations with Coach, Jerry spoke about how good some of his teammates were.

Coach cut him off. "Jerry, those guys were O.K. But when we played Penn, you were the guy we had to stop."

I think this comment really helped Jerry's confidence, and ultimately he had a nice pro career in Israel.

Coach similarly played a huge role in my getting back into coaching after a few years away. I went to the 1996 Princeton-UCLA game with my teammate Dave Sawczuk, and we were part of the post-game celebration, hanging out drinking and laughing at the hotel with the coaching staff and a few others. At some point in the night, Coach Carril said, "Howie, you should come down and coach." Everyone laughed, but a week or two later, Bill Carmody, who had taken over from Coach after the 1996-97 season, asked if I would join the staff at Princeton.

Coach was around from time to time when he was not in Sacramento and it led to a lot of great conversations about basketball and about life. Once after a game I stormed into Conte's complaining about one of our players.

Coach responded, "He's young, Howie, just give him some time and he'll be O.K."

I stood up, turned around. "I think I must be at the wrong table." I didn't remember Coach as an overly-patient guy! It was good advice nonetheless.

He was a great resource for me later as the head coach of Mercer County Community College—some X and O stuff, but more about how best to handle the team and the individual players. He came around a few times and spoke to the team and was very complimentary, as he immediately understood the challenges that we faced at Mercer. His advice to me was invaluable.

One year we had a very good team led by a terrific lefty guard from Philadelphia named David Johnson. David had a difficult time getting to practice and I had to balance the desire to play him with enforcing appropriate behavior. In debating what to do, I turned to Coach. He offered some very practical advice.

"Don't stand too hard on your principles, Howie!"

Based on his advice, I was able to "punish him" in ways that did not hurt our team, and we took an undermanned team to the conference finals. David ultimately was appreciative, learned the right lessons, and moved on from Mercer to lead his next team, Lycoming College, to the NCAA D-III tournament while earning his four-year degree.

In our conversations, Coach expressed growing skepticism about the so-called Princeton offense, thinking that it had lost some of its effectiveness. I disagreed and told him that what had spread throughout the basketball world (thanks largely to what Coach was able to do with Sacramento) was rarely taught with the belief, passion, and attention to detail that he brought to it. Once something is given a name, it implies that it is done evolving. I cannot tell you the number of Princeton offense videos that I have seen that leave me screaming at the television. My view of the offense involves certain principles that are implemented differently depending on the talent you have and the opposition you are facing, and are taught with a high level of belief and attention to detail. I learned from Coach, and I am sure that it still holds true.

I will finish by talking about my relationship with Coach off the court. I considered him a friend, and we shared many moments, happy and sad, together. He played an integral role in my meeting my wife and has been an important figure in our lives ever since. Coach took a liking to my son, Lior, and enjoyed working with him and watching him play. He was so happy to hear of Lior's recent success in Israel. We have celebrated family events with Coach and the DiGregorio and Giles families. We had a nice tradition of celebrating Coach's birthday along with the birthdays of Lior, Zack (DiGregorio), and Christian (Giles), all of whom were born in June or July. It started with the boys' 21st birthdays six years ago and continued through Coach's 90th, when we had a socially-distanced barbecue in our backyard during the pandemic. It is hard to imagine where my life's journey would have taken me without Coach's influence, and I am grateful that he was able to see beyond my deficiencies as a 17-year-old. As he said in a letter that I dug up dated February 3, 1981: "With the kind of dedication that I believe is inside of you, you are going to be O.K." Thanks, Coach!

CHAPTER 22

Jeff Pagano '85

My journey with Coach Carril started after he saw me play at the Five Star Basketball Camp in Pittsburgh. Little did I know that my fateful performance that week in steamy Western Pennsylvania would change the course of my life. It did not take much for Coach to convince me to come to Princeton. I played my high school basketball in rural New York, outside of Buffalo, oftentimes in empty gyms in tiny farm towns. Coach told me that Princeton was the place for me and that we would play big-time teams and make it to the tournament, and I did not need anything more than that.

My career got off to an inauspicious start as the preseason physical uncovered a hernia. The week before the season started I landed in the Princeton Hospital. Fortunately, 18-year-olds heal quickly, and 10 days after my operation I was back on the court and ready to suit up for two big games back to back—BYU and Ohio State.

After a 39-38 Friday night loss to BYU, I got my first sense of what it was like to play major college basketball. My first start came in front of 19,512 fans in a holiday double-header at Madison Square Garden. We played Ohio State in the first game and Rutgers played North Carolina in the nightcap. We got off to a hot start and led the Buckeyes by eight at halftime. I was in awe of the arena, the fans, and OSU players as I went through the motions of our offense. It was at that point that fantasy met reality.

As we started the second-half, Coach yelled out "Knick Play," and I threw the ball cross-court. Soon-to-be-New-York-Knick Tony Campbell intercepted my careless pass, taking it the length of the court and dunking the ball while I sheepishly tried to stop him, ending the sloppy mess with a foul and a place on the bench with Coach two inches from my face shouting every possible profanity one could imagine. This experience haunted me for a long time as I replayed it in my mind's eye over and over again—the pass, the dunk, the foul, and the face-to-face humiliation of a coarse lecture in front of the sold-out crowd. Sadly, we went on to lose that game by four points. The game happened to be our last before a break for Christmas. Prior to departing the Garden, Coach decided to give each of us a progress report. My feedback was concise: "11, you are nothing but a roly-poly fat f##king meatball. You better go home and come back here in shape to play."

We struggled my freshman year and ended the season with a .500 record, which was substandard for Princeton. We suffered through a great deal of frustration and heartbreak: a loss to Seton Hall by one point after losing a 16-point lead in the second-half; a loss to Colgate by one point after they held the ball most of the game; and two losses to Penn by a combined six points. However, one game that was not close was a 52-39 defeat at the hands of Manhattan College. We put in a pitiful performance. In fact it was so bad that when we got back to campus, we were instructed to put on our practice gear. We went at it for another two hours. We earned it and deserved it, but it was painful. When it was over, Coach gave us our marching orders for the offseason, instructing all of us on the things we needed to work on. However, this time he also undertook a self-examination, which he shared with us: "Boys, I generally don't think about myself when it comes to winning and losing, but I thought about it long and hard this year. I have decided that I need to do something this summer.

So I am going to go out to Indiana and spend some time with Bob Knight, so I can learn how to be an asshole again, because I am too f##king nice to you guys."

My sophomore and junior years tested my resolve. I played very little as new players came in and I became a fixture on the "white team." However, we won back-to-back Ivy championships, and I began to understand the bigger meaning of Princeton basketball. Yes, I loved the competition and was dying to be on the court, but equally important was the camaraderie of the team and understanding how to find ways to contribute.

It was through this process that I started to appreciate why Coach recruited the players he did. It was not always about skill. Instead, it was about background, character, drive, and commitment. These individuals came together to form something special—a unit, a team, and a force. We never went into a game thinking we were going to lose, and we did not lose many.

As I struggled to get on the court, I continued to work hard but did not achieve much success. One game that highlighted my plight was against DePaul, then, a national power. We were having a shootaround prior to the game, and as he often did, Coach stopped practice to call out a player. This time it was me.

"Jeff," he said. "You make shots on Tuesdays and Thursdays, but we play on Wednesdays and Fridays. I gotta find a way to get you in the game."

And so with that vote of confidence, I thought, "Wow.... Maybe I have a chance of getting in."

So that night, in front of a sold out Rosemont Horizon, I bided my time and sure enough I got the call—"get in there for Smitty"—so off I sprinted to the scorers' table only to face a sub's worst nightmare: no stoppage of play. Back and forth the ball went up and down the court with no whistle, with the guy I was subbing out scoring twice. Oh no, could it be? Yes. I got called back to the bench not to be summoned again. The call-back in front of 18,000 people was harrowing to say the least, but not to have another chance was a psychological terror. Despite knowing that on any given night only one or two of the subs would get in, we conspired about how to get our names in the box score—a shot, a foul, a turnover, anything to log our place in history. Through it all we came away with two Ivy championships and a basket full of memories.

As senior and a co-captain, I learned a lot. We lost our first five games and never recovered. We were a young team, and we were riddled with injuries and departures. This tested our patience and Coach's resolve. He was as frustrated as we were, and we could not overcome our weaknesses. We own the legacy of Coach's first losing season.

Despite all of the ups and downs of my Princeton basketball career, it remains the most formative experience of my life. Coach taught us how to fight adversity, how to come together as a team, and how to win. These life lessons have served me well over the years and certainly molded me as a parent and a professional. I had the great fortune to lead the Friends of Princeton Basketball for 10 years. Through this experience, I was able to work with three of Coach's successors. It is clear that the legacy of Pete Carril and Princeton basketball lives in all of those who have been fortunate enough to be part of the program—that includes the coaches, the players, the managers, the trainers, and the roommates. They have lived the stories over and over, and many have experienced them in their own unique way.

My teammates remain my closest friends, our shared experiences amounting to a lifetime of memories and the creation of a kindred spirit that lives in all of us. It is our identity. We are Princeton basketball players, and I am eternally grateful to Coach for making that happen.

CHAPTER 23

Joe Scott '87

"What good does it do to be Spanish if you don't tilt at windmills?"

—Coach Carril

I grew up on the Jersey Shore in the early 1970s. I watched Bill Bradley win two NBA titles with the Knicks, and I watched Princeton play on New Jersey Channel 23/52 every year with Dick Landis and Dick Lloyd on the call—Princeton versus Rutgers, Princeton versus Penn—or on the ECAC Game of the Week with Bucky Waters on the call. I remember watching Princeton beat Oregon with Ron Lee and then Providence to win the NIT. I knew the names Taylor, Hill, Steuerer, Omeltchenko, Sowinski, Melville—great players, great games, but one thing always stood out about Princeton: Coach Carril. Columbo, the mad scientist, program rolled up, why are they so tough, how do they keep winning? That Coach Carril.

Fast forward a few years and into my high school gym walks Pete Carril to watch me play against Long Branch. He found my Dad at halftime, shuffled over to him with cigar in hand and trench coat on, and said, "I want to coach him."

He would see me twice more that year, and each time I knew I wanted to play for him. On my recruiting trip I stayed with Bill Ryan—great point guard, great passer, friend to this day—and I remember what he said before I left. "He's not the same—he's different when he's coaching." He was getting me ready for Coach. What followed were four years where every practice was the hardest class I took but enjoyed the most. I was lucky to watch and learn from Bill Ryan because he helped me truly learn what Coach was teaching. I was lucky to play with great teammates because we were a *team*. And we were a team because of Coach and what he taught us daily.

He believed that basketball was the most interdependent sport after football. This meant that everyone's individual happiness was tied up in the team's success. Therefore, everything we did was about the team and its ability to function under the hardest circumstances. Attention to detail, precision, discipline, doing what you are supposed to do when you are supposed to do it, when someone is trying like hell to stop you from doing it, were the keys. Developing that kind of toughness was a daily ritual. As others have said, it was not for everyone, but it was for me. His way of coaching brought the team together and made the players closer. The difficulty of practices, the challenge to your character, the consistency of it were all designed to teach us that we were playing against ourselves. To make the games easier, to make men of us. To give us friends for life.

I have been extremely fortunate to have met, played for, and then coached for and with Coach. Four years as his assistant continued to teach me so much but also showed me so much more about him as a person and man. He was a link to all parts of the University and the town of Princeton. I knew this when I played—from his relationship with professor Bressler to seeing president Bowen sit with him after games in Caldwell as Coach smoked his cigar—but I learned it and saw it first-hand coaching with him each day. Tennis with the former admissions director, breakfast at Mario's with the stonemason, electrician, and history professor, saying hello to everyone to make them say hello back and be in the same world—that was Coach.

All along the way our relationship continued to grow—having beers at Conte's after practice, drawing on napkins, talking about our team, every player, creating new offensive actions, coaching in general. Continuing to learn from his mantras: "Life parts of the game and skill parts of the game." "The thing you are doing at that moment in time is the most important thing in the world. Otherwise don't do it." "Think like a pessimist; work like an optimist." Defining what it meant to play to win. "Everyone wants to win, everyone hates to lose, but who plays to win? Every possession, all possessions. Who does what is required for the team to win? Who has that kind of character, guts, and skill?" That is playing to win.

I always say work "for and with" Coach because we did work together. The responsibility he gave me, the way Bill, Armond, John, and I worked together with him, talking basketball, going over practice every day, why we were doing what we were doing, listening when I spoke, all gave me the framework and foundation for my coaching career. The confidence he showed in me, the manner in which we worked together—the *team*. I took everything I learned from Coach and have been fortunate to be able to coach my own teams and have a career.

My time with Coach has given me so much in life. I met my wife, Leah, who was a great basketball player at Princeton, while we were both assistants at Princeton. Lunch ball were our first dates and Coach had a hand in it. Chris Thomforde became a friend as he would work camp with us. He married Leah and me. All the guys I watched growing up I have met, and in some way, shape, or form have gotten to know. Because of Coach there is a bond that we know we all share (Omo, Armond, Mickey, Peter, Frank, so many more, too many to name). My own teammates are friends for life (Howie Levy, Bobby Scrabis, Dave Orlandini, Alan Williams, John

Thompson, Bill Ryan, and more). With the players I helped coach with Coach—Mitch Henderson, Mike Brennan, Gabe Lewullis, James Mastaglio, Brian Earl—a strong bond was forged. How lucky was I to have had a coach, mentor, and then friend for life? Thank you, Coach, for teaching me how to tilt at windmills. I will never be able to thank you enough!

CHAPTER 24

Kit Mueller '91
Co-Written by Buzz Hollander '91, (Princeton roommate)
and Ellie Mueller '24 (daughter)

Princeton: 29; Georgetown: 21

St. Patrick's Day, 1989. Friday night. No. 16 seed Princeton against No. 1 Georgetown. Those who did not yet know Coach Pete Carril became aware of him that night.

Many people talked about the Princeton offense, but the system Coach created involved teaching his players to play to their own strengths and to take advantage of their opponents' weaknesses. On this particular night, against the best team in the country, one would think there would not be much to exploit.

Most of the fans in the arena or watching on TV, along with parents of the players, as well as the players themselves—O.K., and probably even some of the coaching staff—were expecting Princeton to be destroyed. But we found opportunities. Coach's system was really about discovering and converting these opportunities into points.

It was incredible to me just to be playing Georgetown, not to mention being up eight at halftime. If you could imagine our halftime locker room, it is not tough to picture our shock at the lead. Rather than erupting with excitement, we found ourselves stunned into silence. This group of athletes did not look like a team built to knock off Georgetown. Our 6'2" point guard George Leftwich was a freshman, thrown into his first NCAA action against a team that had just ripped through the Big East Tournament. Coach liked Leftwich's toughness and ability to possess the ball. My roommates, 6'2" Troy Hottenstein and 6'3" Jerry Doyle, shared duties at guard. They had recently joined in getting flattop haircuts with most of the team and looked all of 14-years old. Our leader was 6'3" forward Bobby Scrabis. What height we had belonged to our power forwards, 6'7" junior Matt Lapin and 6'8" freshman Matt Eastwick, who split minutes. I was 6'7" with no jumping ability and growing into the hook shot that Coach had taught me as a freshman center. Coach knew that my high school turnaround jump shot would not fare well against college centers. Sure enough, the first points of the game were off an awkward hook shot over 6'10" Alonzo Mourning. I would not get a lot of easy opportunities against Mourning, the nation's leading shot-blocker that year. We were out of our league physically, to say the least.

Yet… Coach knew just what he needed from us. He took advantage of the few strengths he believed could help us win. He had done this for years and had found no weaknesses impossible to overcome.

Coach would often talk about players from years past who fit well in his system. At times, a current player would fail to do something that others before him had done to Coach's satisfaction. In that moment, Coach would not be able to help himself from becoming extremely frustrated and flustered.

This could lead Coach to blur the names of some of his players. My freshman year, Tim Neff was playing the guard position vacated by Joey Scott, who graduated a few years before and ran Princeton's offense perfectly for Coach. If Tim fell short in aspects of the system, Coach would get so frustrated that he would start calling out things like, "Why can't you see that cut like Joey did?" which would become "Joey, why didn't you make that pass like you always did?" If reminded by someone that the player was *Timmy*, not Joey, Coach might blurt out something like, "Well, you gotta get used to being called Joey!"

Coach had certain types of players and people who he believed would help him win. He talked about recruiting kids whose dads were coal miners. He preferred basketball IQ over book smarts. He would sometimes poke fun at the good students, especially those from prep schools ("three-car-garage guys"), saying things like, "You book-smart guys get your money stolen from guys with street smarts." A common lament: "I got all these Rhodes Scholars, but I want *road* scholars!"

Two teammates, Matt Henshon and Matt Eastwick, had prestigious Morehead Scholarships and came from prep schools with strong academics. Eastwick recently reminded me that Coach liked to call them his "Bonehead Scholars." Both Matts likely had to fight a little harder to get in his good graces for playing time. On the court, above all, Coach looked for tough kids who could cope with the complexity of his system and his desire for its perfect execution.

It was hard to get a basketball team through Princeton's admissions department. As a result, the pool of athletic talent from which Coach selected was already shallow and he had to fight to acquire the best players in this group. Coach's system was so complex that fitting in players within these limitations must have been incredibly frustrating for him. Coach's knowledge of the game was at such a high level that it took thousands of repetitions and focused work for us to operate at a moderately acceptable level in his eyes.

This likely fed into why our practices were so long and rigorous. Coach obsessed over the tiniest details. A minor alteration in the offense could lead to a lower success rate. As a freshman, I recall spending hours repeating the dribble hand-off, a seemingly simple maneuver. My first mistake was my habit of flipping the ball rather than handing it off, affecting the shot of my teammate. Next, I failed to hand the ball off at the correct angle, placing it forward instead of directly to my side, leaving the ball exposed. Then, I handed the ball off inside the three-point line, resulting in a long two, rather than a three. Finally, I would fail to screen after handing the ball off, allowing the defense to slip through. These were all unacceptable and fixing them was a part of moving through Coach's progression. The learning curve was steep for all of us.

In all, the system was brutally challenging to learn. With tens of options throughout a possession, there were consistently opportunities to be missed. I vividly remember reading the defense correctly for one of the first times in a practice my freshman year. I looked off the first cut down the middle, saw the defender fading to the corner, and hit the wing for a three-point shot. He scored and I was so satisfied with the outcome of the play. Seconds later, I heard Coach screaming in frustration. The pass was off—it was too low. The shooter had to pull the ball up from his waist, lowering the probability that he could get the shot off with minimal pressure. Unacceptable. Every detail mattered.

People talk about the Princeton offense as if Coach pulled it from a playbook, but in reality, the vast majority of the system is more of a series of reads and reactions. When I discussed this with Troy Hottenstein, he recalled how we ran these sets so often that we knew one another's next move based on cues, such as a quick look, the angle of a teammate's cut, a defender's step, or the way one of us held the ball. This is the progression that Coach built upon and ingrained in his players over time. Coach had a picture of how *everything* should flow in his mind. His system helped us deal with different scenarios and play against any opponent. Coach taught this through thousands of repetitions of each piece of his offense. When we were clicking as a cohesive offensive unit, 45 seconds of defense was really hard on a team. That was how we controlled the pace of the game and frustrated our opponents to the buzzer.

I played the first game of my career against a Division III team. I had a big half against their center, maybe 20 points. I remember running into the locker room at halftime thinking, "I am making it as a college player!" I could not have been more wrong. Coach spent the entire halftime ripping me to shreds between curse words. In retrospect, he was right—against a weaker team, I could get away with playing outside of the system, playing selfishly, and finishing unrealistic looks. This would not be possible moving forward, and Coach made sure I knew that he would not stand for it. Many coaches would praise a freshman with 20 points at halftime in his first college game. Coach, on the other hand, knew what I needed to do to help us win, and my play in that half would not cut it.

To me, his reaction was jolting at first. But Coach's legacy was built on the high standard of performance that he demanded. Everyone was terrified of disappointing him. From the players to staff to equipment managers to water boys, all those involved feared being the one having an off day. Even during the offseason, if you went to Jadwin to shoot around or play two-on-two, you would always look up high in the stands, and if you saw Coach sitting up there, you would pay attention. If you did not look, you could surely hear him groaning at your mistakes. Anything you did half-assed would circle back to haunt you, even months later.

There was a fear factor for all of us. We knew basketball meant everything to Coach, and he was 100% in on the team. As one example, he would always schedule a practice during the Super Bowl. I have no great explanation for this; there was no standard 6:00 P.M. Sunday practice, but we inferred that Coach wanted to make a point about what should matter most. Coach would start each Super Bowl practice with the same inappropriate joke ending with the punchline, "Honey, YOU'RE IN the Super Bowl." Then we took the court.

Coach's intensity and commitment was not an act; it was who Coach was. He could not stand to see us fail to execute his vision properly. What he created on the court was his life.

I once went to visit Coach's house as an upperclassman. He had a cork board with a family photo push-pinned into it, a fridge full of beer, and he was rolling 8mm film of a very old game. He showed me a play in this game to illustrate an aspect of our system that needed improvement. Midway through this demonstration, one of his previous players failed to go backdoor. Coach fumed. He rolled the film back, becoming angrier and angrier that the player—we shall call him Johnny—continued to miss this cut despite Coach's clear feedback. Rewind again. He still missed the cut. Coach ran the film over and over, pleading with Johnny to change his behavior. Coach reached the point at which he was yelling at the screen: "Johnny, why won't you make that f##king cut?" Coach had a library of film running through his mind at all times, of you and the hundred players before you. It was pretty incredible, and the joy and frustration of these moments fueled Coach's obsession with the game.

That intensity was essential. So was Coach's attention to detail, pre-game preparation, hours of repetition, and his particular genius. This combination gave us, a group of middling athletes going up against a collection of future NBA players, a chance to play them close. Without Coach, there was no chance.

Georgetown: 50; Princeton: 49

Before that night, the Ivy League team had been getting blown out of the first round of the NCAA tournament for years. There was serious discussion about eliminating the small conference's automatic bid to the NCAA Tournament. Hopefully this game played a small part in ending that discussion. Decades later, I am shocked that people still come up to me and can tell me about the bar where they watched that game.

I do not remember much of what Coach said after the game. I was in a fog, a mix of emotions. I mostly remember receiving standing ovations as we walked into bars wearing our Princeton sweats.

One of my teammates, Dave Pavelko, does remember Coach's post-game speech. According to Pavelko, Coach had a few words for the team's senior captain, Bobby Scrabis. But quickly, Coach's frustration began to rise. We made too many second-half mistakes. Coach was talking to a team with a nucleus of young players, one which had just come within a basket of beating the best team in the country. This team would go on to take Final Four-bound Arkansas to the wire the following year and find itself in the top-20 with an eighth-seed in the Big Dance the year after that. Despite this, Pavelko remembers Coach concluding with:

"If things don't change around here, this team could lose 20 games next year!"

That was Coach. The mistakes cannot be unseen. All that imperfection was unbearable. Time to load up the projector again.

CHAPTER 25

Matt Henshon '91

When you first think about playing basketball at Princeton, you become aware of the tradition. Coach Carril is himself a bridge for that history. After all, it is a through-line from the 1965 Final Four to VBK '45 leaving for the Lakers, with Coach as his hand-picked successor. As Faulkner wrote, "The past is never dead. It's not even past."

But getting to know Coach Carril led to a new appreciation of the legacy. On my recruiting trip, Coach brought me to the office, selected a canister from the film library on the wall, threaded the reel into a seemingly Cappy Cappon-era projector, and proceeded to show me the original Princeton vs. UCLA game.

My first college basketball memory was Bird vs. Magic, so I never saw the Wooden Dynasty. By the time I was paying attention, Larry Brown was the coach, and UCLA was playing the role of "Cinderella" in the 1979-80 Tournament.

The film showed the mighty Bruins in Pauley Pavilion. The defending (and soon-to-be-again) NCAA champs. A year removed from Lew Alcindor, but with multiple future NBAers. And a Tiger team trading (two-point) basket-for-basket thanks to Geoff Petrie '70 and John Hummer '70, among others. We were watching the game long after it was played, but for Coach, the outcome was still in doubt, muttering "What do you see?!" at the flickering images. Final score: 76-75, on a Sidney Wicks shot at the buzzer. Same as it was in December 1969.

The sense of history changed again when I got to campus and the season started. In the days leading up to a game, Coach would watch film incessantly. He would try to get current film of the upcoming opponent ("trading tapes" with coaching acquaintances, in the parlance of the time), but also going back into the Jadwin library, especially for league games. And when he came to practice the next day, he would make references to actions that had worked against an opponent, even a half-decade earlier.

Playing at forward, I had to be familiar with all the names who had come before: "Aaron" Belz '86 or "John" Thompson III '88. I was never mistaken by Coach for a former player—it was "Aaron did this" (or perhaps more likely, "Why can't *you* see what John saw?") He was exhorting me to be as adept as the celluloid images he had watched the previous night.

But with other (frankly, better) players, he did conflate the past and present. One of the most prominent was Sean Jackson '92. Sean was a tough, undersized guard with a quick release and deadly three-point shot. He was also a relentless defender. He clearly reminded Coach of Joe Scott '87. And accordingly, the two began to meld in Coach's mind; he sometimes referred to Sean as "Joe" in practice.

On a Saturday night in February 1990 we went up to play Cornell. Just before a game, Coach, building off the film review, would cover the scouting report on the other team—which dangerous scorer "you can't let out of the bag," or which guy "throws all the passes," or which guys "could only go left, so approach that guy from the right side." For the latter, and knowing we attended Princeton, he might add after a pause: "*Your* right side."

The chalk-talk (as he called it) would start about 40 minutes before tip-off and would run about 20 minutes. On the board, he would sketch out the other team's offensive sets, out-of-bounds plays, and full-court press. For the opposing team he would invariably use uniform numbers so we could keep track of which guys we "could not let out of the bag." For our team, he would just use names.

Towards the end of this one, the old films apparently began playing in Coach's mind. Instead of "Sean" and the starters, it was "Joe" and the four other names. Given that this mix-up was a regular occurrence in practice—that we all knew whom he was referring to and the chalk-talk was winding down—there seemed no point in correcting him.

He wrapped up ("Just hold onto your guts tonight, fellas"), and we began standing up, lightly stretching. The managers would tell us when the scoreboard clock began ticking down from 20:00 before tip, allowing us to begin warmups. In the meantime, we waited, talking quietly amongst ourselves.

Many teams would distribute scouting reports to their players. Needless to say, an opponent's scouting report is valuable information. It tells a coach what someone in the profession thinks of his team's strengths and weaknesses, its tendencies, and how to win. And at least once a year a student manager or Jadwin custodian would emerge from the visiting team locker room with a scouting report on the Tigers, inadvertently left behind by the previous night's rival in a wastepaper basket or (dare to say it) toilet stall.

Coach left no such possibility. The scouting report was in his head with a single index card to jog his memory. At the end of the talk, he would carefully fold the card and tuck it in the back pocket of his khakis.

He would then take a fresh towel, disappear into the bathroom, and dampen it completely. While a dry eraser can sometimes leave behind legible 'shadows' on a chalkboard, when Coach was done with the wet towel it was sparkling from top to bottom.

On this night he began his methodical treatment of the board. He started at the upper right corner, even though it had never been written upon. He had just gotten to the diagrams when the manager burst in, with the news that the clock countdown had started. We started crowding towards the door.

"Wait a minute, fellas," Coach said, looking at the half-clean board, and then back at us, his palms up.

"Who the f##k's Joe?"

CHAPTER 26

Sean Jackson '92

I had one of the more unique journeys to Princeton basketball in that I transferred after playing one year at Ohio University (OU). I had not been pursued by Coach Carril out of high school because, at the time, "scholarship" schools were the only options my family considered. Growing up in Wayne County, W. Va., where most of my classmates finished their academic careers at high school graduation, going to college for free was thought of as the chance of a lifetime. In the end, my choices came down to OU, Delaware, Radford, and UNC-Charlotte.

I was often asked why I transferred and why to Princeton. My year at OU was not necessarily that bad, at least not worse than any other freshman basketball player experiences. But spending a year in college did open up my world a bit. I found out that I enjoyed being in an academic environment but also wanted to play high-level college basketball. Ivy League basketball began hitting my radar, and with the discovery that financial aid was available, playing there became more than just a daydream.

The only place I applied as a transfer was Princeton. I had zero connection to the school, did not know anyone who ever attended, and even had to look up what state it was in. But I had heard of

Bill Bradley and figured it must take basketball seriously. After my freshman year at OU in the spring of 1988, my high school coach contacted the Princeton basketball office to inform the coaches of my interest. I am not sure what the reaction was on the other end, but given that they had not seen a transfer before, I suspect it was not given a lot of thought. So needless to say, my expectations of getting in were not that high. Finally, in late June, I turned in my pencil-written application. In early August, as I was preparing to start my sophomore year at OU, I got a call from Coach Carmody saying in a surprising voice that I had been admitted. The next day I received the official letter and thus began a journey that would change the trajectory of my life.

My first recollection of a conversation with Coach Carril was when, after playing pickup with other team members during that first fall, he said, "I'm not a fan of transfers, I feel like they are running away from something." This was my first introduction to his bluntness and brutal honesty. But it also made me think: Was I really running away from something? Whether you agree with Coach's declarations or not, at a minimum they force you to confront and re-evaluate your own decisions and actions. In this case, it did reinforce my belief that I was actually running to and not away from something, and that fact motivated me even more to be a part of the program.

NCAA rules at the time stated that transfers could practice but could not play in any games in their first season. I practiced two days with the team before Coach Carril pulled me aside and said that because I could not play this season, he would not have time for me, and I might as well not show up for any more practices. Most people would have seen that as a big red flag, but I think I was just too naive to see it as anything more than he said. After all, Coach Carril was not known to pull any punches, so I took it at face value. When people ask whether I was at Princeton during the

Princeton-Georgetown game, I say I was, but I was watching it in my dorm room like the other students.

My next interaction with Coach Carril came in the spring of 1989 after the season was over. I had played intramural basketball all winter and had begun playing with some of the other guys on the team during spring pickup games. Coach Carril brought me to his office and said, "Sean, I don't think you are really that good, but Coach Carmody seems to like you, so I will let you try out next year." Really, I am not quite sure if Coach had seen enough of me to make any evaluation, but he did recognize that I was always around the gym and could tell I loved to play. Coach connected with people who loved the game, and I think he was somewhat curious because I had a different pathway to Princeton from other players.

When practice began the next year, I worked my way into the starting lineup after about three weeks. Of course, this also brought increased scrutiny of every little thing I did. After a bad pass or decision, one of Coach's favorite lines was that whoever had recruited me as a point guard at OU must have been drunk when they had seen me play. This progressed from just being drunk to a three-day drinking binge after another bad pass. Of course, his insight was spot on. At a touch under six feet, I had a point guard body, but had never met a shot I did not think I could hit. My main measure of any improvement I made during my career had little to do with points scored or shots made—it was how often I heard the drunk recruiter story.

One of the major differences between the OU and Princeton programs that I noticed immediately was that no one was immune from Coach's critiques. At OU, we had two future NBA players on our roster, and I do not remember those guys ever getting yelled at. So it was a surprise when, during my first year, Coach would call out our best player as too fat. Also, it was not uncommon for players to hear critiques about how they grew up. At OU, coaches would yell at players for basketball-related errors (bad shots, forgetting plays, etc.), but it was much more personal with Coach Carril. To play winning basketball, you needed to have the right skills (passing, shooting, dribbling, etc.), but you also had to have the right character. Someone who was not worried about who got credit; someone who had the toughness to withstand pressure. One of the most memorable lines from Coach was that basketball (and sports in general) do not build character so much as they reveal it. Also, I think Coach figured that if you were at Princeton you had more going for you than just basketball, so he was not too worried about hurt feelings when it came to his critiques.

Despite all the negative comments from Coach, there were moments that reflected his curiosity. I started a chapter of the Fellowship of Christian Athletes at Princeton. One day at the end of practice at our team meeting, he pulled out a flyer we had distributed around campus about an upcoming event. After pointing out a misspelling in the flyer, he started quizzing me about the religious implications of certain basketball scenarios. "O.K., Sean, if you fake a charge, what would Jesus say about that?" I never heard questions like that at OU.

In my three years playing at Princeton, we won three Ivy League championships and I shared with my teammates and coaches a lot of great experiences. But as you were going through it, the work was seemingly never done, and Coach reminded us there was always next year to worry about. I did not fully appreciate the impact Coach had until I was asked to play in three-on-three tournaments with several Princeton alumni years after college. John Rogers '80 was the architect of these teams, which won several national championships and included many Princeton alumni. Looking back, I often wonder if any other collegiate program could have pulled this off. Having alumni spread out over three decades still wanting to play and compete together shows the Coach's binding force. We all felt that we had a unique shared experience.

After graduation, I saw Coach at the occasional alumni basketball game but never really had much of an extended conversation. That all changed when I visited Jadwin in 2017 with my family for my 25th Reunion. We were about 30 minutes early for an event, and the gym was completely empty except for Coach sitting on the sidelines by himself. I had no idea he was even going to be in town and there he was, right in front of me. After saying hello and introducing him to my family, he immediately saw my two boys (ages 15 and 17) and asked if they played basketball. He proceeded to work them out for twenty minutes. Here was Coach, well into his eighties, totally in his element, alone in a big gym, teaching a game he loved.

Later in the day, I sat with Coach for a couple of hours watching some of the alumni play. I heard he had mellowed through the years, which was true, but he still longed to see good basketball being played. I think that is why he was such a perfectionist and demanded our best. It gave him so much joy to see basketball played the "right way" that it was hard for him to tolerate anything less. Most coaches do not have the energy for harping on every little detail because most coaches do not have a bar higher than winning. Coach's expectations were different. I remember many times when a win provided Coach with little satisfaction. And I think that was one of my biggest takeaways. If you want to stand out in any endeavor, it is going to take more energy than the next guy expends. So find something that gives you the joy to make the effort worth it.

CHAPTER 27

Sydney Johnson '97

I am not the best storyteller, so this may serve as a good filler between one great story about Coach and the next. Truthfully, it is funnier for me to listen to my teammates recounting one of our unforgettable experiences with Coach through their eyes. It makes me laugh to this day thinking about guys like Moon, Mitch, Hielscher, J.O., Earl and Jesse and how good they are with putting the perfect accent on the "F" as they describe another colorful use of the word by Coach as he tried to come to terms with whatever asinine decision one of us had made on the court. We were all there for those moments, we live them now, and we will live them forever.

My story is one that gets to the essence of Coach from my personal view. It may not be as comical as those my teammates might share, but it is impactful for sure. My junior year we were pretty good. We spent two years getting our butts handed to us by Fran Dunphy, Jerome Allen, Matt Maloney, and that whole crew from that school in Philadelphia. It was tough losing to our archrivals for my first two years of college and tougher to be reminded by Coach *every day* about how much less of a player I was than former greats Mike Brennan, George Leftwich, Armond Hill, and Billy Ryan. Those guys found ways to win big games—why couldn't I? Coach was right about me relative to the guys before me—but more on that later.

Anyway, the coaching staff had done a brilliant job of recruiting and adding new players. So with a loaded group of underclassmen and juniors and seniors who were battle-tested, we started to get some wins. Coach always scheduled a challenging non-conference schedule and loved competitive holiday tournaments. My junior season we played in Fresno State's Holiday tournament. Fresno State had Rafer Alston and Chris Herren, was coached at the time by Jerry Tarkanian and was a fringe Top 25 program. We put on a clinic against Boise State in the tournament semifinal. Our locker room was right next to Boise State's and their coach spent his entire post-game talk asking his guys why they did not execute like the Princeton guys. The championship game was against Fresno State. The gym was packed. It was a close game and we came out on top. Chris Herren did not play, but Fresno still had a good team, and for a group of guys like us who had been coming up short, it was a great win. We were screaming in the locker room after the game—pandemonium, joy. I distinctly remember a gleam in the eyes of all my teammates, and of course there was me, prone to overstating things and being overly vocal as a captain, yelling, "We sent a message to the rest of the league. We sent a message!"

Mitch Henderson and Brian Earl played outstandingly. The three of us were named to the all-tournament team. The picture of the three of us after the game is one of my favorite photos from my playing days. Coach Carril walked into the locker room with a grin on his face. Barely audible, he said, "O.K., O.K. Settle down. Let me tell you something." We did as we were told, but instead of readying ourselves for another "and 2" or another 15 minutes of scrimmaging, we readied ourselves for the praise that we had been spared almost since any one of us had begun our Princeton careers. Here was the moment that Coach was finally going to say, "Hey, you guys have done well. Maybe we have something."

We could not wait. Instead, Coach said, "Let me tell you something. This team—Fresno State—they wouldn't finish higher than third or fourth in our league." DAMN. Just like that!

There have been only a small handful of times that I can remember seeing and hearing a change of intense emotion sweep through an entire room, and this was one of those moments—elation to despair in a matter of seconds. It let the air out of our balloons and then some.

So why is this my story about Coach Carril? Because for me—and it is important that I make it clear that this is from my perspective—one of Coach's greatest gifts to his players was honesty.

Coach saw everything in the game. He read the game and people so well, and, damn, was he demanding. At every step along the way he was honest about what he saw. He was true. And I cannot say that he loved me, but I do believe that the folks who care for you the most are the ones who are honest with you. And that was Coach Carril. What did that honesty breed? A keep-at-it mindset. The job is not finished. We are here to win the league. There is another game, another practice, another something to be better at, to get better at. Details, execution, precision. As much as young men from 18 to 22 years old can appreciate those ideas, that is what he was teaching—relentlessly. I was not as good as some of the best players who have ever played at Princeton. I know it because Coach never told me that I was. And until I heard those words (which I never did), I was going to bust my ass trying to prove that I was worth my spot on the team. Because my coach was *honest* with me.

We were discouraged after Coach spoke to us in the locker room after winning on the road against a Top 25 program with another Hall of Fame coach on the opposing bench.

And then, a few months later, we beat defending national champion UCLA 43-41 in one of the most memorable upsets in NCAA tournament history.

I know Coach was proud of us after that one—because he told us he was.

CHAPTER 28

Steve Goodrich '98

A favorite memory of mine about Coach Carril is not as vibrant or colorful as other recollections. One day in the locker room before a game, he was explaining to us how reasonable he was and why we would be well-served to listen to him.

"I'm not an assh##e," he said. "I'm not one of those guys who is going to tell you I am right all the time, but I would say I am right 87% of the time." He then wrote 87% on the chalkboard. He considered it for a few moments before erasing it and writing 86% before erasing again and settling on 88%. He was right 88% of the time. There it was. I always found that hilarious—the precision, the candor, the erasing and rewriting, the high self-regard for himself as a truth-teller. To him, the truth he was giving us was an unappreciated gift. It would pay huge dividends down the road. But few of us wanted to be receiving it there and then.

His "gift" ruined some guys. Sometimes it was fair, and sometimes it was cruel and arbitrary. Was it fair to call a kid a c##t for missing layups? Did it really mean that his parents had not raised him with appropriate values and work ethic? Did not getting a rebound in traffic mean a guy was not going to succeed in life?

There was no hiding from his truth. By most definitions I was successful playing for him, but I had a miserable freshman year and felt very much like a failure every day. Having him casually dispense an aside to me like, "Stevie, you're a good kid, but I'm not sure you'll ever be good enough to help us," would wreck me for days. Was I going to fail at this?

"Basketball doesn't build character, it reveals it." He said that dozens of times. "Do you have any guile, kid? Did you ever have to take another kid's lunch money?" "I can't believe how fast you just ran down the court—why don't you do it every time?" And he had a gift for seeing the gaps, the character flaws that were revealing themselves on the court in front of him.

I often wondered if a different bunch of guys would have told Coach to get lost—or worse. If he had a team of future pros, would they have tuned him out or confronted him? I remember talking to him about the Sacramento Kings teams he coached, and he had the same laments. "(Chris) Webber doesn't run the floor every time. We could be so much better if he did." I do not think Webber was too worried about that.

But building teams was another skill of his. His recruiting style was self-selecting. By choosing to establish himself and his program the way he did, he built a series of conditions that could not be replicated. He decided early on to coach in one place and the school he picked did not offer scholarships. He then recruited kids by telling them that they were not as good as the other coaches were telling them they were. So he built teams of kids willing to bypass scholarship offers. Many of his players made big financial sacrifices to come to school and, more importantly, he got kids who were attracted to the idea of playing for a guy who emphasized improvement. So you had people who were relatively low-ego, who wanted to get better, and who had opted into his crucible—even if no one had any idea what that really meant when they signed up for it. I felt lucky to be with guys who liked each other, who were O.K. with this experience, who lived with the idea that being somewhat miserable and getting s##t on every day was worth it.

Everyone who has written about Coach or observed him has mentioned the contrast between the elitism of the institution where he worked and the nature of the steel town where he grew up. He always implored us to understand what was important in our college lives. "Don't pay too much attention to what's going on over there," he would say, waving his arm at the campus beyond the Jadwin parking lot or mocking the goofy costumes and the extended arm gesturing during the singing of the alma mater. "This is what matters! What you do in here. How you play for the other guys in this gym with you."

How did he make us care so much?

Most of his communication to the team took place during "states of the union." He would gather us on the bench and run down the row guy by guy to give an assessment of how the team was doing, how each of us was performing. This ritual goes against everything that any management book would tell you. Every manual I have read encourages leaders to praise in public and coach in private. But Coach's technique was not to waste time on compliments and to coach out in the open. He would search for root causes of your weaknesses. Were you selfish? Scared? Lazy and/or entitled?

"State of the union" could happen before a practice or after a game. It could derail an entire pre-game talk. Rather than getting us ready to play, he would be so angry thinking about something that might unfold that he would spend 20 minutes talking about how one guy was not cutting hard yesterday and he was about to get 'fired' and that was why we were about to lose by 20.

He was brutal and honest, and insightful and mean, and he was very funny.

"Your dad told me your high school coach didn't let you shoot. So you don't shoot, you can't dribble, you don't pass. Did he let you take a good s##t once in a while?"

"We were up in the office yesterday and we drew your balls up on the chalkboard. When they are this big (draws two small circles on the board), you are playing great. But when they get this big (draws larger circles), then you try to do too much, and it gets a little rough."

"Did you work on your jump shot over the summer? Did you say: 'Father, I worked on my jump shot. May I have five dollars, please?' Bulls##t. You are a Division I player, and sometimes your three-point shot doesn't even get to the rim."

I was laughing, I was terrified. I was hoping he would just call me a pu##y and move on. Was it O.K. that I was laughing as he was eviscerating my teammates and feeling deep relief that it was not me being ridiculed?

Playing for him was all-consuming. I was constantly exhausted, physically and mentally. Many of my friends and roommates played varsity sports at Princeton. Why did their experience feel so different? They were competing and being coached. But the stakes and intensity seemed lower. There seemed to be less on the line. It was not the test of character and personal worth that I was wrestling with every day. How did he conflate your performance in basketball with passing a test that would reveal your character and determine your success for the rest of your life? That was the magic trick!

Some interesting psychological tendencies emerged. I remember reading *The Right Stuff* while playing for Coach. When Tom Wolfe wrote about the test pilots convincing themselves that surviving danger and death meant they had that invincible quality, I thought about Coach. Why was I comparing my experience playing college basketball to the life and death stakes of Navy test pilots? It seemed silly.

Is suffering required to get really good at something? Coach suffered too. He never took a play off. Even three hours into a boring practice in the middle of January, he was this angry little ball of accountability who would stop plays every three minutes. "Yo, yo, yo!—what did you seeeeee, a##hole!" The stamina, and inability to let a mistake slide, do not seem remarkable. But that relentless consistency and high standard was a gift, an internal voice that he put on my shoulder. I have not always been able to live up to it.

Pictures of him on the bench during games show that he was so tortured, his face in agony. It affected his ability to coach games. All of the insight and analysis and evaluations of player performance, all of the scouting skills that he had in abundance were virtually impossible for him to summon through the haze of agony he suffered while watching his team play the games. Game management was his weakest area. The accumulated frustration added up and was taking a toll on him by the time my recruiting class arrived. Penn had won the last two Ivy League titles by going undefeated and was bringing back its best team in 20 years. Mike Brennan and Chris Mooney had just graduated, and Coach had watched a team that would have won the league most years lose twice to the Quakers. He may have stopped coaching earlier, but he could not leave with Penn winning so much. He probably recognized that he was a little more disconnected from the kids he was coaching. He would often lament the days when parents would just turn their kids over to the coach to let him handle them instead of having parents around all the time always watching and involved. He cared just as much about holding us to a high standard, but maybe there was a little less of a connection with the kids as his head coaching career was coming to an end. He looked much younger and healthier in his early years as an assistant with the Sacramento Kings, once he had shed the responsibilities of a head coach.

That 1994-95 season, we ended up starting three freshmen, one sophomore and a junior. One member of my recruiting class came from a nationally-ranked high school team. And he spent the first half of my freshman year telling us that high school team would kill us. Meanwhile I was struggling to keep my head above water. I felt like I was failing every day. I came in to play forward and was so incapable of doing that during preseason that I was moved to center. Coach had the quote of the week in *Sports Illustrated* that fall, when asked by a reporter if my shooting range was the reason for moving me to center. "He has the shooting range; he doesn't have the making range."

Coach had decided that he needed to throw his younger players on the floor to see what we could do. I started in front of a senior center who was better than I was. Was that fair? Was the senior, three-year starter feeling O.K. about Coach benching him? Or was Coach doing the right thing for the program by seeing if any of his three freshmen starters were going to be able to help him beat Penn in the next couple years?

In this case he was correct. Having a year of playing as a freshman got me on an improvement curve into Coach's last year, and our young team began to play better. Finally, we were able to get over the hump and beat Penn in the playoff leading up to our UCLA game. I am sure he was relieved. The moments before that game were the most nervous I have ever been, and winning that game must have taken a huge weight off of him. It was a special gift to be able to win the game against UCLA.

Coach was quite charming, and I remember being excited for any connection with him outside of the crucible of games and practice during the season. I always enjoyed taking a recruit out to dinner at Conte's. Coach would hold up the first slice of pepperoni and peppers to check if the crust was crispy enough to hold or if it was going to flop over. Or sitting around drinking beer after the pickup games at summer basketball camps in hundred-degree dorm rooms, and spending a few hours listening to him hold court, relaxed, telling stories with former players and his friends from Reading. The absolute best moments were the earned ones. The best basketball memory of my life was not hearing I had reached the NBA or even contributing to a few victories with the Chicago Bulls and New Jersey Nets. No, it was winning the Ivy championship playoff game by finally beating Penn and riding the bus home from Lehigh singing songs and drinking beer with all the guys and coaches. I really had no idea what I was signing up for when I chose to play for him, but it was one of the best decisions I ever made. I feel so lucky that I had the opportunity to be a part of the community of people that Coach brought to the program. Turns out Coach Carril *was* right. Exactly 88% of the time.

CHAPTER 29

Mitch Henderson '98
Princeton Basketball Head Coach (2011 to Present)

A short time after I was hired as head basketball coach at Princeton in 2011, my former coach handed me an index card with three words written on it.

Think. See. Do.

After Carril handed me the card, he looked at me for what felt like 30 seconds, staring me down with that "Are-you-listening?" glare.

Coach was a teacher before he was a coach. He started out as a history teacher and was clearly heavily influenced by the teachers he knew throughout his life. He would often say the role of a coach is that of a teacher. And if one of us did not know how to do something on the basketball court—make a hook shot, throw a left-handed pass to the corner—his job was to teach us how to do that. We would repeat the moves, over and over, until we got it right. His record here proved that he was a master teacher.

He was always teaching—sometimes by showing us out on the court, sometimes in more subtle ways. My freshman year (1994-95), Coach would occasionally toss a stapled packet of box scores our way. It was a gesture that was clear in its intention. These were box scores of great games from before our time at Princeton, from teams he had coached that were special. These box scores were a snapshot of what a team can and should do together. Even if it was highlighting an individual performance, the emphasis was on how that performance contributed to a key team win. Or better yet, a league title-clinching win.

Eighteen rebounds in one game. Thirty-three points scored in a game. Ten assists and only one turnover! It was his way of saying, "You want to know what doing something looks like? *This* is what doing something looks like." He might have also been saying, "You guys stink!" Even if that was not his point, that is likely what we heard.

We were all very aware that he was nearing the end of his time at Princeton at this point—the looming conclusion to a monumental career he would hint at every now and again, usually in moments of frustration or anger. The team wanted one of those big title-clinching wins too—a victory for us but also for him.

The following season, we were on the cusp of just such a win. We finished with a share of the Ivy championship, which meant we were preparing for a one-game playoff against Penn to decide which team would get to go to the NCAA tournament. The game was to be held at Lehigh, not far from where Coach had grown up in Bethlehem, Pa. To make matters worse, we had lost to Penn several times in a row, including twice already that very season. I do not remember our team ever being so nervous in the locker room before any other game.

But something clicked that night. We beat our nemesis in overtime, and the team and all our fans broke out into a massive celebration. It was huge for all of us, but it felt like something more for Coach. I remember watching Coach entering the locker room silently. He walked right up to the front of that room without saying a word and started very slowly writing on the board in chalk: "I am very happy. I am retiring." We all started cheering and hugging and clapping. Happy was not an emotion we expected often from our coach—when he felt it, we were allowed to feel it too.

Then the party started. Coach loved to celebrate the big wins, especially on the bus. It was finally our turn to celebrate a huge win with him. That bus ride back to Princeton was one of the most fun bus rides we ever had. We all knew he was a great coach and teacher, but I suspect none of us on that team felt quite as connected to him as some of his earlier teams and groups. He had had such a storied career and coached so many greats—those historic box scores he handed out to us every season made us feel like we would never quite match up to our predecessors. But on that ride, we finally felt like the team Coach expected us to be. We sang songs with him and the rest of the staff and loudly celebrated our upcoming trip to the NCAAs.

Anyone who has ever played for Coach knows how tough a road it was. But I can honestly say that my relationship with him became so different from what it was when I played for him. To play for Coach is to see the game like him. And there is not much room for interpretation. He would often ask, "What do you see?" If you were dumb enough to answer, it was at your own peril. The point was that you were expected to figure it out. You had to figure out how to "just play" the way *he* saw the game.

He had patience, albeit limited, for learning, but zero tolerance if you did not try to do your best. If you did try your absolute very best and maximized your potential, it was noted. But that level of effort was not deserving of a compliment. That was just the way it was supposed to be. To get a compliment from Coach as a player, this was the ultimate gift—it was so rare.

The same has been true as my relationship with him changed, from player to collaborator and colleague. Compliments were vanishingly rare, but there was a level of positivity I had never experienced before. Whenever he would tell me that the team was playing well, the words alone, coming from him, were a great reward. Sometimes it was just a nod, but I read it. The nod meant that what I was doing, in his eyes, was right. Maybe for that one night, I was thinking, seeing, and doing—just as Coach had always wanted me to.

I would like to share what those three words— think, see, do— mean to me, those words Coach has been drilling into us all these years.

Think. Think about what the most important thing to do is, and then do that in practice as often as possible. Think through carefully how to work through all of the different teaching points on one side of the court. Then, when it is time, move to the other side. Keep thinking—which way does the player you are guarding prefer to go, right or left? What play does this coach like to run in this exact scenario? Where is the best matchup on the floor right now? And then ask regularly (in Coach's voice), **"Yo! What were you thiiiinkiiing?"**

See. See everything. Watch what they do and then ask questions. Observe very carefully how someone does something and then ask them to do it again. Is it the same this time or different? Why? How? Do not always answer right away. Be sure to let your team know that you believe in change, in growth. What are they doing to make themselves experts? Then ask, all the time, **"Yo! What do you seeeee?"**

Do. Be on the floor, be engaged, and teach them what to do. The "do" part is the work. The goal is to become a worker, to overcome something that is in you and push through it to where you can see change. The "doing" is the moment that stands out. Of course, ask the players all the time: **"Yo! What are you doooooing?"**

Craig Robinson '83 told me about how at the beginning of his senior year, Coach was imploring him to work on a reverse one-foot layup. Craig spent time on this move, and when he made the move and sank the layup in an open gym session that fall, he heard a familiar voice from high up in the Jadwin Gym bleachers. "Yo, CRAIG!" The best kind of "Yo!" you could get—one of approval.

Coach loved to be around people who worked to improve on their own. In the fall, in the spring, down at Jadwin, working hard in an empty gym. He believed "doing" was rare. It was the sign of strong character.

When I became head coach several years ago, he would frequently stop by to watch us practice. Afterwards, when practice was over, we would often talk. He would say, "I have some notes for you from practice." He would pull a piece of paper out of one of his pockets, look down at it, and shake his head. "Well, that's not it. (Long pause) That's my recipe for Spanish rice."

Coach's wisdom never faltered. "Be yourself," Coach told me many times over the years. He would often drop this one on me after a particularly tough loss. You think about what you want to do, watch closely, and then you do it. You lose the stuff that does not work, keep the stuff that does, and above all, *do it in your own way.*

There is so much of Coach in me—so much of him in Bill Carmody, who coached me at Princeton after Carril and then hired me at Northwestern—that what comes out of my mouth should often be footnoted: *Passes must be on the money. Snap your chest pass. Cut hard. Free throws are free points, fellas. We have to get every one.*

It is the way in which these points are delivered that resonates the most to me now. The longer I coach, the more I realize the simple elegance of each teaching point being reiterated regularly.

No one who knew Coach will ever forget his mantra: The most important thing you are doing is the thing you are doing right now. Our coach was practicing "mindfulness" before anyone even knew what that was.

Coach was also a pioneer in basketball analytics, way before anyone else was. This was ironic given that he never crunched a single number on any computer. Bill Carmody once said to *Time* magazine writer Sean Gregory '98: "He didn't understand computers or the people who used them."

He was a singular presence, an unforgettable essence. He was, forever and always, very much himself. When I was a player, it was easy to get lost in the way Coach would talk to me. He was unlike any coach or teacher I had ever had. He was so direct, so honest, and often personal.

Many former players would come back to games or to Princeton reunions and tell some of their favorite Coach Carril stories, some good ones and some bad ones—and there is no shortage of these stories. As players, we have all held on to these stories. We tell them to compare tours of duty, to laugh, to unload, but most of all, to honor our Coach.

Coach would occasionally admit to me that he was not always right in the way he did things. I would watch Coach cringe occasionally as he listened to the stories where he was particularly harsh to someone. Coach was, in short, brutally honest. But he was less so as he got older, and he trended towards the positives, towards building relationships that were about more than just basketball. Of course, he enjoyed talking hoops, but he also loved to drill down on the best Gary Cooper westerns, or what makes for a great breakfast sandwich, or to talk about his own kids and grandkids and what they were up to.

It is not always easy to be taught well. For Coach, praise was the cheapest form of reward. When Craig tells that story of Coach giving him a "YO" from the rafters, he says he felt like he was floating in the air.

In 2017, Ben Cohen came to do a featured story on Coach for *The Wall Street Journal* and Carril's influence on the NBA. This was a very important piece to Coach. He had it framed and hanging on the wall of his apartment ever since it was published.

I remember Bill Carmody telling me a story about how, when he was Carril's assistant, high school coaches would often call the office in Jadwin looking for notes or plays on how to run the Princeton offense. Coach would answer the phone. There would be silence for a few seconds. Then he would say, "Figure it out like I did." And then he would hang up.

Good spacing and good players who play together. Who are the X's and who are the O's? What are you doing on every possession to make the guy next to you better? Fellas, I am preparing you to *win the game.* Not to be close. We must make practices harder than the games. You are what you do in practice! (Basketball as a metaphor for life.)

Coach did not like the term Princeton offense, and he told reporters like Cohen and anyone else who asked as much. For him, it was about five guys playing well together, thinking together, speaking the same language. Coach believed that any shot, regardless of distance, in which you are not guarded, is easier than the shot that you are guarded. He constantly asked us: What are you doing on every possession to make your teammates better? If you commit to that, the ball will find you.

Coach wanted his centers to play the game like Bill Russell. He would tell us that there were lots of players that were better than Russell—better shooters, or dribblers, or passers. But no one took away more things from the other team than Russell. No one made you win like Russell.

To celebrate Coach is to talk about his direct influence on us on the court, on sharing the ball, on playing together. But playing for one another is just one part of his legacy. There is a notable influence that Coach has had on the game at every level—everyone from Golden State Warriors coach Steve Kerr to former Boston Celtics coach Brad Stevens counts Carril as an important influence on their careers. With so many of us former players and assistants now coaching, Coach has to have one of the most expansive coaching trees in the country.

His profound influence on the game of basketball itself is sometimes hard to fathom. In the first two years since the advent of the three-point shot, which started in 1987, Coach's teams shot 30% of its shots from behind the arc. Two years later, it was 42%. Two more years later, nearly half of Princeton's shots were threes. (As a point of comparison, in that same year—1991—the percentage of shots taken from beyond the three-point line in the NCAA was near 20%, the NBA below 10%.) Carril, ever the outlier, had those Princeton teams shooting near or above 45% from beyond the arc, not to mention 50% from the field. His 1991 team was nationally ranked most of the season.

Coach was elected to the Hall of Fame in 1997, accepted the very first time he was eligible. He got in on his impact on the game of basketball—his impact on the game, on his players, on the character of the game. Coach understood that he was a dose of reality. He was not the guy in the three-piece suit, never a self-promoter. He stayed true to who he was. This resonated.

In that same *Wall Street Journal* article, Coach was asked if it was easy for him to enjoy watching the NBA's best teams—because the NBA's best teams now played like his old Princeton teams.

Coach responded, in trademark fashion, "You'd have to be blind as a bat to not see that."

Thank you, Coach. Think. See. Do.

We think about you every day. We see you. And we love you.

CHAPTER 30

Brian Earl '99

I had two very different experiences with Coach Carril. My first was as a recruit and player in the mid-1990s. The second was 15 years later as an assistant coach at Princeton. The common thread of both those experiences was Coach's commitment to the truth, although his process of delivering it was different.

He saw the game—and your character—in definitive terms. As a head coach, he would not shy away from telling you in often colorful ways. I had some scholarship options outside of the Ivy League as a high school recruit. Usually, other coaches would explain how they would fit my skill set into their system. I remember one coach coming to my house in a suit and tie during the summer. He was making his pitch and began sweating profusely. He said that I was one of the best high school shooters that he had seen and that I would immediately impact his program. He praised my court vision, hustle, and winning mentality. He sweated through his suit. Shortly after this I went to see Princeton and Coach Carril to hear what he had to offer. Coach simply said, "You're too skinny, you don't play any defense, and you are not as good a shooter as you think you are, but we will take you." All of it true.

I only played one memorable year under Coach—the 1995-96 season that ended with the classic UCLA win. My teammates will probably cover most of the more unforgettable memories. I do know that the most indelible and nerve-racking moments for me were when Coach would go down the line. He would sit us down and pick a few of us to criticize. Everything from your basketball limitations to your character faults, and often the overlapping of the two, were on the table to be aired in front of your teammates. From telling a player he would not rebound because he grew up with a three-car garage to asking if my parents fed me growing up—nothing was out of bounds. The truth was unfurled in public for all to judge.

As a current college head coach, I am afraid to use this tactic with my teams in today's environment. Usually, we have one-on-one meetings with players to discuss these things. But something is lost when guys do not hear the truth in front of their teammates. After a one-on-one meeting they can distort what has been said or deliver it in a different way. After being criticized down the line—among your peers—it is very difficult to go to the locker room and say, "But I am not an assh##e" if your friends know otherwise.

Coach delivered one of the greatest compliments of my life when I mentioned to him years later that maybe I was a little soft as a freshman. He looked at me incredulously, offended that I had misinterpreted his coaching. He said, "No, Brian. You were never soft. I never thought you were scared. You were just too small as a freshman, but I never doubted your toughness." I will keep that compliment forever.

I got to know Coach much better in my years as an assistant coach at Princeton. He retired back to Princeton after his years with Sacramento and began visiting the office a few times a week. Coach and I settled into a comfortable friendship after an initial thawing period. We would grab a soup, head to Conte's after a game, or he would come over for a dinner with my family. He would come to the office, and I would transfer video from my television to the big screen so that I could try to soak up whatever he would see.

I was always hoping that he would tell me exactly what he saw while scouting an opponent or watching video of a recruit—as he did when we were players. It was my way of trying to get the answers before the final. But that was not the Coach Carril I experienced during these years at Princeton. He was a calm, thoughtful, and funny genius who usually made me talk my way through the things I saw and let me make my own mistakes. I can remember opposing fans and writers mockingly referring to him as "Yoda" back in the day in reference to his appearance. But I experienced his Yoda-like teaching and am very grateful for it.

I can only remember two times when he snapped back to his old self. The first was when we were facing Pennsylvania, and we had trouble guarding their mountain of a post player. I watched hours of video. While watching film one day with Coach over a soup, I entertained fronting the post. Coach responded that they had almost won a game against Arkansas and Oliver Miller by just staying behind him and making his shots hard. I talked about doubling from the baseline. He said it was hard to get nine guys to understand the rotations—even NBA guys had difficulty. I started to expand on my next idea. Coach snarled, "Just put Hans (our undersized center) behind his fat ass and you will be alright." We were.

The second time was while we were watching our elite prospect camp where the campers usually come to be recruited by Princeton. We were watching the games with glazed eyes and Coach ambled over to me and pointed to a kid. Coach called him K-A Russo, "as in Kick Ass Russo." We were familiar with the prospect, who was only 6'4," had no left hand, and could not shoot but somehow got things done on the court. Coach brought up K-A Russo to me, head coach Mitch Henderson, and the staff numerous times and we sort of brushed him off. Finally, Coach got our attention and said,

"I don't give a s##t who else you are recruiting, that f##king kid is better than them all." We got the message, and the kid, whose name turned out to be Henry Caruso, not K-A Russo, became a first team All-League and an All-how-does-he-do-that guy.

    I would occasionally bring up with Coach funny stories of how hard he was on guys. They were memories of my year or stories that the players who were older than me would tell over a few beers. Coach did not love talking about his harsher days. He would say that it was important that guys who want to get better hear the truth. He would even admit that he was wrong sometimes. "You know Brian, I used to act like I was right 100% of the time," smiling wryly. "It was more like 90 or 95%, but you didn't have to know that." I am not sure about that.

CHAPTER 31

Gabe Lewullis '99

Coach was brutally honest. He never sugar-coated his thoughts about us as players. More often than not, when he had a comment or critique about your play on the court, it also seemed to have implications for you as a young man and the core of who you were. That really upset me in the moment. I constantly tried to prove him wrong at practice. But, man, that guy was rarely, if ever, wrong.

Phlegmatic

Not a word I heard often, if ever, growing up in the Lehigh Valley, but I will forever associate Coach with being phlegmatic.

It was a mid-season practice and we were on the side court of Jadwin. Everyone hated when we had to be on the side court. It just always seemed like a more difficult, agonizing practice. Side court at Jadwin was one thing, but at times we would practice at Dillon Gym. Yikes! We did not know what would happen there with Coach—perhaps he would let out a large roar and rip his polo shirt after an errant Jesse Rosenfeld pass hit him in the head and knocked his glasses off. The rest of practice he coached and yelled with his polo shirt ripped at the collar with gray and black chest hair flowing out of the torn shirt.

Back to being phlegmatic. In the 1995-96 season, my freshman year, we were scrimmaging five-on-five half-court. I did not think I was playing all that poorly that day, but Coach stopped practice with his standard "Yo, yo, yo!" He then proceeded to explain what I looked like playing basketball and equated it to spitting out phlegm.

"Hey Gabe, do you know what phlegm is?"

(No response from me of course. I learned real quickly from other players you were wise to allow these types of questions to remain rhetorical in nature).

"Well, you are like phlegm out here. Phlegm, you know, you spit it out and it just jiggles on the ground. Nothing firm, just jiggles. That is what you are like out here—phlegm—you are a phlegmatic pussycat from the Lehigh Valley."

After the standard, but, in this case, very strange Coach Carril rant, there was silence and confusion among all in the gym. But then practice just picked up where we had left off and moved forward.

So then I wondered what the hell he was telling me. Obviously, he did not like how I was playing. Maybe I had to be more firm, more decisive on the court, particularly with my cuts. It was hard for me to cut hard when I ran like I had a piano on my back (another Carril-ism used to describe my running style and speed during his recruiting trip dinner in my parent's dining room while eating my mother's lasagna). I decided to work harder on my cuts after that practice.

Did that grossly odd description of my basketball game alter the course of that season, my basketball career, and Princeton hoops history? Maybe it did, maybe not. But that five-minute rant from Coach in front of our entire team sure as hell motivated me. I wanted to prove him wrong. But again, that SOB was right. I was not cutting hard enough. I was not playing decisively enough. I still ran with a baby grand on my back, but I definitely focused on cutting firmer and faster with a purpose. Thank you, Coach.

Lehigh Valley

Any player who played for Coach learned very quickly that his father worked at Bethlehem Steel and that his dad never missed a day of work in his life. He had a work ethic and pushed through the tough days in life. Coach demanded that you give your all during practice no matter the circumstance. That was simple for him to say. It was not always easy for us to do.

Coach made sure to remind me that he had grown up in the tough neighborhood of south Bethlehem, a neighboring town from my hometown, Allentown. Those two towns, along with Easton and many other small communities, comprise the Lehigh Valley. During his recruiting trip to see me, he made sure to show me a newspaper clipping from his years at Liberty High School. It was a photo of him and stated that he was an All-State center that year. A center—really? I had heard he was a tough-as-nails player just as he was as a coach. I always had that Lehigh Valley bond with Coach, and I embraced it. I did not want to let my fellow Lehigh Valley people down.

In March 1996 we played an NCAA play-in game in Stabler Arena at Lehigh University in Bethlehem against our archrival Penn. We won a hard-fought game in overtime. We were going to the NCAA tourney! Princeton friends and fans stormed the court, and we cut the nets down. What a euphoric moment that I had only dreamt about. And it was all happening in the Lehigh Valley. Assistant coaches Thompson and Scott corralled all the players from the chaos and brought us back into the locker room. Coach announced his retirement, writing on the chalkboard in the locker room, "I'm retiring. And I am very happy."

Coach is happy? Wow. I had never heard that all season. After we got back on the bus, the bus took us to a random small cheesesteak spot in downtown Bethlehem. My teammates and I ate cheesesteaks in the backroom, and we then got back on the bus. That one-and-a-half-hour bus ride back to Princeton was unforgettable. Coach let loose and walked to the back of the bus and sang songs with us. He sang the verses while we sang the chorus. I am leaving out some other details intentionally but I had never seen him like that and never did again. Best bus ride ever. Thank you, Coach.

The Three Stooges

During our freshman fall, before official basketball practice started, we would work out and play half-court or full-court. New to campus life, I found myself hanging around a lot with fellow freshmen Brian Earl and Mike Carr. Coach apparently took note of that, as he notes all sorts of things. As we were walking out of Jadwin in the lobby one evening, we crossed paths with Coach. Coach commented, "What, you guys like the Three Musketeers?"

Before I could think about my response, I blurted out, "More like the Three Stooges."

Coach laughed and said, "O.K., you're gonna be all right."

That was such a cool interaction with Coach. He seemed like a grandfather figure with a great sense of humor. I was a bit off on that one. That was something I never would have said after having one official practice with him. He did not use that sense of humor with us when we played for him.

As a freshman, I did not stay up at night, lying in bed thinking about the advanced calculus class in which I was struggling. Instead, I could not figure out what to do when I caught the ball at the top of the key during a low-post play. When I would make a mistake at practice, Carril would shout, "And you wanna be a doctor? You're gonna kill your f##kin' patients!" Upon graduation from medical school, I sent him my graduation notice and reminded him of those comments. He replied and told me that I was going to make a great doctor and that he was proud of me. I still hold on to that letter.

Looking back, I am very glad he retired after my freshman year. His absence allowed Coach Bill Carmody and his assistants to expand the Princeton offense and to adapt to our talented team. I do not think we would have achieved the success of the following years if Coach had still been on the sidelines. He knew it was his time to hand off the program to Coach Carmody. That is a testament to what he instilled in my teammates and the coaching staff. He was a huge part of all those wins during the following years.

I am forever blessed to have had the experiences playing for Coach. He instilled in me the power of accountability and attention to detail. The strength of a team is more powerful than the individuals. I use these lessons daily as an orthopedic surgeon. I learned more valuable lessons in the classroom of Jadwin Gym than in any other building at the University. Thank you, Coach.

CHAPTER 32

Marvin Bressler
(Former Princeton Sociology Department Chair)

In January 2002, a book was being considered commemorating 100 years of Princeton basketball. Renowned Princeton Professor Marvin Bressler, the 20-year Chair of Princeton's Sociology Department, was asked to share some "pearls of wisdom." Excerpts from his draft appear below.

On Timeouts

Anyone grown weary of earthly woes need only poke his head into the huddle of the Princeton basketball team during a time-out with the score tied in the waning moments of a Penn game and intone merrily, "What the hell, it's only a game." He will be assured a swift passage to eternity. There are no coaches and players, and virtually no fans who regard basketball as a mere diversion from the serious business of life.

On Princeton Players

Princeton players . . . are totally miscast as "dumb jocks." Basketball alumni are well represented in education, journalism, law, government, and business, and during my thirty-seven year tenure as faculty adviser to the team, I have rarely known players who regarded the classroom and library as alien territory, were estranged from words and numbers, and exhausted their spiritual capital in post-game expressions of gratitude to "the man upstairs." My conversations with present and former players in a variety of settings about all manner of intellectual and personal issues have been among the most rewarding of any that I have experienced during my time at Princeton. The term student-athlete, then, is no oxymoron and there are lessons to be learned on both sides of the hyphen.

The Culture of Princeton Basketball

The culture of team sports, and of Princeton basketball in particular, is not adequately captured by the recitation of the military virtues or the simple propositions that winning is better than losing, playing well is better than playing poorly, and that playing "hard" is better than surrender. The basketball team is among other things a debating society. Every practice and game invites reflection and discussion about a wide range of issues which in their larger meanings are also prominent in the curriculum of the social sciences and the humanities.

What do players owe to their teammates, their studies, and to themselves? Is it important for players to like each other so long as they cooperate in their assigned tasks? How much can character and a strong work ethic compensate for limited athletic talent? Do players who perform well in practice do well in the game? What accounts for inconsistencies in individual and team play? Should all players be treated alike or do some need "a kick in the rear" and others "a pat on the back?" Which is the more effective form of motivation, praise or blame? What is permissible to tell others and what secrets should never leave the locker room? Should players learn how to "do it right" or do "whatever works for them?" Does leadership consist of words or deeds? Are the best five players always the best winning combination? Are most referees "homers" who are unfair to visiting teams? Is it all right to foul if you don't get caught? Should coaches trust their hunches or always "go by the book?" Is it proper to run up the score on overmatched opponents?

Student-athletes are not of one mind on such questions, and as carriers of both the shared values and internal conflicts of their complex culture, they bring distinctive experiences and perspectives to class discussions about such paired couplets as nature and nurture, talent and desire, discipline and creativity, passion and restraint, pride and humility, specialization and versatility, authoritarian control and democratic values, collective welfare and private ambition, group solidarity and internal competition, perception and reality, free-will and determinism, prediction and chance—and the list could be expanded.

The culture of basketball speaks to teaching as well as learning and a succession of coaches have provided a model of instruction, which deserves the serious scrutiny of everyone involved in undergraduate education. It is a curious hybrid of conservative and liberal educational philosophies that combines concern for "the whole man," commitment to the meritocratic principle of equal rewards for equal performance, insistence on the superior claims of the collective welfare over self-interest, and devotion to the Puritan ethic of hard work, character, and personal integrity. Its pedagogy is informed by the Deweyite creed of "learning by doing," reliance on nineteenth century traditions of repetitive drill, and sustained contact over a four-year period with the same mentor, the coach, who is at once a father, priest, psychiatrist, commander, and a guide to the perplexed in all seasons.

Education, so conceived, may suffer from the defects of its virtues. The student-teacher relationship can be compromised by a coach too hungry for victory and careless in the use of power. These risks remind us yet again how well Princeton has chosen its coaches.

On Princeton's Basketball Coaches Through Pete Carril

Butch van Breda Kolff, the happy warrior of American basketball, has coached with fierce dedication and an irrepressible sense of fun at every level from high school to the NBA. He played for the still-revered Cappy Cappon and coached Pete Carril at Lafayette before returning to Princeton, where his teams won four Ivy League championships and reached the Final Four of the NCAA tournament. He may be justly described as the patriarch of all Princeton-trained head coaches of the modern era; the father of Pete Carril and Gary Walters; the grandfather of Bill Carmody at Northwestern, Armond Hill at Columbia, Jan van Breda Kolff at Pepperdine, and Joe Scott at the Air Force Academy; and the great-grandfather of John Thompson III, who as the heir of the wisdom passed on from the fathers to the sons is carrying on the family business in the same tradition of excellence established by the founder. Mike Brennan, Howard Levy, Craig Robinson, Mitch Henderson, and Chris Mooney now serve as assistant coaches at Princeton or elsewhere.

Pete Carril always knew deep within the recesses of his dark and brooding Castilian soul that the world would not yield anything that was not truly earned. This knowledge is at the root of his characteristic mood of mixed exaltation and despair. His philosophy may be briefly stated as, "The fates are cruel, the fates can be overcome, and isn't it beautiful that the fates are cruel so that they can be overcome?" It was his custom on the eve of each season to issue his annual communiqué predicting that "we'll be lucky to win three games this year," the better to remind himself that if you relaxed your guard even on a moment then all was lost.

I remember an evening in 1975 at a Spanish restaurant near Madison Square Garden on the night before the final game of the NIT after an improbable week of consecutive victories that Coach Carril recalls as the best basketball that he coached at Princeton. The entertainment featured singers of sad songs full of lamentations about the innocent who die young, sailors lost at sea, betrayed lovers, children cruelly separated from their families, and so on into the night without neglecting a single personal or natural catastrophe that might befall the lot of man. I have never seen Coach Carril happier; tomorrow he would be tested again in the uneven struggle between angry gods and human resolve. Thus fortified by his deepest forebodings, the morose magician willed his team to the NIT championship, 13 Ivy League titles, over 500 victories and, protesting all the while, was inducted into the Hall of Fame.

Like Coach, Marvin was a unique Princeton asset and legend. When Marvin died in 2010, Coach Carril tossed a basketball in his grave and softly said, "Best assistant coach I ever had." The following remarks of former Princeton athletic director, Gary Walters, delivered at Marvin's 2010 funeral, perhaps best sum up the relationship between Professor Bressler and Coach Carril:

> "During my six-year (1967-73) hiatus from Princeton, the Professor and the Coach had become close friends, united in temperament by wit, wisdom, and passion, as well as by a dueling flair for drop shots and lobs on the tennis court, tactics which prompted acerbic commentary from each about the other's lack of tennis ability. Although The Professor generally won the rhetorical exchanges, he would readily concede that he was always better at talking a good game than playing one!
>
> The friendship and respect that The Professor and The Coach had for each other, combined with their mutual love for pedagogy, led The Professor to become the unofficial advisor, rabbi, friend, and mensch to the basketball players for four decades. Paradoxically, this magical

relationship with the players gained traction and authenticity because Marv himself took the initiative to show sincere respect for the athletic and cognitive abilities of the players. In doing so, he sparked the players to open their souls to the life of the mind, thus enabling them to become better student-athletes on both sides of that connecting hyphen. The Professor also bridged the racial divide, becoming a champion for Black student-athletes on this campus. His influence moved the players beyond their comfort zones, to another version of "Elsewhere," that place where social and intellectual barriers go up in smoke, where diversity is actually practiced and where the concept of cognitive bandwidth is not limited to the narrowly academic.

The Professor was above all a social force, the personification of a Tipping Point, whose teaching example served as the spark for The Princeton Academic-Athletics Fellows program that is now the envy of universities "elsewhere and everywhere." (Teach for America!!)"

CHAPTER 33

Gary Walters '67
(Princeton Athletic Director, 1994-2014)
(Assistant to Coach Carril, 1973-'75)
(Played at Princeton under Butch van Breda Kolff)

Having grown up in blue collar Reading, Pa., where I attended Reading High School, it was my good fortune to play high school basketball for Coach Pete Carril—who also doubled as my senior year "Problems of American Democracy" teacher, a subject often referred to as civics. Coach Carril was as fine a teacher in the classroom, absent the expletives, as he was on the basketball court. As a high school student-athlete, I could not have had a better mentor.

As a 10th and 11th grader, I was aware that Coach had been a very good player at Liberty High and subsequently Lafayette College, where he had played for Coach Willem ("Butch") van Breda Kolff (VBK) in his senior year. He became a very close friend and protégé of VBK, who himself became an admirer of Carril's coaching.

Coach Carril was named the head coach at Reading High School in 1958. He coached at Reading for eight years and established his coaching bona fides by dominating the Central Penn Conference, employing a suffocating defense and an offense highlighted by back-door action.

His achievements did not go unnoticed. In the spring of 1966, Lehigh, a college then known for its wrestling excellence and basketball irrelevance, hired Coach Carril to turn around the basketball program. And turn it around he did. The year before he assumed the reins, Lehigh was 4-17. In Carril's first year, he led the Engineers to an 11-12 record, punctuating the season with a monumental upset of Rutgers, one of the best teams in the East. He was now on the national radar screen that identified the best young college coaches.

During the 1966-67 season, Princeton and Lehigh basketball were operating on parallel tracks. Led by VBK in my senior season, we achieved a 25-3 record, won the Ivy League and finished ranked fifth in the nation, having lost in overtime to North Carolina in the East Regional—a team we had previously beaten in Chapel Hill.

When we returned to Princeton, very disappointed by our loss to UNC, I had to focus my attention on completing my senior thesis. However, in mid-April I received a call from Coach Carril asking me if I would like to become his freshman\assistant coach upon graduating. Needless to say, I was honored and accepted the job immediately. On the same call, he subsequently asked if I would be willing to play some pickup basketball with his Lehigh players. I readily agreed and suggested that he invite Chris Thomforde too. Coach jumped at that idea, and as fate would have it, our trip to Lehigh would soon play a major role in Coach Carril's future.

Coach drove Chris and me to Bethlehem and then back the next day to Princeton. The shared time we had in the car enabled Chris and Coach to exchange thoughts, opinions, and stories, thus enabling them to bond. We all had a great experience that would subsequently prove to be important.

Approximately a week or two later, the players on the team were asked to assemble at Dillon Gym for an important meeting. Much to our surprise and disappointment, Coach VBK told us he had accepted Jack Kent Cooke's offer to coach the Los Angeles Lakers. As a soon-to-be graduated senior, I felt badly for the returning players, all of whom had been recruited by VBK. Having said that, however, I still had some skin in the game.

Not surprisingly, VBK and I shared the same thought about who his successor should be—Coach Carril, of course. But we had to overcome a major obstacle: VBK and director of athletics Ken Fairman '34 had a very strained relationship. Notwithstanding the fact that Coach Carril had impeccable coaching bona fides, Fairman didn't want another basketball coach with VBK's temperament, compounded by the fact that Carril was a VBK protégé.

A day or two after the VBK-to-the-Lakers announcement, I received a call from Fairman, who asked me to come to his office to discuss the coaching acumen and character of Carril. Understanding that Mr. Fairman's potential anti-VBK bias could extend to Carril, his protégé, I made one of the smartest decisions ever in my life: I recommended that Fairman include Chris Thomforde '69 in the meeting. Chris was the center on the team, was a very smart player, had an impeccable reputation on campus and had spent substantial personal time with Carril on our visit to Lehigh. I could give testimony to Carril's coaching, and Chris could share his evaluation of Carril's character. Fortunately, Fairman took my advice and invited Chris.

As is said, the rest is history. Chris and I were able to convince Fairman that Coach Carril would be the perfect successor to VBK. Twenty-nine years and 514 wins at Princeton later, Coach Carril was enshrined in both the National Collegiate Hall of Fame and the Naismith Memorial Basketball Hall of Fame. And irony of ironies, I transitioned from being his point guard and assistant coach to becoming his boss for two years when I was appointed as athletic director at Princeton in 1994.

I will conclude with this saying from Walt Whitman, which is relevant to Coach Carril's distinguished teaching and coaching career:

"I am the teacher of athletes,

He that by me spreads a wider breast than my own proves the width of my own,

He most honors my style who learns under it to destroy the teacher.

I teach straying from me, yet who can stray from me?

I follow you whoever you are from the present hour,

My words itch at your ears till you understand them."

    Coach, your words will always itch at my ears and those of others you taught. That is your legacy. You passed it forward.

CHAPTER 34

*Jason Garrett '89
(Former Princeton and NFL Quarterback, NFL Coach
and Current NBC Sports Analyst)*

Like all great teachers and coaches, there is always wisdom. Always a takeaway. Always a nugget. Always a lesson.

Lesson 1: Throw It Away from the Defense (The Willow and the Oak)

The first of many lessons I received from Coach Carril came in the winter of 1987. Some of my football teammates and I were working out in the middle of the track at Jadwin Gym. There was a handful of us. A couple of quarterbacks and three or four receivers running one-on-one routes against the defensive backs. Walking around the track wearing an old gray hoodie with Princeton Basketball across the chest was Coach Carril. He was getting in his workout. I was a huge fan of Coach Carril from afar. We were in school during a really fun era of Princeton basketball—the Howie Levy, Joe Scott, John Thompson, Bobby Scrabis, Kit Mueller, etc., years. There were excellent players, and some fantastic teams. We loved going to the home games and even went to some of the road games. The Penn game at the Palestra was a can't miss game for us! While we could not get enough of watching Carril coach his team, we did not really know him very well. Occasionally he and I would cross paths in Jadwin as I was going in for a workout and he was going to play tennis with Marvin Bressler, getting ready to get after 'em in lunchtime hoops, or heading to practice. The conversation was brief and always the same. "Hey Red! How're ya doin'?" I'd always reply, "Great, Coach!" and keep moving. Then, as he walked away, he would always shake his head from side to side and say, "I'd rather be dead than red," and chuckle to himself.

This was the extent of my relationship with Coach until that day at the track in Jadwin. While he appeared to be walking around the track not paying any attention to us, he was the kind of guy who, when he was there, the effort level and the focus and the concentration of everyone involved in the workout picked up. We all wanted to impress him, even though he was not our coach, and we were not quite sure he was even watching. On about his third trip around the track, I threw a pass to the sideline that was broken up by the defender. It was an out-breaking route against an outside leverage defender, and the ball got knocked down. As the pass hit the ground, I heard Coach Carril holler at me from the curve on the track behind me. "Hey Red! Hey Red!!" I turned back to look at him, and he asked in a loud voice, "Hey Red, why did you throw it there?" I explained to him that we had an 18-yard comeback route called, and I threw it to the spot 15 yards down the field and five yards from the sideline where the receiver should be coming out of his break. "I wouldn't do it that way!" he said with conviction. I asked him how he would do it. "I'd always throw it away from the defender! If the defender is outside, I'd throw it inside. If the defender is inside, I'd throw it outside. You and the receiver need to see the defender together and throw it away from him. That's what we do in basketball. Quit banging your head against the wall and throw it away from the defense." Then he turned away and kept walking around the track.

Many years later, I read an article in *The New York Times* about Princeton basketball in which Carril's longtime assistant, coach Bill Carmody, described the Princeton offense as "a lot of yin stuff—oak tree, willow tree…you know." It made me think of that day in the middle of Jadwin's track when Coach Carril was urging me to throw the ball away from the defense instead of into the teeth of the coverage. The idea stuck with me. Coach was conveying that in football, in basketball and in life, there are times when it is best to be a willow and bend and adjust and stay flexible. He would later tell me there are other times, however, when it is best to be an oak and stand strong and be firm and stay true to your convictions. What he was teaching was the idea that the people who thrive in this world have a bit of both the willow and the oak in how they approach things in life. They know when it is best to be flexible like a willow and when it is best to be firm like an oak. This Carril concept is one that I have reminded myself of over and over again in my life. Whether it is trying to attack a defense in football, where you balance "taking what the defense gives you" with "doing what you do best," or just as in everyday life when interacting with family, friends, or colleagues, it is so important to be flexible like that willow without ever forgetting to have a little oak in there too.

Lesson 2: Accuracy Matters (Lead by Example)

I got to know Coach better and better over my last couple of years in school, but it was not until after I graduated and my wife, Brill, and I started hosting a football camp at Princeton that we became friends. Every June for the last 20 years some of my former classmates and teammates from Princeton, as well as players and coaches from college and pro football, descend on Princeton's campus for a football camp for student-athletes from disadvantaged backgrounds in the Tri-State area. It is a one-day football and life-skills camp with a dinner and a leadership forum the night before for all of the out-of-towners. Our staff quickly became a mix of many of our favorite people from in and out of football, including former Princeton basketball great Howie Levy. Prior to one of the early camps, I asked Howie if he thought Coach Carril might be interested in being on the panel at the dinner the night before the camp to discuss leadership. It would be a panel of four people and I would act as the moderator. After talking to Coach, Howie called me back to let me know that Coach did not care much for the pontificating that went on with most panels, but he was excited to come to the dinner and was happy to be part of the discussion.

One of the best parts of the leadership forum is that the people in the audience come from different walks of life and have different insights and perspectives on leadership that benefit us all. One of the biggest challenges of the leadership forum is to keep the discussion on leadership and not on politics. Politics, as we all know, can cause people to get emotional, and the discussion and questions from the audience can become partisan and not very productive. Not only would Coach Carril not bite when it got political, it almost appeared like he was not even listening. At one point, I was trying to make a point about the importance of charisma in leadership and used President Kennedy as an example. I referenced the Nixon-Kennedy debate in 1960 and how those who listened on radio thought Nixon had won and those who watched on television thought Kennedy had won. I was quietly very proud of the point I made, and I asked Coach what he thought—does having a charismatic personality like JFK help you as a leader? He responded by telling me he "didn't hear a word that I had said, had no idea what I was talking about and asked if there was someone in the room who could get him a nice, cold beer." The crowd erupted in laughter! Once the laughter died down and we returned to the conversation, he shared some wisdom with the room that I will never forget.

He asked a simple question. "Where have all the statesmen gone? We need leaders who are statesmen. Guys like FDR and Eisenhower. Doesn't matter the political party. Statesmen! They are leaders who act the right way, with dignity and respect. Statesmen! They are leaders who are concerned about the interests of all, not just the interests of their own party and peddling their own agenda. Statesmen! They are leaders who get the job done." Then he turned to one of his fellow panelists, my former teammate with the Dallas Cowboys, and NFL Hall of Fame quarterback Troy Aikman. "Like you, Aikman. You're a statesman! You led by example, didn't you?" Troy nodded. "Worked harder than everybody, didn't you?" He nodded again. "And when you put that ball right on the money, that helped your leadership too, didn't it?" Troy nodded again, and he and everyone laughed. "Don't tell me about charisma! Set the example! Act the right way! Work hard. Dignity. Respect. No agendas. Get the job done. That's leadership!" The crowd gave him a huge round of applause. The forum was complete. Coach just got up and walked over to the bar and got himself another cold beer.

Lesson 3: One Play at a Time (Focus on the Task at Hand)

Great teachers and coaches understand what is most important, boil it down, and convey it to their students and players in a way that resonates and they always seem to remember.

One of my favorite examples of Coach Carril's prowess in this area happened at our leadership forum dinner in 2017. Coach was not officially on the panel that year, but we always liked to make sure he was seated up close, and when the question-and-answer session began, we tried to get him involved to share some of his insights. The keynote speaker that year was Dr. Sandi Chapman, who started the Center for Brain Health in Dallas. Dr. Chapman made a wonderful presentation and shared different things we all can do to help make our brains healthier. She talked extensively about how our brains respond much better when we focus on one task at a time until it is complete instead of trying to focus on doing many different things at once. She referred to the former as "sequential tasking" and explained that it was much better for our brain health than multi-tasking.

She argued that our brains cannot actually do two things at once, so when we are multi-tasking what our brain is really doing is going back and forth and back and forth between and among the different tasks. The consequence of that approach is that we do not do each task as well as it can be done. The other byproduct of all that back and forth is our brain gets extremely tired and is not as healthy. The point was well-made, but the question came up that sometimes we cannot help but have to do a few things at once, say if you are a mom, an air-traffic controller, or even a basketball coach. Sometimes the situation will not allow us to "sequentially task," and we have to figure out how to handle more than one thing at a time. At this point, as the moderator of the discussion, I thought it was a good idea to ask Coach his opinion on this topic. He responded quickly and loudly by saying, "I agree with the Doctor! She's great and she's exactly right! I'll give you an example. Last night I was making some chicken soup at the stove, and I had to go to the bathroom. As I turned away from the stove, the phone rang. I tried to pick it up and before you know it, I hung up on my daughter, I burned the soup, and I pissed all over myself!" The entire audience burst into laughter! "Focus on one thing at a time!" Coach Carril always seemed to be ahead of the discussion and knew exactly what the conclusion was going to be. Then he had a fantastic way of conveying that message in a manner that you never forgot!

Lesson 4: The Power of Friendship (The Bonds are For Life)

Coach Carril's coaching philosophy was all over the program we built with the Dallas Cowboys. Every year, I would share some of Coach's wisdom with our staff and our team. Whether it was distributing copies of his book, sharing articles on him from *The New York Times* or *The Wall Street Journal*, or simply telling some of my favorite Carril stories, Coach's DNA pervaded our team. Everything from helping our players to "be good at things that happen a lot in the game" to reminding them that it's our job as coaches to notice every little detail and tell our players when it is not right and help them get it right.

Coach's impact on me personally continued to grow each year we did our camp. Not only did he come to the leadership forum, he also came to our post-camp staff gathering: Pizza, beer, and Frankie Crow playing guitar and taking requests into the night. The image of Coach sitting in a chair holding court with a slice of Conte's pizza in one hand and an ice-cold beer in the other while a dozen people circled around him, locked in on his every word, is vivid in my mind. Only to be outdone by him going up to the mic and singing every word of Bob Dylan's *Like A Rolling Stone* and by him dancing to Van Morrison's *Brown-Eyed Girl* with my wife and her crew. Friendship.

When Howie and I went to see Coach the day before our camp in June 2022, I thanked Coach for making such a big impact on me and our team. I also shared with him that some of my favorite memories in my life were the visits he and I had during the camp, especially the Friday afternoons we spent talking in the Caldwell Field House training room. Coach was in the training room doing his daily workout, and I was there to help my wife and others get ready for the camp. Invariably, Coach and I would sit down on those round black stools that the trainers use to go from athlete to athlete, and we would simply talk—sometimes for two to three hours.

I would ask him questions about coaching or basketball history or the NBA Finals or what was happening in college basketball. He always shared such great wisdom and insight.

He would then ask me questions about what was going on in Dallas. What always struck me about our conversations was how well-informed he was about our team. He knew the principals really well—the owner, the coaches, the players, who was someone we could count on, who was someone we needed to keep an eye on, the dynamics between and among different parts of the team, etc. He seemed to know it all. When we finished those conversations, I was always astounded by how much he knew about our team and what we were doing. I always chalked it up to his being such a brilliant coach that he naturally just knew that stuff even though he was not around our team at all.

During our recent visit, when I shared with Coach how impressed I always was with his knowledge of our team, he said something that made me emotional, something I will never forget. He said, "Red, I cared a great deal about the coach! I was following very closely every day. Pulling hard for you!" While I still believe he has unique wisdom, what I found out was even more special—that he was an incredible friend who truly cared about what was happening in my life. And what I have come to find out from many of my Princeton basketball friends is that my story is not unique. He had that same kind of relationship with so many of his former players. He cared about what they are doing. He followed them. He pulled for them. He was always there to provide wisdom and support when needed. Coach Carril was hard on his players and challenged them to live up to incredibly high standards during their time together. The players might not have always liked it, but that environment made them better as players and people. The bonds they formed with their coach and with each other as a result of this experience are life-changing and remain incredibly strong. The friendships they made are for life.

Thanks, Coach! Know how appreciative Brill and I are to have formed some of those same bonds with you through the years. We are forever grateful for your friendship.

    Howie and I wrapped up our visit with Coach by taking a selfie, giving him a hug goodbye, thanking him for everything, telling him that we loved him and that we looked forward to seeing him again soon. He said thanks for stopping by, that it meant a lot to him. He also told us that he loved us and that he would be there when we came back around. Then he said, "See ya, Howie! See ya, Red! … Red. I'd rather be dead than red." We could hear him chuckle to himself as the door closed behind us.

CHAPTER 35

Selected Managers (Calvin Roberts and Chris Palermo)

Calvin Roberts '74

"Winning builds character. Losing just stinks!"

It has been 50 years since I was a basketball manager for Pete Carril but some memories are just indelible.

I was a basketball manager at Princeton because I loved to play basketball, but I was most definitely not at the talent level to play on the team. Still, Coach Carril understood my love of the game, would allow me to work out with the team in practice, and gave me a key that opened the one door at Jadwin gym not connected to the alarm system. That allowed me to come on the basketball floor at any time of the day or night, turn on the klieg lights above the main court and shoot and fantasize for hours. What happy memories I have of those solo workouts.

The Coach's demands on people were proportional to his expectations for their performance. For potential stars, it was exceedingly high. For role players, it was modest. For managers, it was succinct:

1. Learn the responsibilities from your predecessors;
2. Master the business side of basketball;
3. Navigate the administration of the department of athletics;
4. Anticipate the needs of the team and the coaches;
5. Get along with everyone.

Much of the responsibilities of managers in the 1970s is now done by professionals in the department of athletics. But in those days, we were responsible primarily for team travel to away games. This involved buses, planes, hotels, meals, practice schedules, tickets for guests, and post-game beer.

Every era has its unique challenges, and my tenure as basketball manager was dominated by the OPEC cartel-generated energy crisis of the early 1970s. Not only was gasoline availability limited, but also the price of gasoline went quickly from $0.29 a gallon to $1.25. For our coaches, driving to scout potential recruits was key, and part of the manager's job was to wait in long gasoline lines to keep their cars' tanks full.

As a 20-year-old, I was surprised by how much trust Coach had that I would handle my responsibilities effectively with truly minimal supervision. While l felt like a kid, Coach always trusted me and treated me like an adult. Consequently, I tried to act like one and to be as professional as I could. These were early lessons that I drew upon later as a young physician, when despite my lack of experience, I still asked patients to trust me with their care.

Coach Carril always liked to have company. It was not a requirement to converse; it was more one to listen. We would speak in his office or in his car, but most often it was at the bar at Andy's Tavern, where the Coach had a soulmate—the bartender, (Uncle) Joe Fasanella. Coach would discuss his frustrations with certain players who were not achieving what he believed was their potential. Long before Donald Trump, Coach would often say, "I should fire him!"

He also loved to talk about the admissions process at Princeton and how certain recruits who wanted to come to Princeton never got past the admission requirements that Coach believed were more arbitrary than specific. His well-known name for the admissions office was Heartbreak Hotel.

A friend of mine who played basketball at Penn once told me a story about a Penn-Princeton basketball game. Penn at the time was coached by future Hall of Famer Chuck Daly. At halftime of a close game, Daly finished his halftime speech by saying, "You guys better go out and outplay Princeton since you can be sure that they're going to outcoach us." My friend just looked at Coach Daly with disbelief.

The famed broadcaster Howard Cosell once said, "Sports is a microcosm of life." To Coach Carril, basketball was his microcosm of life. He often said to me that you cannot separate the person from the player. You cannot expect someone with bad habits off the court to have good habits on the court. That is why he always tried to visit his recruits at their homes before he watched them play. He was looking first for good young people and second for great basketball players.

One day Coach invited an Israeli sophomore to come to the gym for a workout. While he was tall, he was neither particularly strong nor skilled. When asked why the Coach was interested in this young man as a potential player, he said, "I can teach someone to shoot. I can teach someone to dribble. I can teach someone to play defense. I cannot teach someone to be 6'9"."

The relationship between Coach and the university was always complicated. He reveled in the academic prestige of the university. It meant so much to Coach that he was the coach at Princeton, the elite academic institution. He was so proud of his relationships with renowned professors like Marvin Bressler, Henry Bienen, and Hal Feiveson. He would read and truly study their writings, so that in their company he would sound intelligent and scholarly. He wanted to be known as an intellect and not just as a great basketball coach. With me, he eagerly discussed world events, national politics, and science. He would always remind us that he was a high school history teacher before becoming a basketball coach. His teaching career was always important to him, and he wanted it to define him as much as basketball. I often heard him refer to himself as a teacher of basketball rather than as a coach.

Similarly, Coach was very proud of his players' academic achievements. He would ask them repeatedly about their thesis topics and the progress of their independent research. He totally rejected the concept of the dumb jock and quickly would rebut any critic with a litany of his players' academic achievements.

The only game I missed in my four years at Princeton was one that was scheduled for the evening before the organic chemistry final exam. When I explained to Coach why I felt it was more important for me to be cramming for the final exam than to be at the game, he emphatically agreed and then made sure that future basketball game schedules would never interfere with finals.

Coach always had a great relationship with the press because he provided them with great copy. In 1972, we went to a Christmas tournament in West Virginia. Our first-round opponent was Florida State, which was ranked No. 2 in the country, while host Marshall University had a much weaker first-round opponent. At the pre-tournament banquet, the tournament organizer spoke at great length to explain that the pairings were the result of a random draw. When it was the Coach's turn at the podium, he said, "I don't doubt for a second that the pairings were a random draw. My question is how many times did you have to randomly draw until you got these pairings?"

After we beat Florida State in the first round, when these same West Virginia reporters surrounded Coach for an explanation of Princeton's successful strategy, Coach said, "In this world, the strong will conquer the weak, but the smart will conquer the strong."

My heart will always ache for several of my classmates who were great basketball players but who could not form a relationship with Coach. He coached in an era in which scolding and berating was an acceptable way to motivate players. Certain players either responded positively to Coach's criticism or were able to block it out, while others found it to be too much. His style would not be allowed in today's cell phone camera era when everything one says is recorded. It may be unfair to judge him by today's standards rather than the standards of that day.

Coach's players meant the world to him not only during their playing careers but also after graduation. His memory of players' names, their parents' names, their high schools, and their achievements in high school, plus what they did after graduation, was encyclopedic. In later years, when we would reminisce, he much preferred to talk about his players than to talk about particular games. If I knew something about a former player that he had not yet learned, he was always excited and wanted to hear more.

My relationship with Coach continued after graduation as I became his ophthalmologist and later performed Lasik surgery on both his eyes. Per his nature, Coach asked very few questions about his surgery and simply trusted that I would achieve the results he desired. He was very appreciative of his enhanced vision and was sure to tell everyone how much I had helped him. Several Princeton professors made the journey into Manhattan for their eye surgery solely upon Coach's recommendation.

Coach was also eager to heap praise on us. At my 50th birthday, one of my friends collected remembrances from important people in my life. Coach sent a handwritten note on Sacramento Kings letterhead: "The quality of his work, regardless the endeavor, is tribute enough. He needs no words or mementos from me or anyone else to add to everything he does. He was and is thoughtful, sincere, careful about his work and experiences with others. He was the first of many good young men I met during my tenure as coach at

Princeton. He loved the school and the players and was always there to meet their needs. There's not much more to say. They don't come any better than him."

Sometimes the praise can be uncomfortable, like at the 2018 Friends of Princeton Basketball annual golf outing. At the post-golf cocktail hour, coach Mitch Henderson spoke about his current team and then turned to Coach to speak about the team from the 1990s that was being honored that day. Coach was barely 30 seconds into his comments when he looked at me and then spent the rest of his time talking about me! Well, it was quite awkward as everyone was turning to see who it was that was receiving such high praise.

I love Coach and will forever appreciate all that he taught me about basketball and professionalism and all that he continues to mean to me. But I was not a player, and Coach judged me by a set of standards entirely distinct from his players. Yet he considered his managers as part of the team, and that is why, 50 years later, I remain so committed to Princeton basketball.

Chris Palermo '84

I had the good fortune to be a basketball team manager all four years at Princeton, and with that had the best seat in the house for three Ivy League titles and three NCAA Tournament wins. Fun times, filled with wisdom from Coach Carril that I have tried to carry with me ever since. My senior year, the *Nassau Weekly*, in what must have been an extraordinarily slow news week, ran an article on team managers that accurately quoted me saying something along the lines of, "Most students come to Princeton to study under great professors, but for me it's ended up being an opportunity to study the game of basketball under Coach Carril." I am sure those words warmed my parents' hearts as they paid my tuition. But it was true. Coach was the best and far and away the most impactful teacher I had at Princeton, giving valuable life lessons and instilling the belief that with hard work, creativity, vision, staggering attention to detail, and a willingness to be unselfish and put your teammates in position to succeed, you will have a chance to achieve great things.

Unlike recruited players, I had never met or seen Coach before I started managing the team. All I knew about the state of Princeton's basketball program at that time was that they had just upset a nationally-ranked St. John's team and, I was told, had a "great, young" coach named Pete Carril. Armed with that minimal description, I went down to Jadwin Gym. Sure enough, there was a young coach who fit the image one might have of a Princeton basketball coach: tall, athletic, short haircut, Princeton Basketball golf shirt. That had to be the guy, I thought. Right out of *This Side of Paradise*. And then there was this other guy—older, short, smoking a cigar, wearing a frayed, well-worn Princeton sweatshirt, every now and then yelling, "YO! YO! YO! YO! YO!" "Cut hard!" "Go through!" "Stay wide!" The more I watched, the more I realized that all the players were watching and listening intently to the old guy.

Coach paid incredible attention to detail. He agonized over every pass that was too low or not to the shooter's hand, or thrown to the player who was not in good position to catch it or do anything good with it if he did catch it. Be good at things that happen a lot, he used to say, which meant that every single practice began with layup drills, since the offense, when executed well, resulted in a lot of layups. And it was important to make them. All of them. He watched the layup drill with an intensity I have never seen, literally rocking forward as he stood there when the ball left each player's hand, as if doing so might help will the ball into the basket. God forbid somebody missed one—a bad way to start practice. And just to be clear, we are talking about practice. Not a game. We are talking about practice.

Coach constantly preached the importance of preparation—scouting the other team and knowing its players' tendencies. Force this player right; make that guy dribble; do not let him catch and shoot; let that guy shoot from there all night if he wants. Hard work and preparation were the keys to having a chance to succeed. Few coaches worked as hard as Coach to prepare. Senior year, forward Kevin Mullin '84 scored 38 points in a nationally-televised preliminary round win in the NCAA Tournament against the University of San Diego. After the win, we prepared to play our first-round game against 13th-ranked UNLV, coached by the legendary Jerry Tarkanian, with our second team quickly learning the Runnin' Rebels' offense and defense and pushing our starters to give us the best chance to win, as always. Against that background, I was shocked when Coach Tarkanian came over to me at the scorer's table, moments before tip-off, and asked, "Which one is Mullin?" Coach never would have been so unprepared. Most games, we knew what the other team was trying to do better than they did.

Coach was tough on his players, and his criticisms could often be personal. I had the sense that he reserved his harshest words for players he thought had the greatest potential. I can think of a player who, to this day, I am astonished was willing to put up with Coach's diatribes the entire four years he played at Princeton. That takes a thick skin. My lone regret about my interactions with Coach came my senior year when, after one practice during which he was particularly critical of one of the underclassmen, he asked me if I thought he had been too harsh. I was so surprised he asked me that I quickly said, "No, not at all." In hindsight, I should have given him the same blunt honesty he gave his players and told him that he was picking on the wrong guy and that there might not be a right guy for that approach on that team.

Coach stressed the importance of knowing your strengths and limitations, joking that nobody would ever mistake him for Cary Grant, a name I took to calling him from time to time. He also knew he could be over the top at times, and every now and then he let his players know that he knew that. One of the starting forwards my junior year was Gordon Enderle '83, who was so wholesome that his nickname was Opie, after Andy Griffith's son on the old *Andy*

Griffith Show. After ripping into Gordon fairly mercilessly for an entire practice, Coach concluded practice as he often did by commenting at length on each player that day, saying, "Gordon, I don't know when it will be, but one day, one day, you're going to get a call from my wife telling you I passed away. And you're going to ask her, 'Was he in pain? Did he suffer?' And she'll say, 'Oh, yes. He suffered horribly, and he was in terrible pain.' And do you know what you're going to say when you hear that, Gordon? Do you know what you're gonna say to my wife? You're gonna say, 'GOOD!'"

As a manager, I suspect I had a different relationship with Coach than his players did. I did not have to endure his seemingly constant critiques and sometimes brutal candor. Still, he expected precision on and off the court, and I was by no means immune from his sharp tongue or his expectation that those working with him would be prepared. Sophomore year, after a tough loss, Coach Carril invited me to join him and the assistant coaches at the bar on our road trip. I was more than happy to be a fly on the wall, and he was buying. But to my surprise, after talking to the coaches, he asked me what I thought they should do. I lobbied for more playing time for a player who among other things was a great scorer. Although Coach did not specifically say I was blind, as he so often told players who could not spot open teammates at practice, he might as well have, pointing out in great detail the many things I missed, getting increasingly animated as he explained why I was wrong, like a great professor in a precept (albeit with beers in hand).

Some have asked me whether Coach was a curmudgeon. My answer is an emphatic no. He might well have been the funniest person I met at Princeton. And he definitely knew how to have fun—his end-of-year parties at Jadwin, the Sunday before reading period, were epic, fun as any house party. They began early in the afternoon and went until early the next morning. Senior year, when we returned from the NCAA Tournament, Coach ordered pizza and beer for the team, and we stayed at Jadwin well into the night. Coach loved every minute of it—a surprising Ivy League championship season, won after starting the Ivy season 0-2 for the first time in his career. At one point, as the festivities were winding down, he said to me simply, "We can't let this thing end." So much did the game and his teams mean to him. Coach also regularly broke into song, including occasionally singing *Blue Bayou* (or *Blew By You*) in practice when someone decided (in Coach's words) to sign a non-aggression pact and play no defense. And he could actually sing. Curmudgeons do not sing.

Legendary Princeton sociology professor and longtime formal and informal Princeton basketball academic advisor Marvin Bressler, in describing Coach, used to say that a key ingredient to being enormously successful at anything in life is to care about whatever that thing might be in complete disproportion to its overall importance to the universe. And this was true of Coach, whose passion for coaching winning team-basketball was boundless.

During the 1981-82 season, we played Seton Hall on the road and led at halftime by 18 points, 42-24. Alas, in a frustrating season in which 12 of our 13 losses were by five points or less and seven were by a total of 13 points, Seton Hall came back to beat us 75-74, when Danny Callandrillo, who finished third in the country in scoring that season, hit a last-second jumper off a missed shot that we should have rebounded. Coach came into the press conference afterwards, and a reporter asked when the last time was that Princeton had scored 42 points in a half, which he dutifully tried to answer. Another reporter then asked when the last time was that one of his teams had blown an 18-point halftime lead. To his great credit, without cursing, he simply said, "I think you guys don't want to talk to me. You want to talk to our sports information director." He then returned to the locker room, picked up one of those old-style, two-sided, wooden chalkboards on wheels that was bigger than he was, lifted it above his head and threw it against the wall. No one ever had to wonder whether Coach cared.

At the end of the season my senior year, Coach took all the seniors down to an Italian restaurant in Trenton for dinner and to watch the NCAA championship game. On the drive back, he commented about each of the seniors (two of whom ended up being NBA draft picks), as he often did about each player at the end of practice. As usual, Coach was brutally honest. After commenting about each of the players, he turned to me. What might he say after my four years as a manager, time spent keeping the official scorebook, handling game tickets, travel and meal money, and dutifully looking for the occasional lit cigar Coach left on the (wooden) bleachers at Jadwin? Nearly 42 years later, I still remember exactly what he said: "Chris, in the 30 years I've been coaching basketball, you have the ugliest jump shot I've ever seen." Howls of laughter and protest exploded from my classmates in the car. This precipitated a heated debate about whether various Princeton players had uglier jump shots, with Coach insisting, correctly, that several players whose names quickly came up did not count because they did not have a jump shot.

Coach's legendary coaching career earned him the respect of coaches at every level and a richly deserved place in the Basketball Hall of Fame. His style of play is emulated by many, even at the NBA's highest levels. More than 25 years after he retired from Princeton, five of his former players are coaching Division I programs. More should be. Beyond all of his success, through his loyal devotion to Princeton, his passionate commitment to doing things the right way, with preparation and hard work, he created a culture of high expectations and a bond among those who played for or worked with him. That bond continues to this day, with those who now play at Princeton aspiring to achieve the success of those who played before them, and those whose playing (or managing) days are over caring deeply about each other and about the success of those who follow, and missing Coach greatly now that he has passed away.

Coach once said, "I am committed by my style and principles of life to make the best of whatever the situation. It has been the way

I have done things my entire life. I get my happiness out of seeing things done right, out of being successful, out of seeing the interaction of people working together for a good cause, spilling their hearts out on the floor, giving you the best of what they have."

That's a helluva legacy for the "great, young" coach I first saw down at Jadwin more than forty years ago.

CHAPTER 36

Selected Sportswriters' and Authors' Tributes to Coach Upon His Passing

Pete Carril died on Aug. 15, 2022. Numerous media tributes were immediately written across the country. This chapter includes five such tributes.

Pete Carril, Engineer of the 'Princeton Offense,' Was Decades Ahead of His Time

The blue-collar coach always deflected praise toward his players, and believed their character and intelligence were a result of how they approached the game.

ALEXANDER WOLFF '80
AUG 15, 2022

As originally printed in SI.com

> The coach approved the postgame stop at the 7-Eleven, agreed to the purchase of the beer, even signed off on the conversion of his hotel room into a speakeasy for that beer's consumption. And drink his players did, well into the Shenandoah night,

spilling out into the hallway on account of their delegation's high spirits and in spite of their low numbers—numbers that, as we'll see, are part of this story.

Around midnight the commotion roused a hotel guest, a woman who confronted the presumptive adult in charge, who stood in that corridor wearing a T-shirt and black boxers.

"May I ask what you're doing?"

It's said that Pete Carril, the Hall of Fame basketball coach who died Monday morning at age 92, sent a cloud of cigar smoke her way before delivering his answer: "I'm wallowing in success."

That moment was uncharacteristic of the man who presided over the program at Princeton for nearly three decades. No coach more hastily declared virtually every one of his 525 victories "ancient history." Yet Princeton's 55–50 win at Virginia 47 years ago deserved a little wallowing. It's a game from which he was ejected, yet years later he would call "the highlight of my life as a coach." It carries a lesson for teachers of all types, and stands as a worthy lens through which to look at the life and coaching career of Pete Carril.

On the morning of Feb. 25, 1975, Carril's Tigers had headed to Charlottesville in a strange psychological limbo, at once gaining confidence and wobbling in their faith. They had strung together six wins in a row thanks to a core of average-sized upperclassmen that included future NBA guard Armond Hill, as well as Mickey Steuerer, Tim van Blommesteyn, Brien O'Neill and Peter Molloy. A couple of rapidly maturing big men, Barnes Hauptfuhrer and Lon Ramati, supplemented them with size and muscle. But only one weekend of Ivy League play remained, leaving Princeton with quailing hopes of claiming the conference's automatic bid to the NCAA tournament.

The Tigers had split their home-and-home series against Penn and stumbled at Brown. Lagging a game behind the

Quakers, Princeton knew that even a sweep of Brown and Yale on the final weekend of conference play would mean little unless Penn lost to one of the same two opponents. And without winning at least 20 games, the Tigers weren't likely even to land a bid to the National Invitation Tournament, which still held prestige during an era when the NCAA field accommodated only 32 teams.

Worse, Princeton had traveled south exhausted and depleted. The game was set for the Monday after the Tigers negotiated the Columbia-Cornell bus trip, the Ivy's toughest. The team took only nine players because of injury and illness. Except for a trainer and a team doctor, Carril would be the only person on the bench in civvies. He feared the trip would be such a fool's errand that he had dispatched his top assistant, a former Princeton player named Gary Walters, to check out a high school prospect in Kentucky, while his other aide, Bob Dukiet, coached the Tigers' freshmen against the Army plebes.

So, still weary after the eight-hour ride back from Ithaca, the Tigers flew from New Jersey that morning to the seat of Mr. Jefferson's University, where not 36 hours earlier Virginia had beaten nationally ranked North Carolina. Late in the afternoon, the Princeton players took their pregame meal, then filed out of the hotel to board the bus for the short ride to University Hall. In the parking lot an impeccably groomed woman began to heckle them. "She was maybe mid-forties, a Southern belle, but one of these rah-rah, Wahoo Virginia fans," Hauptfuhrer remembers. "She was saying things like, 'Our Cavaliers are gonna whoop up on you folks to-*night*!' I guess she was expecting Coach Carril to say something back. Coach just stared at her. She waited for him to say something, but he kept staring. Finally she got uncomfortable and turned to walk away. That's when Coach yelled, 'Hey!' She turned back around like she'd had a shock to her system, and he went, '*Grrrrrrrrr!*'

We watched all this while getting on the bus, laughing so hard we were guaranteed to come out loose."

Taking the floor before the customary Virginia sellout, Steuerer couldn't help but notice the Cavaliers' bench—"an endless line of players," he remembers, with lieutenants in matching orange blazers flanking coach Terry Holland, then in his first season at the school. Many of the 7,450 fans in the stands wore orange too, but only a scattering matched theirs with black, Princeton style.

The two teams spent the first eight and a half minutes shadowing each other, which emboldened the visitors, who knew the long odds Princeton faced by drawing a homestanding Atlantic Coast Conference power for what was a third road game in four nights. Hauptfuhrer sank an 18-foot jumper that pulled the Tigers to within a point at 11–10.

And that's when the lights went out.

Suspicious by nature, Carril believed someone on the Virginia bench had signaled an electrician to break whatever spell was causing the home team's slow start. After a 20-minute wait for the mercury vapor lighting to come back on, play resumed with Virginia inbounding the ball on the sideline—whereupon van Blommesteyn darted in front of the pass and sailed in for a layup. On the Cavaliers' next possession, Hill poached into the passing lane on the wing to make a steal of his own, scoring another layup. The first boos tumbled from the upper reaches of the home team's roundhouse arena.

Hill picked off another pass and converted, and moments later he swanned in for two more points after another steal. When van Blommesteyn added yet one more steal and layup of his own, Holland, furious, called timeout to rip into his guards, who seemed still to be basking in the defeat of Carolina over the weekend. The Cavaliers' coach subbed in an entirely new backcourt. "The first play after that timeout, they throw another pass to the wing," Molloy recalls. "And Timmy intercepts it too and goes in for *another* layup." The Tigers ended the half with an 11–2 stretch. Turning six stolen passes into snowbird baskets, they left the floor with a 31–21 lead. The second half would deliver even more remarkable events. But of those first 20 minutes Holland would later say, "I'll never watch something like that again. If I have to, I'll get thrown out myself."

Pete Carril was born in Bethlehem, in Pennsylvania's Lehigh Valley, in 1930 to a father who had emigrated from Spain to work in the steel mills. A coal yard across the street served as young Pedro's childhood playground. First in high school, then at Lafayette, he played run-and-gun, the furthest style possible from what he would become known for as a coach. By '67, Princeton had seen its two high-profile Bills kite off to the NBA: All-American forward Bill Bradley to the Knicks and coach Bill "Butch" van Breda Kolff to the Lakers. On van Breda Kolff's recommendation, the school hired Carril, who had just finished coaching his first collegiate season—a losing season—at Lehigh.

During Carril's early years, Princeton played an offense lively enough to produce, in Geoff Petrie and Brian Taylor, NBA and ABA rookies of the year, respectively. But by the mid-1970s, escalating tuition costs and the Ivy League's long-standing refusal to permit athletic scholarships began to price the Tigers out of the market. As he struggled to attract first-rate athletes, Carril chose to hunker down. He developed a set of offensive principles based on the old "pivot play" popularized by Dutch Dehnert and the Original Celtics back in the '20s. His teams would wait out an opponent, carefully moving the ball around the perimeter, until a defender, lulled or careless, turned his head. Then, suddenly, some Tiger would "pull the string" and cut through the open middle to the basket, taking a pass and converting a layup.

Carril's teams would go on to use "the Princeton Offense" to engineer a series of signal NCAA tournament victories and near-misses, most notably a one-point, down-to-the-wire first-round loss against Alonzo Mourning and Georgetown in 1989, which until UMBC's upset of Virginia in 2018 was as close as any No. 16 seed had come to upsetting a No. 1. But the final victory of Carril's career—the game that seared him into the minds of the public and probably ensured his enshrinement in the Hall—was Princeton's 43–41 upset of defending-champion UCLA in the first round of the '96 NCAA tournament. Victory came on a backdoor layup in the dying seconds, after Carril, during a timeout, had urged forward Gabe Lewullis to circle back and try "pulling the string" again if he couldn't at first get his defender to bite on a backcut. That's precisely how Lewullis freed himself for the winning shot, a basket that became a monument to Carril twice over: as the Tigers' signature play, to be sure, but also as a demonstration of the stubborn faith their coach placed in it.

Carril detested praise, both the collecting and dispensing of it. "The cheapest kind of reward," he called it. Late in his final season, right after Princeton had held Dartmouth to 39 points, someone asked him about his team's defensive performance. Carril sensed a trap. Surely Dartmouth deserved no praise, but he had found plenty to be desired in his own team's play. The coach's answer was a rhetorical backdoor pass, threaded past the premise of the question to score a point of its own: "They have guardable players. And we guarded them."

Throughout his career, Carril used his working-class beginnings as a touchstone. He made an obsession out of the truism that material comfort rarely confers advantages on those who play basketball. The game instead rewards guile and deception, traits bred on city streets and at lower social strata. So he brought the sons of cops and firefighters and holders of union cards to the Ivy League school. He didn't consider basketball to be a builder of character; it was instead, he believed, a revealer of it. How someone played the game told Carril everything he needed to know. Indeed, his greatest flaw was a tendency to believe that a player came to him with character fully formed, and thus it wasn't always worth the effort to change him for the better.

In Carril's worldview, beer had its place. He considered it a restorative drink, the reward due a man after an honest day's work. He winced when he saw his players eating candy. Children ate candy. He wanted his players to be men, and men drank beer. This veneration of proletarian life helped him survive on an Ivy League campus—to cope, as a *Sports Illustrated* headline once put it, with being "a blue-collar coach in a button-down league."

Like van Breda Kolff before him, Carril in 1996 nominated his own successor. He did so with an ad lib at a postgame press conference after clinching the league title at the end of his final season, declaring that his longtime assistant, Bill Carmody, would replace him—"after a brief search." (At this, Gary Walters, by now Princeton's athletic director and nominally Carril's boss, watched from the back of the room with the blood draining from his face.) Two years later, under Carmody, the Tigers lost only twice and were ranked No. 8 in the country. The season's emblematic moment came in Madison Square Garden, during a defeat of Niagara in the ECAC Holiday Festival, when Princeton scored every one of its 21 field goals on an assist. With the Tigers briefly flummoxed by the Purple Eagles' switch to a zone defense, Carmody called timeout. In the huddle, his players looked at him searchingly. Carmody could have been channeling his old boss when he told them, "You're smart guys. You figure it out."

The home team's sluggish start, the blackout, the ease with which Hill and van Blommesteyn made sport of the Virginia guards—all combined to make for a bizarre first half. But the strangest moment came slightly more than five minutes into the second, after which the Princeton players were indeed left to "figure it out."

Virginia's offense involved running its All-American forward, Wally Walker, off a series of screens to spring him free. Until late in his career, when they played virtually nothing but zone, Carril's teams rarely conceded any pass, and the man guarding Walker on this night, Hill, contested every cut and fought through every screen. As the Cavaliers struggled to catch up, Walker became more and more frustrated. Finally the two stars' private battle came to a reckoning. Walker cut off a back screen. Hill scrambled over its top, beating Walker to his intended destination on the wing. That's when—in the Princeton telling, anyway—Walker shoved Hill out of the way, sending him, as Hauptfuhrer remembers it, "under the scorer's table."

Referee Lou Moser had to blow his whistle. But then Moser, a veteran ACC official, did something that left the Tigers in disbelief. He ruled not that Walker had shoved Hill, but that Hill had shoved Walker, thereby committing his fourth foul. What happened next, Steuerer says, was "like out of a movie." Carril flung his program to the floor and lit out after Moser "with his full Spanish red temper on high," Hauptfuhrer recalls. "He was already in a foul mood from the lights going out. When this happened, his cork popped."

After the game, Carril would sound Churchillian in his indignation, calling Moser's call "the most flagrant act against fair play I've seen in 20 years." But his response in the moment was a cartoonish stream of profanity that left his players so slack-jawed they failed to perform the task that normally fell to Princeton's absent assistants—restraining the head coach so he wouldn't get tossed.

No transcript exists of exactly what Carril said to earn his only ejection in 29 seasons. But according to the recollections of several players, Moser whistled the first technical foul after Carril called him a cheater. He whistled the second after Carril called him a redneck. In those days it took three, not two, T's for a coach to get ejected. And so:

"Say one more word and I'll give you a third!"

"You're a @#$%*&%^$# cheating redneck!"

"It was funny, really," Molloy recalls. "It was like when you tell your kid, 'Say one more word and you're grounded,' and your kid says, 'Word!' Coach really did do everything but slug the guy."

Once Moser had banished him, Carril began to consider the consequences. "He wouldn't leave," Steuerer says. "We're like, 'Coach, you've gotta go.'" But Carril believed he couldn't go—not so much because he had no assistant to coach the team, but because he didn't want to leave his players to the tender mercies of someone he considered to be "a @#$%*&%^$# cheating redneck."

As it happened, the other official whistling that night's game—college basketball hadn't yet adopted the three-man officiating crew—was a veteran well known to the Princeton party. Hal Grossman worked often in the Northeast, and Carril had actually grown up with him in the Lehigh Valley. "Hal sort of calmed me down," Carril would recall years later. "Said I was embarrassing him. That's sort of why I agreed to leave the court."

A couple of Princeton players clearly remember one other thing Grossman told Carril: "You tell your boys to hustle. If they do, they shouldn't have anything to worry about."

Carril appointed Molloy, a 5'10" junior reserve from Merrick, N.Y., as acting coach and took his leave. A calm quickly settled over the bench. "Carril wasn't the world's greatest game coach, because he'd get so worked up that smoke would be coming out of every orifice," says Richard Stengel, another reserve guard on that team. "What struck me was how calm and focused Peter [Molloy] was. It's like with horses: If you're calm, they're calm. He spoke clearly and softly and told us to do the simplest things."

Before departing, Carril ordered the team to give up its aggressive man-to-man and instead play a 1-2-2 zone, with Hill planted safely at the point to avoid his fifth foul. Then, flanked by security guards, the coach took up position in a tunnel leading from the court.

Molloy says he faced only one difficult decision the rest of the game: whether to sit Hill down or risk that fifth foul. But Steuerer disputes this. "Lon Ramati hardly ever took a shot, and within 30 seconds after Coach gets thrown out and we decide we're slowing it down, Lonnie jacks up a turnaround airball from 20 feet," he says. At that, Hauptfuhrer remembers looking over at Carril in the tunnel and seeing the coach draw an index finger across his throat. Whether or not the team's new player-coach saw the gesture, Molloy made his move, replacing Ramati with O'Neill, a guard, and ordering the Tigers into a forerunner of the Princeton Offense.

In January, Carril had installed the alignment, a four-guard set he then called "the Open Offense," to cover for his team's lack of size. By late February, it had evolved from a jerrybuilt fix into an effective weapon. If they seized a lead, Carril would sit Ramati, as erratic a foul shooter as he was an offensive player. With Hill, Steuerer, van Blommesteyn and O'Neill or Molloy arrayed around the sweet-shooting Hauptfuhrer, Princeton would prosecute each possession with patience. Controlling the ball, snapping off passes and cuts, staying wide to keep the lane vacant (hence the name "open"), they waited out backdoor opportunities and spotted up for jump shots if a defender became too mindful of his flanks. The Open Offense had an additional virtue: Four guards created at least two mismatches. "No forward was fast enough to guard Armond [Hill] or Timmy [van Blommesteyn]," Molloy recalls.

And so Princeton minded the clock—the game clock, for the shot clock hadn't yet been introduced. The Tigers' 35–29 advantage upon Carril's ejection flowed to eight and ebbed to two but never entirely evaporated. Molloy called only two timeouts, the first with 5:11 to play. "It was either to remind the guys that we were trying as much as possible to hold the ball," he would say years later. "Or it was just to catch our breath. There were no TV timeouts back then."

The game turned on a moment right after the first of those stoppages. Since Carril's ejection, Grossman had served as Princeton's guardian angel. "If there were 15 close calls down the stretch, we must have gotten 14 of them," Molloy says. "Grossman would step in and wave the other ref off."

With slightly more than four minutes remaining, the black stripes on Grossman's shirt looked more than ever like those of a Tiger. Hill drove down the gut of the Virginia defense, flipping in a shot while sending the Cavaliers' Mark Newlen into a heap on the floor. You couldn't find a more explicit charge in an indictment, and Lou Moser stood poised to make the call. But Grossman freight-trained on to the scene. He whistled a block, counted the basket, and sent Hill to the free-throw line, where he added the point that pushed Princeton out to a 48–40 lead. Hill's full-contact layup would be the Tigers' final field goal of the game. From there the Cavaliers could only foul, and Princeton sank seven of 11 free throws, including a couple by Molloy who, after van Blommesteyn fouled out with 2:20 to play, had finally put himself in the game.

As Princeton's victory became more likely, several Virginia fans gathered along the railing overlooking the tunnel to bait and throw things at Carril down below. "Policemen chased everyone back to their seats," the coach recalled in 2001, still sounding surprised that the cops had afforded him any protection at all. By the time the buzzer sounded, he had already retreated to the safety of the Tigers' locker room, where he greeted his jubilant players. "Muggs [Molloy] and Mickey [Steuerer] were soaking their knees in ice," he remembered. "Everyone was asking, 'How in heck did we ever do this?' There was a moment of silence, and Mickey said, 'Well, we finally got ourselves a coach.'"

Firing up a cigar, Carril met the press to make the case of a man wronged. "My guy got pushed 20 feet," he said, "and they called the foul on him!" Then he urged reporters to interview "our real mastermind."

"The kid wants to be a coach," he said of Molloy. "I'm trying to get him to be a lawyer. He's got 1520 board scores and his old man is spending 6,000 bucks to send him to Princeton. To do what? To be a coach?"

The Tigers swung by that 7-Eleven on the way back to their hotel, making sure the cashier knew the lettering on the marquee outside—a pregame message that still read "CAVS OVER TIGERS"—needed revision. Then the team repaired to Carril's room. "The beer went in the bathtub," the coach recalled. "And they sat me up on the bed, like a king."

A year later, Molloy, the Tigers' coach-in-a-pinch, would find himself featured again, this time in one of Princeton's tantalizingly unavailing efforts in the NCAAs. With his team up a point and four seconds to play, the Scarlet Knights' Eddie Jordan fouled Molloy, a 90% free-throw shooter, sending him to the free-throw line for a one-and-one. Rutgers called a timeout, and another timeout, desperately hoping to preserve with some magic spell an unbeaten season that for the moment lay out of its hands. Finally, Molloy squeezed off his shot, the last competitive one of his life. It clanked off the back of the rim.

Afterward Carril and his one-time understudy headed to the coach's favorite dive, Andy's Tavern, on the fringe of campus. Together they drank beer into the small of the morning. "Believe me," Molloy says, "more people remember Rutgers than remember Virginia."

But considering how it fit into the grand scheme of Princeton's 1974–75 season, the Virginia game should earn Molloy a more flattering kind of immortality. That victory in Charlottesville, followed by a sweep of Brown and Yale the following weekend, did win the Tigers, despite an 18–8 record, a place in the NIT, where they took out Holy Cross, South Carolina, Oregon and Providence in what became one of the program's great accomplishments. For much of its postseason run, including most of the second half of the NIT final, an 80–69 defeat of the Friars, Princeton used the same offensive set that had so bamboozled the Cavaliers and would become Carril's great legacy to the sport. "The crispness, the ball movement, the cutting, the way we broke the press—everything we did in Madison Square Garden [during the NIT] followed from that game," Hill remembers. "The Virginia game began everything, with five guys being mentally together."

A year later, the morning after the loss against Rutgers and suddenly free from Carril's ban on facial hair, Molloy let his beard go. It lasted into the next century. He did leave Princeton with the vague idea of becoming a coach, and briefly signed on as an assistant at his old high school on Long Island, St.

Agnes Catholic School in Rockville Centre. But as Carril would have it, Molloy wound up going to law school, and then into the title insurance business in Mineola, N.Y., where he and his wife raised four kids. He limited his coaching to CYO ball. Over the years, Molloy became amused at how often his old coach would mention that game he failed to finish. "I think it became part of his shtick," Molloy says, "because the story's not really about him."

Of course, in the end, the story is entirely about him—about how soundly he taught the game. Is it any wonder that a Chicago-based team composed of various former Tigers, including Barack Obama's brother-in-law Craig Robinson, became a perennial three-on-three champion, regionally, nationally and even internationally? As Carril conceived and imparted it, the Princeton Offense was basketball at its most stripped down. By the end of the century, it had spread throughout the sport, with teams at every level adopting its principles because they could be so effective, no coach required. "I've always said the test of a teacher is how the students do when the teacher isn't around," says Hill, who after a pro career installed the Princeton system as coach at Columbia and went on to win an NBA title in 2008 as an assistant with the Celtics. "He did such a good job drilling us. There were times he'd ask us to do things and we'd ask why. Against Virginia, we found out why."

Or as Steuerer puts it: "We didn't need as much coaching because we were older and pretty experienced. But it just goes to show that if you prepare properly, a game is no different from practice. It's the team whose coach tries to get everyone all pumped up that's in trouble, when you should really be doing just what you do every day.

"I don't remember ever getting a motivational speech from

Coach—anything like, 'C'mon, play hard.' Play hard is what you're supposed to do."

What Carril ceaselessly urged his players to do was play smart. "That game was the most beautiful display of knowledge I've ever seen," Carril would later say of that February night, delivering himself of that rarest of things, a compliment. "The fellas played so smart, it was unreal."

Praise may indeed be the cheapest kind of reward. And Carril's long wallow in how smart his men played that night was, in a roundabout way, a kind of bouquet to himself. But with that game his pupils delivered a lesson of their own. *He that by me spreads a wider breast than my own proves the width of my own,* goes the stanza from the 47th section of Walt Whitman's "Song of Myself," a poem about teachers of athletes that Walters shared with each of his coaches after he became Princeton's athletic director. *He most honors my style who learns under it to destroy the teacher… My words itch at your ears till you understand them.*

The best teacher, Carril's players demonstrated that night, is the one who engineers his own redundancy.

How Pete Carril of Princeton Changed Basketball, the NBA— And Me

SEAN GREGORY
AUGUST 15, 2022

As originally printed in TIME

It was the summer of 1994, and my mom popped into my room to deliver a message: Pete Carril was on the phone. I walked out into the kitchen to grab the old landline receiver, nervous about what this conversation could possibly be about, and a bit awestruck that it was even going to happen.

By then Carril, the innovative Hall of Fame basketball coach who died, at 92, on Monday, was known throughout the hoops world as a near-slayer of giants: five years prior, on St. Patrick's Day, his 16th-seeded Princeton team put a scare into top-ranked Georgetown Hoyas in the first round of the NCAA tournament. Princeton lost, 50-49. But at a time when the college basketball powers-that-be were considering eliminating automatic March Madness bids for the small conferences, the Georgetown-Princeton game restored faith in Cinderella's charm. It was the highest-rated hoops game in the history of ESPN. The little guys kept their spots and CBS bought the rights to the whole NCAA tournament. The NCAA men's basketball tournament is now an $8.8 billion enterprise, and the March office pools a national pastime.

I now had a chance to be a part of all this. Carril recruited me to play for Princeton very late in my senior year of high school, and I'd be heading down to New Jersey come fall. There was one problem, the subject of this phone call: at 6'3", 155-pounds, my dimensions were not optimal for banging under the boards with, say, former Georgetown center Alonzo Mourning, who willed the Hoyas to victory over Princeton back in 1989. Forget Mourning: those dimensions weren't ideal for going up against 99% of Division 1 players. I needed to put on weight, fast, and Carril was calling to make a very specific suggestion.

"Yo, Sean, here's what you need to do to get bigger: drink a six-pack of beer and eat a ham sandwich, before bed, every night. Got that kid?"

I laughed. Carril didn't. He was deadly serious.

Up to this point, I had known Carril only as so many people from the outside viewed him: as the Yoda-like sideline genius whose deliberate style of play, which emphasized passing and movement and more passing until a worn-down defense gave up an easy shot, enabled an undersized team like Princeton to hang tight with Georgetown, Arkansas, Villanova, and Syracuse in four straight NCAA tournaments from 1989-1992. As I'd soon discover, Carril was so much more. What he lacked as a nutritionist or a purveyor of modern-day "load management"—all his starters often played nearly 40 minutes a night—he made up for in viewing the game, and life, in the maddeningly effective terms of a pop philosopher. See what's around you. If you can't see, you can't do. Share the ball. If you're closely guarded, go backdoor. Don't spend too much time reflecting on the past, because what does that really do for you in the moment, and in the future?

Michelle Obama's brother, Craig Robinson—1982 and 1983 Ivy Player of the Year at Princeton—had Carril in mind when inviting her new boyfriend, Barack, to a pickup game in Chicago in order to size him up. *If a guy is an a-hole on the basketball court, he's probably an a-hole in real life.* This Obama guy, Craig knew after playing with him, was all right.

Carril abhorred new-age tools. "He didn't understand computers or the people who used them," says Bill Carmody, Carril's longtime assistant at Princeton, who succeeded him at the school and went on to coach at Northwestern and Holy Cross. But going back to the 1970s, Carril foresaw analytics before anyone—especially him—even knew what that term meant. His Princeton teams were essentially basketball's version of the *Moneyball* Oakland As. While finances constrained the small-market Oakland from competing with the New York Yankees for high-priced baseball talents, Princeton's strict admissions requirements, and lack of athletic scholarships, constrained the Tigers from signing All-American recruits. So Carril had to look elsewhere for competitive advantages.

He found it, in an offensive designed to secure two of the most efficient ways of scoring: open three-point shots, and easy backdoor layups. He prized players, overlooked by most big-time schools, who could hit open threes and throw crisp passes for those two-point shots. Princeton's teams almost never took contested mid-range two-point shots. Those attempts were inefficient; their smaller players were better off shooting further away from the stronger defenders. Plus, those shots were worth another point. Carril's math added up.

Once Carril left Princeton in 1996 after 525 career victories in 29 years there and one year at Lehigh —his last college win was a memorable 43-41 victory over UCLA that secured his spot in the Hall of Fame, and whose winning basket, a signature backdoor layup, plays on a highlight loop every March—he brought his philosophy to the NBA, as an assistant to the Sacramento Kings. In 2002, Carril's Kings nearly met the New Jersey Nets in the NBA Finals; Nets head coach Byron Scott was also an assistant with Sacramento in the late 1990s, and he installed some of Carril's passing concepts with New Jersey, who at the time employed the best passer in the game, Hall of Fame point guard Jason Kidd. A 2017 *Wall Street Journal* article pointed to Carril's continued influence in the NBA: like Princeton, teams like the champion Golden State Warriors seek out efficiency through valuing the three-point shot, easy layups, and eschewing mid-range two-pointers.

Warriors general manager Bob Myers was a reserve on the UCLA team that lost to Princeton in 1996 (I was also a reserve in that game, for the Tigers. Myers outplayed me, 4 minutes to zero.) He's seen Carril's influence up close. "I will never forget losing to Pete's Princeton Tigers my junior year at UCLA," says Myers. "His team's back door cuts and passing out of the high post are something that the Warriors and the entire basketball world has benefitted from."

'You'll Miss'

When I got to Princeton, I also soon learned Carril wasn't for everyone. Upon his retirement from Princeton back in 1996, he admitted he was "a little too rough, too severe" for a then-younger generation. The son of a Pennsylvania steelworker, Carril held the privileged background of some players against them, even if they didn't completely deserve such animosity. Many were just trying to succeed at basketball. He drove some players to quit, and in quieter moments in later years, would admit he'd handle some relationships differently.

But damn if he wasn't entertaining. One of our players threw an errant pass in practice that cracked Carril's glasses. He ripped his shirt off in anger, exposing tufts of gray chest hair. His crooked frames stayed on his face the whole time, and the drill resumed. He smoked cigars during practice: the indoor track teams who shared the gym with us had to sprint through the stench. Carril once told a player he planned to write the word "layup" across his own chest. He'd dare the player to punch him. "You'll miss!" he screamed.

Carril, who was a "Little All-American" at Lafayette College in the early 1950s often played basketball at lunchtime, well into his 60s. He had a funny set shot that somehow went in more often than not. During one game, a football coach blew out some ligament and was writhing in pain.

Carril sauntered over to him. "I suppose," he said, "this is a bad time to tell you you traveled."

He asked a friend about a prospective recruit. The friend told him that many respected scouts said the player had a bad summer. Carrill leaned back in his chair and took a puff of his cigar. "Frankie," he said, "we play in the winter." He wanted our biggest player to get faster. So he had him chase around our smallest player around the court for about a half hour. "Catch him!" he'd yell. "CATCH HIM!!!"

Before or after many practices, he'd go "down the line," pointing out the fatal flaw of each and every player, in front of everyone else. This exercise often involved ranting and raving and colorful language. When I was helping coach my son's 7th-grade basketball team a few years back, in a private moment with him I channeled Carril, and acted out what he would probably say about each of his 12-year-old teammates—and him. He laughed.

And damn if he wasn't right about a lot of stuff. Focusing on the past is largely counterproductive. Failing to take a charge, or dive after a loose ball, is probably a character flaw. All that takes is some bravery. He'd add five-to-10 feet to a player's shooting range by encouraging him to shoot the ball while rising in the air, instead of at the peak of the jump. You get more leg strength that way. (Stephen Curry never played for Carril. But he shoots like that).

After Princeton's current coach, former Tiger player (and teammate) Mitch Henderson, was hired for the job in 2011, Carril handed him a card. It said, "Think. See. Do." Carril stared at him for five seconds. "It felt like 30," Henderson says. "It was one of those, *are you f-cking listening?*' looks." Message received. He's won 63% of his games at the school.

And he was probably right about my diet. I tried the ham and cheese and six-pack combo once or twice, but it didn't really sit. I never really put on enough weight to be a serious college player. But I can trace most good things in my life—friends, wife and family, occupation—to Carril's decision to give me a shot. He labeled me "Bones" my freshman year, and it stuck. I swear some friends and classmates still don't know my real name. And while that's not a great name for a wanna-be hoops player, I'd love to try to get away with it come middle age.

Thanks, Coach.

Every NCAA tournament Cinderella owes a debt to Pete Carril

John Feinstein
August 16, 2022

As originally printed in The Washington Post

The first time I appeared on ESPN's "The Sports Reporters" was March 19, 1989 — two days after Georgetown and Princeton met in a historic NCAA men's basketball tournament game.

Georgetown was the No. 1 seed in the East and — informally in those days — the No. 1 seed in the tournament. Princeton was the No. 16 seed in the East and — just as informally — the No. 64 seed in the 64-team bracket.

Georgetown won, 50-49, surviving when Alonzo Mourning got his hand on a last-second 15-foot jump shot taken by Princeton center Kit Mueller. It appeared that Mourning got a piece of Mueller's wrist, but there was no call, and the Hoyas escaped.

That Sunday morning, host Dick Schaap turned to me to open the show and said, "Did John Thompson get out-coached by Pete Carril on Friday night?"

"Yes, he did," I answered. "But everyone gets out-coached by Pete Carril."

Four days later, when I showed up on the practice day for the East Region semifinals in the Meadowlands, I ran smack into Thompson as he was walking onto the court with his players. When he stopped directly in front of me, I knew I was in trouble.

"I heard what you said on that TV show about Pete out-coaching me," he said. "It's about damn time you said something that was true." He was laughing now. "You're right. Everyone gets out-coached by that little SOB."

Princeton and Carril — who died Monday at 92 — lost that night, but the game is seen as one of the most important in NCAA tournament history. Then — as now — the powers-that-be in the sport were talking about eliminating automatic bids for one-bid conferences to give more spots to power conference schools.

Princeton's oh-so-close loss was later dubbed "The game that saved March Madness" by *Sports Illustrated*. All the stunning little-guy upsets that have come since then — including the Saint Peter's run this past season — grew from Carril out-coaching Thompson that night in Providence, R.I.

Thompson's respect for Carril was already well known: He had sent his son John III to play for him. He liked the idea of a Princeton degree for his son. He loved the idea of him playing for college basketball's Yoda.

At 5-foot-7, constantly rumpled on and off the court, Carril actually looked a lot like Yoda, and he trained his young Tigers to play as if the Force was with them — even when the opponents came loaded with Darth Vaders in the form of future NBA players.

They ran his Princeton offense, which made defenses dizzy because one misstep would result in a backdoor cut to the basket for an open layup, often with the shot clock under five seconds. When the three-point shot arrived in 1986, Carril adjusted to include pop-out jumpers from the wing, and the offense became even more dangerous. Cut off the backdoor pass, and you might find very good shooters killing you with threes. Take away those threes, and you were back to getting repeatedly beaten for layups.

Carril finished with 525 wins and 273 losses in 30 seasons in an era in which teams played far fewer games than they do now. He coached for one season at Lehigh, where he had the only losing record of his career, going 11-12. During the next 29 years at Princeton, he won 13 Ivy League titles and finished lower than third once. In 1975, when the NIT was still a big deal, Princeton won the tournament after finishing second to Pennsylvania in the Ivy League.

In 1996, his final season, Princeton had to play archrival Penn in a playoff game to decide the league title and automatic NCAA bid. Princeton, which had lost to Penn eight times in a row, won in overtime after Carril, with his team in foul trouble, switched to a zone defense — which he loathed.

Afterward, he went to the whiteboard in the locker room and wrote: "I am retiring. I am very happy."

He wanted his players to know first.

Five days later, they faced 1995 national champion UCLA in the first round of the NCAA tournament in Indianapolis. As with the Georgetown game, the opponent was bigger, quicker and more athletic. But Princeton controlled the tempo all night. Even so, the Tigers trailed 41-34 with five minutes left. UCLA didn't score again.

During a timeout with the score tied at 41, Carril told freshman Gabe Lewullis to expect to be stopped the first time he cut to the basket. Sure enough, UCLA's Charles O'Bannon was waiting for him. Lewullis returned to the wing, then, as his coach had instructed, made the cut again in the final seconds. This time, O'Bannon wasn't ready, and Lewullis caught a perfect pass from Steve Goodrich and laid the ball in for the winning basket. Princeton won, 43-41.

O'Bannon was one of four players on that UCLA team to play in the NBA. Lewullis is now an orthopedic surgeon. That evening, he was a Jedi Knight following Yoda's instructions.

That was Carril's last victory — in the second round the Tigers lost to Mississippi State, which ended up in the Final Four. Carril went on to work as an NBA assistant coach for 10 more years, installing the Princeton offense in Sacramento during the most successful era in that franchise's history.

When he finally retired for good, Carril frequently made trips to D.C. to watch two of his former players, Thompson III and Mike Brennan, coach at Georgetown and American.

"He loved taking guys aside in practice and talking to them about their game," Brennan said. "He worked with our stars, but he also worked with anyone he thought he could help play the game better."

There was no better example than an AU player named Gabe Brown, a 7-foot-1 kid from Long Island. Brown came to American in 2014, so thin he looked like a middling breeze could blow him away.

Carril took one look at him and made him his project. He labeled Brown "the impossible dream" and "never stopped trying to make him better," Brennan said.

College coaches often have trouble getting into the Basketball Hall of Fame because it is so NBA-centric. Carril was voted in the year after he retired from Princeton.

His peers, such as Thompson, didn't mind getting out-coached by Carril. It was just what he did. And his players didn't mind getting yelled at by him — which they did, quite frequently — because they knew he was right.

Reporters didn't even mind being lectured by him — which also happened often — because they understood that they were learning and that it was an honor to have him take the time to lecture you.

"It meant he thought you had the potential to learn," Brennan said. "That was a big deal."

Carril loved nothing more than talking to coaches young and old about basketball. But anyone who was around him learned something: from John Thompson to Gabe Brown and everyone in between. And while there were coaches who won games from him, no one ever out-coached Pete Carril.

"Yo-yo-yo." Pete Carril, we won't see your type again

Brad Wilson
August 15, 2022

For lehighvalleylive.com

The world will hear "Yo, yo, yo, yo, yo, yo, yo," no longer.

At least not in the unique way Pete Carril said it when he was trying to get your attention. Which he always deserved.

Carril, a Bethlehem native, a Liberty and Lafayette graduate, a former Easton teacher, Basketball Hall of Fame member, and Princeton men's basketball coach for a memorable, passionate 29 years, died Monday at age 92.

Then again, a lot of what Carril did fit neatly into "unique," if into no other catch-all basket.

That "yo-yo-yo" cry will ring around Jadwin Gym for a long time. It was how he got your attention, and, believe me, he sure did get your attention with it, usually waving his hands, which more often than not carried a cup of strong coffee and a powerful cigar – indoor smoking bans were not kind to Carril.

I had a special view of the great man, as I was a manager for his teams in 1981-82 and 1982-83. The first year was one of Carril's least memorable seasons (outside of a win over Duke), as the team struggled to reach .500 (which it did, preventing his first losing season, and indeed he never had one as Tigers coach). The second saw the Tigers win the Ivy League, beating Penn in a showdown at The Spectrum in Philadelphia, and went on to top Oklahoma State in the NCAA tournament – much better.

I could tell a lot of stories about Carril – his sharp eye for error, his rapier wit, his broad smile that could light the gym up when something went right, his attention to the tiniest detail, his devastating, sometimes coruscating criticism, his capacity for friendship, his passion for doing things right, his commitment to be the best – but the best of them still feel like they should stay in oral history fashion, not be written down, to keep the great man alive in our thoughts and lives rather than dimming memories written in dusty history books.

Carril, who also was a head coach at Lehigh and Reading High School, was above all a teacher. He taught basketball. He taught life lessons. He taught how to be a man.

He taught physical education classes, too, usually in racquetball. (Bet John Calipari never had to do that.)

He had some odd ideas. He hated to substitute players, as he thought a substitution should be an improvement, and the better player was playing already, yo, right?

Substitute for a tired player? "Yo, yo, yo, how can a young man in his prime physically be tired playing a game?" he'd say. "Yo, yo, yo, I'm an old man. I'm allowed to get tired."

Carril was probably most famous for his legendary deliberate offense, with its back-door cuts, weaves and "point centers" running offense.

But don't you dare call it a stall. Oh no. "Yo, yo, yo, we're just looking to get a good shot, and if that takes a while, so?"

The definition of "good shot" was open jumper or open

layup, and you better not miss the latter. One player passed up a layup for a dunk once, missed the dunk by slamming the ball off the back rim, from where it shot all the way back to halfcourt, and the opposition turned it into a layup. Carril was so hot he was steaming and that player anchored the bench for a long while.

Carril was flexible, though, and could change with the times. He would have preferred to have a team where he could run the floor for transition layups and play more aggressive defense, and the first few days of practice were often like that until he'd realize there was no way Princeton could hang with its killer schedule (more on that later) and it was back to the "Princeton offense."

When the shot clock and 3-point shot entered a lot of folks predicted doom for Carril, but he knew better. By 1982, it was getting harder and harder for Princeton to recruit the kind of athletic, powerful players who were changing the game. "Yo, yo, yo, but 6-3 guards that can shoot jump shots?" he'd say. "I can get those." And he sure did, as the next 10 years showed.

He saw, by 1983 or so, that coaching in the Ivy League would just get harder and harder, as costs spiraled. In the 1970s, Princeton could offer players such as Armond Hill or Brian Taylor or Geoff Petrie packages that were close enough to what scholarship schools could offer that the extra frisson and prestige of the Ivies made up the difference.

But in 1983, the difference had ballooned into thousands and thousands of dollars, and Carril himself would tell parents of really good players who wanted to come to Princeton that if they got a scholarship offer from, say, William & Mary, to take it.

Carril could have made his life a whole lot easier by going somewhere else, but he never did. He liked the challenge, and he also respected the university's academics. He could be disdainful of the people "on the other side of the road" – meaning the faculty and administration, located on the west side of Washington Road; Jadwin is on the east side – but academics always came first.

And I mean always. Long bus road trips (it seemed to take as long for us to get to Ithaca as Odysseus did) were quiet as everybody read or did work. Practices during reading period or exams were optional, and he meant it – "Yo, yo, yo, you got studying to do? You stay home and study; we'll be fine." If a professor called Carril to complain about your classroom performance, even the best back-door cut couldn't save you from a memorable lecture.

He was, to be put it delicately, dismissive of the academic endeavors of some of the Tigers' non-Ivy foes (and even some Ivy ones). When told of a well-known player's decision to go pro for the betterment of his family, Carril said, "Who taught him to spell that?"

But, yet, Carril wanted to play the best he could play, regardless of academics. His non-conference schedules were stacked with top 25 teams. He once dismissed the idea of playing local schools such as Drexel or Rider by saying, "If I'm going to play a scholarship team, I want to play Virginia (who had Ralph Sampson at the time)."

The problem for Carril was, within the rise of double-round robin conference play as the be-all and end-all, many of the teams he liked to play – St. John's, for one – wouldn't schedule Princeton any longer. Getting good teams – or any teams – to come to Jadwin, like Duke and BYU did in 1981, was almost impossible.

By the early 1990s, he was playing up-tempo Loyola-Marymount and powerhouse UNLV, and wrote in a letter to boosters that year that "anyone wanting to coach in those games, give me a call."

Carril wanted to play those teams because he thought they could be beaten, if Princeton played his basketball the way the Tigers were capable of. He never, ever thought otherwise and he never coached otherwise. With attention to detail, perfect execution and complete mental focus, he always thought his team could win, in any game, anywhere.

This was why he looked so agonized along the sideline, hair askew, gripping his rolled-up program, gesturing to the skies – to him, basketball was easy and his players made it hard. That, he never quite got, that his ideas and teaching could be anything but basic, easy, in the learning and the application.

He was indifferent to stats of all kinds. Once, after running Cal out of its own gym, somebody noted the Tigers had been massively out-rebounded. "Yo, yo, yo, if you don't miss many shots, there aren't any rebounds." Quite so.

In 1982, we were desperate to win our final game at a frigid Barton Hall at Cornell to get to .500 and save coach a losing season. We did. He couldn't have cared less. It was just a stat.

He could also be indifferent to anything outside his immediate circuit. I once watched him walk past the outstretched hand of Princeton president William G. Bowen after a 1983 loss to Penn without the slightest acknowledgment. Media outside the locals who covered him for years could be cursorily dealt with. Receptions and parties were not his style. Athletic department officials could be treated with, well, indifference.

And there were times when he seemed a little lost in the world. One night in that difficult 1981-82 season he asked me to run to the Wawa to get some Jiffy-Pop popcorn for his dinner. I did, but always felt like I should have invited back to the dorm cafeteria for a real meal. When he was inducted into the Basketball Hall of Fame in 1997, he seemed amused at all the attention, with that wry, knowing smile of his cutting through any pomposity.

By then he'd left Princeton and was working for the Sacramento Kings of the NBA, where Petrie, a former player, was in the front office. Asked gently whether the pros paid attention to him, Carril said, "The ones that don't, I don't teach. The ones that do, I teach."

The latter ones were the lucky ones, anywhere "Yo, yo, yo" could be heard.

That was always the case. And if they learned, Carril was thrilled. After the memorable 1989 NCAA loss to No. 1 Georgetown, 50-49, a game where Carril could very easily have been off-the-chart angry at the officials, he was laughing and joking afterward with the press, tousling the hair of team leader Bob Scrabis (who WAS fouled – twice – at game's end by Alonzo Mourning, we'll always believe), because his team had done what it was taught so well.

Of course, winning was always better, and Carril could be the merriest little elf after wins over (especially) Penn and Rutgers. No one who watched it will ever forget the joy he radiated after Allentown Central Catholic grad Gabe Lewullis' perfect back-door layup stunned defending national champion UCLA in the NCAA tournament in March 1996.

That was Carril's last win of his 525. It couldn't have been more appropriate. It was a team that had been taught to play basketball Pete Carril's way and win Pete Carril's way.

For my money, there was no better way. Yo, yo, yo, coach – we can never forget you.

'All of us knew he was a genius.' Remembering Pete Carril.

Matt Drapkin
August 30, 2022

As originally printed in The Daily Princetonian

> "I am the teacher of athletes,
> He that by me spreads a wider breast than my own, proves the width of my own;
> He most honors my style who learns under it to destroy the teacher ...
> My words itch at your ears till you understand them."
> —Walt Whitman

When asked about legendary men's basketball coach Pete Carril, longtime Princeton athletic director Gary Walters '67 points to Walt Whitman's "Song of Myself" to illustrate his grief.

"For those of us that played for Coach Carril, I hope that we expanded the breadth and width of his own, while at the very same time being reminded that his words continue to itch at our ears," Walters told *The Daily Princetonian*.

Carril, the former Princeton's men's basketball head coach who is known as one of the most influential minds in basketball history, died on Aug. 15 at age 92. After coaching at Princeton from 1967 to 1996, he joined the NBA's Sacramento Kings as the assistant coach for 13 years. Carril's "Princeton Offense" revolutionized the game, putting an emphasis on ball movement, backdoor cuts, and reliable outside shooting.

His core offensive philosophies are still embraced by a number of teams at all levels to this day, including the University of Richmond at the NCAA Division I level and the NBA's Los Angeles Lakers in the early 2010s.

Carril's story started on July 10, 1930 in a single-parent home in Bethlehem, Penn. His father raised Pete on his own while working as a steelworker at Bethlehem Steel. Pete said that his father never missed a day of work in his 40 years employed.

That commitment to hard work was seemingly ingrained in the Carril genes, evident in Pete's love for and dedication to basketball. Carril began his playing career in his hometown of Bethlehem for Liberty High School. He found early success, earning all-state honors for Pennsylvania before committing to continuing playing at Lafayette College.

Jerry Price, the senior communications advisor and historian for Princeton University Athletics, shared a 1950 article discussing a game between Princeton and Lafayette that saw Pete Carril's name printed in *The Daily Princetonian* for the very first time:

"Little Pete Carril, former All-Stater from Pennsylvania, and Captain George Davidson were the only Leopards who were able to score against the tight Tiger defense consistently," the article read.

There have since been over 2,400 editions of *The Daily Princetonian* that have mentioned Pete Carril. That was the last one to mistakenly address him as "Little Pete."

"He was about 5'6," but he was really a larger than life figure," Price told the 'Prince.'

Carril graduated from Lafayette in 1952. After briefly serving in the U.S. Army, he received a master's degree in educational administration from Lehigh University. But it didn't take long for Carril to find his way back onto the hardwood.

In 1954, his coaching career began through humble

beginnings. He took the position of junior varsity coach at Easton High School, where he was mistaken for the school janitor on his first day. In 1958, he moved onto coaching varsity at Reading Senior High School.

The lack of glitz and glamor never phased Carril. In a 2007 article published on the Princeton Athletics website by Price, Carril reflected fondly on his early coaching experiences.

"I consider my time as a high school teacher and coach very valuable," he said. "That's where I first learned to teach things from a very basic perspective."

In 1966, Carril took his first coaching gig at the collegiate level with Lehigh University. The following year, he opened the chapter to one of the greatest coaching stints in college basketball history when he took the head coaching position at Princeton University.

During his 29 years with the Tigers, Carril led the Princeton men's basketball team to over 500 wins. In addition to his cumulative .663 winning percentage — the highest in Ivy League history — he led the Tigers to 13 conference championships and 11 NCAA tournament berths, as well as the National Invitation Tournament title in 1975.

"He was a cigar smoking, beer and pizza loving, barrel chested force of nature," Geoffrey Petrie '70 told the 'Prince.'

Petrie, one of the earlier players in Carril's college coaching career at Princeton, spent all three years of his varsity basketball career under Carril before being drafted eighth overall to the Portland Trailblazers in the 1970 NBA Draft.

"I had a fair amount of natural ability, but he's the guy that really molded it into what it needed to be in order to be a pro player," Petrie said of Carril. "I wanted to play in the NBA, and he was able to set my sails in the right direction."

In 1994, Petrie was hired by the Sacramento Kings as

president of basketball operations. Just two years later, Carril joined the organization.

"I played for him for three years, but I spent a lifetime with him," Petrie said. "I was a gym rat, so I spent summers with him working on my game. We stayed in touch after I graduated and had some success in the pros. We spent another almost 15 years together after he retired from Princeton, working in the NBA."

About a decade after Petrie played for the Tigers came a new wave of Princeton Basketball, led by power players such as John Rogers '80 and Craig Robinson '83. By now, the famous Princeton Offense had developed into a well-oiled machine.

"When he coached us in 1967, there was no Princeton Offense," Petrie explained. "That was something that he developed over time."

Rogers was the captain of the 1979–80 co-champion Princeton Tigers. Before arriving on campus for the first time, however, he still remembers one of his first encounters with Carril.

"When I was arranging my visit to go visit Princeton, they had me call Coach Carril at Andy's Tavern," Rogers said. "That was pretty unique… To call up the head basketball coach at Princeton and have the head of a tavern answer the phone. To have to ask, 'Is Coach Carril there?' That was Coach. That was the norm."

Sean Gregory '98 further illustrated Carril's quirks in a recent retrospective piece for Time Magazine that covered his own experiences playing under the coach. Gregory recalled his straightforward advice for putting on mass during the recruiting process.

"Yo, Sean, here's what you need to do to get bigger: drink a six-pack of beer and eat a ham sandwich, before bed, every night. Got that kid?"

'He's like the Oracle in The Matrix'

One of the most notable recipients of Carril's trademark candor is Robinson, who is the fourth leading scorer in Princeton Basketball history. Standing at a towering 6'6," he dominated for the Tigers in the 1980s. He shared his story of receiving Ivy League Player of the Year honors two years in a row under Coach Carril with the 'Prince':

"My junior year, I was the leading scorer on the team, and was voted Player of the Year in the Ivy League," Robinson recalled. "Afterwards, Carril said to me in front of the entire team, 'I don't know how you ended up winning that award, because I didn't vote for you. I don't think you're the best player in the league. You can't do this, you can't do that…' He went on a litany of things that I couldn't do — why he was surprised that I got Ivy League Player of the Year, and why I didn't deserve it."

"He said, 'If you want to be good, you have to do all of these other things.' The next year, I went back and I worked on my game. I averaged fewer points, but did more of the other things. I won Ivy League Player of the Year again," Robinson said. "For the first time, I thought he was satisfied with something I did. But, he waited until I was a senior on my way out to let me know that."

John Rogers shared similar experiences trying to play up to Carril's high standards:

"To have this genius telling you things about your weaknesses, things you need to work on, things you need to get better at, things that you never get better at no matter how hard you try," Rogers told the 'Prince.' "That's the first time anyone ever told me, 'Johnny, you're legally blind, and I can't teach you to see.' But he was right."

"All of us knew he was a genius. So, when he was telling

you the truth, it wasn't just a coach. It was a genius telling you the truth. You just knew that this genius and this future Hall of Famer was telling you things that were accurate," he said.

Gregory shared one of his most memorable Carril stories with the 'Prince': having his entire game critiqued before even making it to college.

"I remember in my senior year of high school, Coach was driving me to the Princeton train station. He just kept reiterating — 'You've got to work hard. It's going to be really tough for you. You're going to have to put on a lot of weight, and you're going to have to lift a lot of weights. You're not the best passer we've seen. Work on your long range shooting. Work on your dribbling.'"

"He's like the Oracle in The Matrix," Robinson said. "He'll tell you exactly what you need to hear."

Candid. Bold. Unapologetically real, sometimes, so much so that the lines between tough love and counterproductive chastisement became blurred. The New York Times recently published a piece highlighting some facets of Carril's philosophy that were harder to fall in love with.

"Practices, before the NCAA imposed limits, typically went for four grueling hours. Carril frowned upon stretching, grudgingly allowed water breaks and was even more parsimonious with compliments, afraid that his players would become complacent," the Times wrote.

Playing for Carril required immense mental toughness and resilience. While reactions from his players differed based on underlying personalities, the pressures he imposed often strengthened the teammates' relationships.

"We all have this special bond, and I think it's because we all persevered through some really tough moments," Rogers explained. "All of us who played for him, we feel like we're part of some special club."

"When he was coaching in the NBA, he happened to be in Atlanta at the time of the Final Four," Rogers continued. "A bunch of the Princeton guys also hang out and go to the Final Four games together. All of a sudden, we're all in the same city again. There's about 12 of us that ended up in his room. We're sitting on the floor, surrounding him in bed, all drinking beer together. We're all telling stories, and Coach is like, 'No, I never said that. I never did that.'"

"These old players still wanted to be around, just telling stories. Just continuing to learn from Coach. I don't think you see that with [Former Duke Head Coach] Coach K. or [Former Indiana Coach] Bobby Knight," Rogers added.

"Because we all were going through the same thing and practices were so tough, we all felt like if we could get through it — we had sort of been through this hazing period," Robinson explained. "It made everybody who's been through it even closer. Some of my best friendships are guys who I played with at Princeton."

"He ended up with a great love affair with a lot of his ex-players," Petrie told the 'Prince.' "He certainly wasn't politically correct by today's standards, but he was very honest, very direct, and just believed in hard work and commitment. It wasn't for everybody, but for a lot of them, it gave them life lessons that carried over into the rest of their life."

At times, Carril's willingness to bluntly speak his mind may have been difficult to endorse from the receiving end. Throughout his career, however, he would earn national attention for what his gritty style produced on the court. His popularity rose on a monumental scale as his Princeton teams consistently performed at a high level during March Madness.

In 1989, one of the biggest games of Carril's career took place in the first round of the NCAA tournament. His Tigers matched up against the star-studded lineup of the Georgetown

Bulldogs, featuring future NBA Hall of Famers Alonzo Mourning at 6'10" and Dikembe Mutombo at 7'2."

Carril knew that the powerful post presence could present matchup difficulties for his outsized Tigers offense; no Princeton player stood taller than 6'8." To prepare accordingly, in the practices leading up to the match, he gave his assistants broom sticks to hold up high for his smaller players to practice shooting over.

Carril's clever preparation proved extremely effective. Although in the end, the Tigers came up short 50–49, the unexpectedly intense matchup sent shockwaves through the NCAA. The effects were two-fold.

First, the entertaining back-and-forth between a No. 1 and No. 16 seed helped persuade CBS to sign a deal with the NCAA to televise every game of the tournament — not just the later rounds.

Perhaps even more important for schools like Princeton, the attention the showdown garnered proved that the underdogs deserve a chance. At a time when discussions of removing automatic bids for smaller conferences (like the Ivy League) were gaining traction, Princeton's impressive performance squashed the chatter. *Sports Illustrated* dubbed the Princeton-Georgetown matchup "The Game that Saved March Madness."

'Coach's fingerprints are all over the modern game'

Carril's final victory as an NCAA head coach would come seven years later. In 1996, Princeton defeated UCLA in the first round of the NCAA tournament in what is today known as one of the greatest upsets of all time.

ESPN included the 43–41 victory in their list of the greatest upsets in March Madness history, writing, "You know why the backdoor [cut] was invented? So 13 seeds could sneak by the defending champs in the first round."

At the time of his retirement, which came after a second-round loss after the win over UCLA, Carril was the only active NCAA Division I head coach to reach 500 victories without the opportunity to offer scholarships to his players. "Without the ability to recruit," Petrie reflected, "he was such a creative mind, figuring out how to compete with a different type of player."

For Carril, "different type of player" usually meant wealthy Princeton students, who he didn't think were cut out for the hard work he demanded. The Coach once said, "Basketball is a poor man's game, and my guys have three cars in the garage."

"It's no secret how acerbic Coach Carril could be when he was admonishing his players," Robinson told the 'Prince.' "He felt like he had to toughen us up because we were Ivy League kids going up against some of the better teams in the country."

"It's not every guy like that," Price explained, "but he could take guys who came from more privileged backgrounds and show them it doesn't matter where you come from. You have to work hard. You have to improve. You have to be a teammate and you have to do what's best for the team. We're all equal here."

These were two of his most clear-cut values: equality and grit. One of Carril's favorite maxims was "you can't separate the player from the person." Looking back at the legacy he left behind, the same can be said about the coach.

You could see equality in the Princeton Offense, all five players sharing the ball to get the best shot for the team. You could see it in practice everyday, him criticizing each player's weaknesses regardless of talent or accolades. And, you could see it in the way he was raised.

"I think the way he grew up in Bethlehem with his father working in the steel mills, clearly had a profound impact on him as a person," Rogers told the 'Prince.' "When you're at

Princeton, you know, you don't have a lot of folks who have that kind of background."

"He talked about his dad a lot," added Price. "He talked a lot about growing up poor and the impact that that had on him. There's no question that that drove him and fueled him."

In 2009, Princeton named Carril Court in Jadwin Gymnasium in his honor. After retiring from his role as an assistant with the Sacramento Kings in 2011, Carril could not scratch the itch that called him back to Jadwin Gym. "He came to practice for almost 10 years straight," current Princeton men's basketball Head Coach Mitch Henderson '98 told the 'Prince.'

In just the past few decades, so much about basketball has changed, with the transition towards positionless play, the movement outwards towards the three-point line, the need for all five players on the court to be able to pass, dribble, and shoot. Carril envisioned and implemented these principles long before they became the standard. With his typical stubbornness, Carril didn't capitulate to the pull of the norm, but instead molded the norm into his own reality.

In 1997, Carril was inducted into the Naismith Memorial Basketball Hall of Fame. He is just one of two Princeton-affiliated figures to ever be inducted. The other was former NBA player and New Jersey Senator Bill Bradley '65.

"Coach's fingerprints are all over the modern game," Henderson continued. "He was a visionary. Sometimes it's hard to separate my own thinking from what Coach saw."

'A coach's teaching is his immortality'

The sheer number of people Pete Carril impacted is incalculable. While his teaching primarily was done on the court, it seems the lessons passed down directly translated to life altogether.

"Were it not for him, I probably would not have gone to Princeton," Gary Walters told the 'Prince.' Walters' lifelong journey with Carril began early, when he played under Coach at Reading High School. "He taught the game in such a way as to enable his players to understand that the whole is greater than the sum of the parts."

In 2008, Rogers was awarded the Woodrow Wilson award for embodying the school's famous motto, "Princeton in the Nation's Service." The award was given in Jadwin Gym.

"When I spoke at the event, I said, 'Coach, you are the best teacher that I ever had,'" Rogers shared. "I'll be watching the game now — NBA game, WNBA game, high school game, whatever — and watching on TV, I'll see someone who's running down the ball. I'll see someone who throws a pass that's off. I'll see someone that didn't cut back door when they're overplayed. I can see it before it actually happens. I can almost feel it in my stomach."

"That's what a great teacher does. They teach you something that is so embedded in you, you know it for the rest of your life."

Today, Rogers is the founder, chairman, and co-CEO of Ariel Investments, the nation's largest minority-run mutual fund firm. He says that he's instilled the values of teamwork and cooperation into the company culture because of the lessons he learned from Carril.

"We have a conference room here named after Coach Carril. It's to remind everyone that works here that you think about your teammates first."

"When Barack Obama got elected president, we were the temporary transition headquarters for three days," Rogers continued. "For three days, President-elect Obama was in the Coach Carril room, calling world leaders and starting to form the government. It just shows you the impact that it's had for us to build our firm around those values of thinking about your teammates first."

After playing for Princeton, Robinson went on to a lifelong pursuit of coaching basketball himself. He held positions at five different schools across a 26-year career before settling into his current role as Executive Director of the National Association of Basketball Coaches. Robinson reflected on how Carril shaped his own perspective as a coach.

"I learned sort of how to play basketball cerebrally, as well as the philosophy of playing against guys who are as good, if not better, than you are," Robinson said. "That served me well when I got into coaching, because I was able to take some of those tenets that I learned from playing for Coach Carril into my own coaching toolbox."

Petrie said that playing for Coach Carril was not a gift which could immediately be appreciated.

"You didn't know it at the time, but you realize it later. For Coach, every day in practice, every game," he said, "it was a reflection of who you were, what your character was, how competitive you were, how willing you were to sacrifice, how committed you were to getting the most out of your ability."

In teaching the X's and O's, the defensive schemas, and the principles of a free-flowing motion offense, Carril knew exactly what he was doing. Carril was giving his players the tools they needed to live life the way it should be lived, by the ethics he valued most: teamwork, strong work ethic, and a never-ending commitment to excellence.

And, when the job was finished? A little bit of fun, as well. In 1975, after a 55–50 victory against Virginia — a game that saw Coach Carril ejected in the second half — he let his team go crazy in the hotel following the big win.

All of the commotion got the attention of one annoyed guest. When the woman confronted the rowdy group of college kids, the man in charge stepped forward, donning a T-shirt and black boxers. According to *Sports Illustrated*, the woman snapped, "May I ask what you're doing?"

Carril puffed a cloud of cigar smoke her way before answering plainly: "I'm wallowing in success."

"He loved to dance, he loved music, he loved good food," Petrie said. "He would go up to the piano bar at this one Italian restaurant and sing this Frank Sinatra song ... He loved life. I will miss him terribly, but he was a lifetime gift to me and to so many that crossed his path."

"Coach's legacy will always live on," Gary Walters said. "At the end of the day, a coach's teaching is his immortality. The whole concept of passing it on — it's what he did, and it's what those players who played for him will continue to do."

CHAPTER 37

Sports Illustrated

Anyone who grew up in the 1960s, '70s, '80s or '90s understands that *Sports Illustrated* (*SI*) was a magazine like no other. I could watch some super-exciting sporting event on a weekend, but could not wait to read about it in *SI* a few days later. The writers made you feel the weekend joy all over again, but they also transported you to a whole new world: a world in which you could experience even greater enjoyment some 48 hours after an event was over. The writers were that good.

This brings me to the connections between *SI*, Princeton and Princeton basketball. I suppose the *SI*/Princeton basketball connection started when *SI* decided to do a story on blossoming legend Bill Bradley '65 in its December 17, 1962 issue, when Bradley was just beginning his sophomore season. It continued when *SI* did a December 7, 1964 story on Bradley and his Princeton team, and put Bradley on its cover again. These articles were written by the most esteemed of *SI* writers, the late Frank Deford '61. The connection further continued with *SI*'s story on Princeton's magnificent 1966-67 basketball team in its February 27, 1967 issue featuring Princeton stars, Chris Thomforde and Gary Walters, on its cover.

I am pleased to say the connection between *SI* and Princeton basketball extended throughout Pete Carril's era. After interacting with longtime *SI*-ers Peter Carry '64 and Alexander Wolff '80 on this book, I can report that this connection is alive and well today. While I had no idea this was true when I started working on this book, upon reflection, I am not surprised. These legends (Carril, Carry and Wolff) share an unusual trait — they see things that escape mere mortals. They remind me of chess grandmasters who see two or three steps ahead. They remind me of my teammate, Armond Hill, who had similar vision and made everyone around him better.

I have always believed that vision was the most underrated asset a basketball player could have. The *SI* writers had it in abundance and still have it today. They display it through their literary skills and their passion for sports and stories. It has been a privilege for me to interact with Peter and Alex on this book and have COACH graced by their talent.

While I try in the Acknowledgments, I can never thank Peter and Alex enough for their individual contributions to COACH. Hopefully, however, the inclusion of this chapter in the book and the following *SI* article about Coach in some small way expresses my appreciation for their time and talent.

Blue Collar Coach in a Button-Down League

Kent Hannon
January 2, 1978

> Billy Omeltchenko tells the story best, although any of his teammates seated around a table at The Pub, Princeton's on-campus watering hole, could relate a similar encounter. This one took place several years ago when Omeltchenko, now a starting guard on the Princeton basketball team, was a senior at Great Neck (N.Y.) North High School and was being recruited by a few colleges in the East.

"One night I was told that Pete Carril, the Princeton coach, would be in the stands to watch me play," Omeltchenko recalls. "During the game I noticed this bald little man lying down on the bleachers with his head propped up on one elbow. He looked like a bum. He was wearing gray corduroys with suspenders and Hush Puppies with white socks, and he was sucking on a cigar butt that was maybe an inch long. After the game, my coach came by my locker and said, 'Billy, I want you to meet Coach Carril.' And it was him, the guy in the bleachers! I mean, he looked like Columbo. I didn't see how he could be from Princeton. He said, 'Nice to see ya, nice to see ya,' and then spent the next 20 minutes tearing my game apart. I couldn't get over him. He was wonderful. So here I am at Princeton, paying $6,500 a year to play basketball for him."

Omeltchenko's recruiting tale describes the predicament that Pete Carril finds himself in while trying to foster winning basketball at a rich man's school. It also hints at how he has gone about assembling such successful teams as his present group, which is attempting to make the Tigers the stingiest defensive team in the nation for the third season in a row and which will be aiming for Princeton's third straight Ivy League championship when conference play begins this week.

First, Carril stuns a prospective player with his "I'm no Clark Gable" appearance (though he does have Gable's ears). Then he gives the recruit an honest—some might say brutal—appraisal of his talent. "When Barnes Hauptfuhrer came here," says Carril of a former Princeton center who was drafted by the pros in the third round, "I told him all he had was a good handshake." Next. he mentions the fact that freshmen are too busy studying to play varsity ball in the Ivy League (although they will be eligible next season) and that the annual tab for a Princeton education is $6,500, not counting any crew-neck sweaters a player might purchase at one of those quaint little clothing shops along Nassau Street.

As a parting shot, Carril will throw in some poetry, usually something about the struggles of life that he can relate to his arduous task at Princeton. One of his favorite lines comes from Thomas Hardy's The Convergence of the Twain, which is about the sinking of the Titanic: "And as the smart ship grew/In stature, grace. and hue,/In shadowy silent distance grew the Iceberg too."

Carril likes to pose as an intractable, if somewhat bumbling, sidewalk philosopher who is at once a congenial and rigid advocate of conservative values. But he is a little too aware of what's going on to pull it off. He is sophisticated enough to appreciate both sides of almost any argument—whether it involves a fight between him and the admissions department over getting a good high school player into Princeton or something more substantial, like the mining of Haiphong Harbor—and this torments him. As a result, Carril, who is a genuinely funny man when he wants to be, goes back and forth between comedy (a willingness to poke fun at even his most sacred ideas) and tragedy (a foreboding that the world is going to pot around him) so often that nobody around him thinks anything of it. He worries about everything, including who is going to go out to pick up the vegetable soup for lunch. When Princeton beat a good St. Bonaventure team 59-55 to win last year's Kodak Classic, Carril came to the big alumni victory party in Rochester, N.Y. wearing a frown. "Aren't you ever going to be happy, Coach?" asked his star player, Frank Sowinski. "I don't know, Frankie," said Carril. But then he ordered the new trophy filled with beer, and everybody got a little drunk.

This is hardly the stuff of which ordinary basketball coaches, most of whom are unabashed backslappers, are made, but

Carril's odd personality must be persuasive, because the Tigers have won 35 of their last 36 Ivy League games while continuing a Princeton tradition of knocking off a couple of powerhouses, a Notre Dame or an Alabama, every season. The Tigers have done all this despite a recruiting budget of $3,800 a year, which, as a North Carolina assistant coach recently told Carril, "is what we spend on telephone calls." Also working against Carril's chances for consistent success are Princeton's entrance requirements, which would prevent most good players from going there, even if they were inclined to. Sowinski, the leading scorer, maintains close to an A average in engineering. His college-board scores coming out of high school were 1,230, good enough so that few admissions departments outside the Ivy League would have thought twice about his qualifications. But, of the three categories—likely, probable, unlikely—into which Princeton puts applicants during the initial phases of the admissions process, Sowinski was listed as a probable.

The case of Bill Bradley notwithstanding, the Tigers have uncovered few athletically skilled intellectuals over the years. To be sure, since he took over as coach in 1967, Carril has produced four first-round pro draft picks—Geoff Petrie and John Hummer (1970), Brian Taylor (1972) and Armond Hill (1976)—but even with those players in the lineup the Tigers had to scratch and claw for everything. They succeeded because of the passion Carril instills in them for defense (they held their opponents to 51.7 points a game in 1976-77, relying mainly on old-fashioned half-court man-to-man) and the brilliance of his tightly disciplined offense. Since the speedy Taylor signed with the Nets, Carril has become even more conservative, slowing the pace of his offense to a walk.

"Depending on how much talent the other team has, we might run through a series of plays three or four times before we even look for a shot," says Omeltchenko. "It isn't that we can't get a shot the first time through. Coach Carril's philosophy says that we should make our opponents play defense longer than they're used to. That makes them anxious; they commit dumb fouls on defense and mental mistakes when they get the ball back. The only thing wrong with our system is that it puts quite a lot of pressure on the player who finally takes the shot for us. He better make it."

Princeton's simple style of picks and rolls, screens and backdoor plays lulls a lot of people to sleep—and not just Tiger opponents. "Some of our games are pretty boring," says Center Bob Roma. "I remember when I was on the freshman team I didn't even go to all the varsity games."

Basketball at Princeton is strictly light entertainment, providing students and faculty with an early evening respite from the writings of Darwin or Plato. There is no rush for season seats among townspeople; most of them buy tickets at the door. As Carril says, "The real superstars here are in the library. In fact, some of them take their sleeping bags into the stacks so they can study off and on all night long. My son is one of them. He's more interested in whether the bald eagle will become extinct than whether the basketball team will win. He came by the house late this fall, shook my hand and said, 'Good luck during the season, Dad.' The president of the university has a $228 million fusion project to worry about. Does he have time to think about the basketball team? Truthfully, I think we occupy our proper place here. But that makes my job pretty difficult."

The other day Carril went out for a leisurely afternoon drive and decided to take a visitor on a sightseeing tour of the campus.

"Hold it," barked a uniformed guard at the rear gate. "Where are you going?"

"I just thought I'd show this fellow the campus," replied Carril.

"I'm sorry, but your sticker has expired."

"I know," said Carril, who seemed to enjoy the fact that the guard obviously did not know who he was. "But...."

"That means you can't drive on campus until you get a new one."

Carril turned to his passenger and, half laughing and half sneering, said, "Do you think Dean Smith has to put up with this? Further evidence that around here you learn humility."

Being beset by genuine obstacles on all sides does not satisfy Carril; he works at making his problems seem worse than they are. As he walks slowly onto the floor before a game at Jadwin Gymnasium, he appears near death. Ah, the burden of it all has finally broken the little guy down. But, no, the ball is in the air, and he erupts into a sideline coaching act that is pure theater—reminiscent of Zero Mostel's strange metamorphosis in Rhinoceros. Carril wants every call from the officials. He bitches and moans, stomps the floor, yanks at his shirt and all but cries when things fail to go in Princeton's favor.

When the Tigers win, you would never know it from looking at Carril as he walks off the floor dragging his coat. Actually, he doesn't walk; he trudges. His large, sad eyes and dark complexion seem to hark back to Old Castile, the region in Spain where his father was born and where for centuries Moors and Christians battled for the right to live on barren soil in an unforgiving climate. If ever there were someone whose background seemed ill-suited to collegiate Gothic and Ivy League pretense....

Carril was born in Bethlehem, Pa., on July 10, 1930, and lived for the first 20 years of his life at the corner of Third Street, directly across from the Bethlehem Steel works where his father found a job after immigrating. The family's day-to-day existence was rather grim, but Carril recalls how grateful his parents were to have a weekly paycheck during the Depression and how much fun he had down at the Bethlehem Boys' Club.

It became Carril's second home. He acquired his great love for pool by hustling games there after school, and he played on the club baseball team with Chuck Bednarik, a neighborhood hero who later became a football Hall of Famer with the Philadelphia Eagles. Dues were 50¢ a year, and young Pete could sometimes make that much on a summer afternoon selling watermelon to the workmen at the Bethlehem drop forge. In those days there was no fence to keep passersby off the factory grounds; but one was erected in 1941, a time, Carril recalls, when he looked out his window one day and saw National Guard tanks rolling up to quell the violence caused by the national steel strike.

"In that part of Pennsylvania people lead especially isolated lives," says Carril. "I can remember taking a 10-mile bus ride to Easton for a high school basketball game and thinking I was going overseas. Nobody ever leaves that area. There is a statue of a bugler on top of a building in the center of Easton that, according to local legend, keeps calling to those who have strayed until they return. I'm not sure that bugler is ever going to get me, but when I took the coaching job at Princeton, my wife's parents sent us two huge flower pots full of soil. They didn't trust New Jersey dirt."

Neither Carril's players nor the Tigers' opponents will believe this, but in high school he was a 5'7" run-and-gun guard whose coach believed that a good team should take 100 shots a night. Princeton averaged 46 shots a game last season. Back then, Carril says, he shot enough to make his teammates mad.

He was a smart, quick player who made a small man's All-America team when he was a senior at Lafayette College.

Carril's first college coaching job was stickier than the one he has at Princeton, because the school was located in his hometown. The Lehigh varsity was 4-17 the year before he arrived, and the freshman team was worse. Carril put those same players through the wringer and somehow came out with an 11-12 team that pulled several upsets. Still, Lehigh is Lehigh, and under normal circumstances Carril's small-time heroics merely would have qualified him for another year there. But that spring Carril's old college coach, Butch van Breda Kolff, having taken Princeton to the threshold of an NCAA title with Bradley, was leaving to coach the Los Angeles Lakers.

"I know a guy who is the best coach in the world," van Breda Kolff told the Princeton athletic committee. "But you'll never hire him, because he doesn't fit the Ivy League image. He's balding. He's got floppy ears. He doesn't dress Ivy. He's just plain Petey Carril."

Van Breda Kolff was no button-down type himself. He violated the canons of sartorial good taste by wearing cut-off sweat pants on the Princeton golf course, and he was a chain smoker of cigars—a nasty habit he picked up from Carril during an evening of player-coach beer drinking at Lafayette. But van Breda Kolff's record—four Ivy titles in five years—proved that neatness was not essential to winning at Princeton. When the committee got a glimpse of Carril, they rightly assumed he was simply a sawed-off version of VBK.

Carril's first Princeton team won 20 games, tied for the 1967-68 Ivy title and managed to keep its poise during a string of nine consecutive road games—something that was to become a scheduling trend. What makes Carril's 190-81 record during 10½ years at Princeton even more remarkable is that the Tigers have averaged 15 away games per season. Many of those matchups have been with powerful non-conference opponents, who, not surprisingly, have a combined record of 57-73 against Princeton.

Carril's next team won the Ivy championship outright. Then in a game that is still talked about by basketball buffs, the Tigers came within a whisker of knocking off UCLA at Pauley Pavilion in the finals of the 1969 Bruin Classic. It took a 12-foot jumper by Sidney Wicks with :03 left to play to give the eventual NCAA champions a 76-75 victory. In 1971-72 Princeton bombed North Carolina 89-73 when the Tar Heels, with Bob McAdoo and Bobby Jones, were on the way to finishing third in the NCAAs. The next season Florida State, with four starters back from a second-place NCAA team, fell by a 61-59 score. The list of David and Goliath encounters goes on and on, including the Tigers' victories over Holy Cross, South Carolina, Oregon and Providence on their way to the 1975 NIT championship. Alabama was victimized 61-59 during the 1975-76 season. And last year Notre Dame, ranked second in the country at the time, was embarrassed by a 76-62 score.

Predictably, these achievements have produced a great deal of admiration for Carril among his colleagues, and his reputation has also spread to the pros, to which two of his players—Petrie and Taylor—came so well prepared that they were Rookies of the Year. John Killilea, the former Boston Celtic assistant coach who is now with the Milwaukee Bucks, remembers being in Los Angeles and watching Princeton work out before its '69 meeting with UCLA. "I listened while Carril went over his game plan," says Killilea, "and that night Princeton played practically a perfect game. They did everything the way Carril outlined it and lost on a physical feat by Wicks. It's the best example of following a game plan I've ever seen."

Chuck Daly, for years Carril's rival at Penn and now an

assistant coach with the Philadelphia 76ers, once gave a pep talk to his Quaker team in which he said, "We have to play our hearts out to win this game. Princeton is a tough team. And they're better coached."

Praise, even when it comes from his peers, does not sit well with Carril. He is too preoccupied with his Princeton-is-like-no-place-else malaise to take solace in old victories or pats on the back. He feels no kinship with the majority of coaches in the country, who can offer players full athletic scholarships worth thousands of dollars a year, while the Ivy League hands out aid only according to need. This has sentenced him to some depressing evenings in places like Mansfield, Pa., listening to Tom McMillen's mother tell him, "We have been tremendously impressed with Princeton but, tell me, why don't you give scholarships? It doesn't seem fair for us to have to pay all that money when Tommy can get a scholarship somewhere else."

Ah, the irony. McMillen, destined to be a Rhodes scholar, was unwilling to pay to play at Princeton and ended up at Maryland. Ron Haigler, who made Carril's life miserable as a player at Penn, wanted to go to Princeton and could have qualified for a lot of aid, but found it was the only Ivy League school that would not accept him.

The admissions department has been known as Heartbreak Hotel to Carril ever since 1970, when he learned that Jan van Breda Kolff, a good student and the son of the former coach, was not going to be accepted at Princeton. The incident set off a bitter feud such as had not taken place since Hamilton and Burr, a Princeton alumnus, shot it out above the Palisades in 1804. Van Breda Kolff's college board scores were borderline by Princeton's standards, but he went on to become a B student at Vanderbilt and was named Southeastern Conference Player of the Year as a senior. Carril has never gotten over the van

Breda Kolff case, and his resultant cynicism seems to have affected his relationships with people he used to be close to.

"I consider Pete to be a friend of mine," says Brown Coach Gerry Alaimo, who played pinochle with Carril before Princeton-Brown games until Pete suddenly announced he was not playing anymore. "But there are things I don't like about him. I think he intimidates officials. I don't know if it's because of his size—he is a little squirt—or his reputation. But he gets away with a lot."

Which he does, sometimes. But ref baiter or not, Carril's reputation suffers mostly because until this year he never belonged to the National Association of Basketball Coaches. This means that during those lively sessions in the crowded hotel lobbies at the NCAA finals he has never been kidded by his fellows about such matters as his treatment of officials. The coaches' meetings are always held at the tournament, but Carril prefers to stay home and watch the games on TV.

"I am tough to referee a game for," Carril admitted recently, while puffing on what was left of an El Producto and checking out the paint that was peeling off the ceiling of his den. "I want them to be totally fair. I don't want them to influence the game in the least. You have to remember that with our players we have to do so many little things to be successful. If we are off by just this much, many of our close wins would turn into close losses. That's why I don't have time to worry about being friends with coaches. Too many of them want to talk about how your wife and family are before the game, and then 10 minutes later we're trying to knock each other's heads off. I say forget about the buddy-buddy stuff until after the season. Then maybe we'll go over to Andy's Tavern and have a beer together."

Andy's is the little place across the tracks where Carril goes to unwind and avoid what he calls "the intelligentsia—those who don't want to see us get too big." When Joe Fasanella, the proprietor, was alive, he rode herd on anybody who came in and pestered Carril about basketball while the coach was trying to eat pizza or play cards. If Uncle Joe got wind of an importunate questioner, he would ring a large bell behind the bar, and the intruder either shut up or was escorted to the street. If Carril was going to be out late on a recruiting trip, Fasanella had a midnight snack waiting for him when he got back to town. After losing to Kentucky in last year's NCAA tournament and staying up all night celebrating the end of the season with his players, Carril walked into Andy's at 7 a.m. and Joe forthwith served up cognac and scrambled eggs.

When Fasanella died in September, Carril was crushed. At the wake he pressed a small package into Joe's hands. Wrapped around it was a note that read, "Wherever you're going you might be able to use these." Inside the slip of paper was a pinochle deck.

Fasanella, a blue-collar guy who ran the dumpiest bar in town, was typical of Carril's friends. Andy's is not merely an escape for Carril; it is more a way of life to him than Princeton University is. The rest of his cronies include Red Trani, a stonemason who takes a nap in Carril's office every morning while he runs game films (who wouldn't be put to sleep by those?); Georgie Boccanfuso, the Princeton athletic maintenance supervisor, who reputedly keeps $900 in cash in the trunk of his car, $500 in half-dollars in his refrigerator and an undisclosed number of coins buried in his backyard; and Marv Bressler, who is head of the sociology department at Princeton but is excluded from Carril's list of intelligentsia because "he isn't pompous." Bressler says, "Pete is the last Calvinist. His teams win because it's his will against the players'. And he is tougher."

Despite Carril's endless complaining that nobody on campus gives a hoot about his basketball team, it seems of late that he has acquired a following of friends and admirers who do not care all that much about winning and losing, but who appreciate someone who produces amid adversity. The *Daily Princetonian* recently conducted a survey to find out who students felt best fulfilled the objectives of his position at Princeton. President William Bowen did not come out on top, nor did either of the university's two Nobel laureates or the physicists who run that expensive fusion project. Just plain Petey Carril did.

APPENDIX 1

Coach Carril's Record at Princeton

Year	Overall Win/ Loss Record	Ivy League Win/ Loss Record	Ivy League Finish	Post-Season Tournament Results[1]
1967-68	20-6	12-2	T-1st	
1968-69	19-7	14-0	1st	NCAA First Round
1969-70	16-9	9-5	3rd	
1970-71	14-11	9-5	T-3rd	
1971-72	20-7	12-2	2nd	NIT Quarterfinal
1972-73	16-9	11-3	2nd	
1973-74	16-10	11-3	T-2nd	
1974-75	22-8	12-2	2nd	NIT Champion
1975-76	22-5	14-0	1st	NCAA First Round
1976-77	21-5	13-1	1st	NCAA First Round
1977-78	17-9	11-3	T-2nd	
1978-79	14-12	7-7	3rd	
1979-80	15-15	11-3	T-1st	
1980-81	18-10	13-1	T-1st	NCAA First Round
1981-82	13-13	9-5	T-2nd	
1982-83	20-9	12-2	1st	NCAA Second Round
1983-84	18-10	10-4	1st	NCAA First Round
1984-85	11-15	7-7	T-4th	
1985-86	13-13	7-7	T-4th	
1986-87	16-9	9-5	T-2nd	
1987-88	17-9	9-5	3rd	
1988-89	19-8	11-3	1st	NCAA First Round
1989-90	20-7	11-3	1st	NCAA First Round
1990-91	24-3	14-0	1st	NCAA First Round
1991-92	22-6	12-2	1st	NCAA First Round
1992-93	15-11	7-7	4th	
1993-94	18-8	11-3	2nd	
1994-95	16-10	10-4	T-2nd	
1995-96	22-7	12-2	T-1st	NCAA Second Round
	514-261	320-96		

1 The NCAA expanded its tournament field from thirty-two teams to sixty-four teams in 1985.

APPENDIX 1

APPENDIX 2

Selected Highlight Wins, Heartbreaking Losses

Coach Carril's 29-year tenure at Princeton is often remembered by fans for two "David versus Goliath" NCAA tournament games: the 1989 50-49 loss to Georgetown, and the 1996 43-41 win over UCLA.

For those who are familiar with the totality of Coach's tenure at Princeton, however, there are many more highlight wins and heartbreaking losses. With apologies to players who may feel that other "big games" should be included in this appendix, here are my top nine (with the four games of the 1975 NIT lumped together).

1. **1969 Princeton beats Columbia 60-59 (at Columbia) to clinch Ivy Title**
   - Feb. 28
   - Columbia finished the prior 1967-68 season ranked seventh in the country and its biggest stars had returned
   - Columbia stars included Jim McMillian (LA Lakers) and Heyward Dotson
   - Princeton finished undefeated in the Ivies this year (the first team ever to do so)
   - Princeton players included Petrie, Hummer, Thomforde and Sickler

2. **1969 Princeton loses to UCLA 76-75 (at UCLA's Pauley Pavilion)**
   - Dec. 29
   - UCLA team would finish 28-2 and would go on to win the NCAA that year
   - UCLA stars included Sidney Wicks, Curtis Rowe, Henry Bibby and John Vallely
   - Princeton players included Petrie, Hummer, Sickler and Bird
3. **1971 Princeton beats UNC 89-73 (at Jadwin)**
   - Dec. 6
   - UNC team would go 26-5 that year and finish second in the nation
   - UNC stars included Bob McAdoo, Bobby Jones, Dennis Wuycik, George Karl and Bill Chamberlain
   - Princeton players included Taylor, Manakas, Rimol, Berger, Bird, Dufty and Sadlosca
4. **1972 Princeton beats second-ranked Florida State 61-59 (in a Christmas tournament at Marshall)**
   - Dec. 15
   - Florida State was the NCAA runner-up the prior season with most players back
   - Florida State stars included Ron King, Reggie Royals, Lawrence McCray and Otto Petty
   - Princeton players included Manakas, Rimol, Sullivan, Berger and Vavricka
5. **1975 Princeton wins NIT (in Madison Square Garden)**
   - March 16, 20, 22, and 23
   - Opponents included Holy Cross, South Carolina, Oregon and Providence
   - Princeton finished the season ranked 12th in the country
   - Princeton players included Hill, Steuerer, Hauptfuhrer, van Blommesteyn, Molloy, Ramati, Hartley and O'Neill

6. **1976, Princeton loses to Rutgers 54-53 in the NCAA tournament**
   - March 13
   - Rutgers was undefeated heading into the NCAAs and ranked second in the nation
   - Rutgers stars included Phil Sellers, Michael Dabney, Eddie Jordan, James Bailey and Hollis Copeland
   - Princeton players included Hill, Steuerer, Hauptfuhrer, Sowinski, Slaughter, Molloy and Omeltchenko
7. **1977 Princeton beats Notre Dame 76-62 (at Jadwin)**
   - Jan. 3
   - Notre Dame would end the season 10th in the nation
   - Notre Dame stars included Duck Williams, Toby Knight, Dave Batton and Bruce Flowers
   - Princeton players included Sowinski, Omeltchenko, Roma and Slaughter
8. **1989 Princeton loses 50-49 to Georgetown in the NCAA tournament**
   - March 17
   - Georgetown was the number one seed in the East Regional and would finish the season ranked second in the nation
   - Georgetown stars included Alonzo Mourning and Charles Smith
   - Princeton players included Mueller, Scrabis, Leftwich, Lapin and Doyle
9. **1996 Princeton beats UCLA 43-41 in the NCAA tournament**
   - March 14
   - UCLA was the defending NCAA Champion with many stars returning
   - UCLA stars included Toby Bailey, Charles O'Bannon
   - Princeton stars included Johnson, Goodrich, Henderson, Doyal, Lewullis and Earl

Each game is discussed in more detail below by a player (or players) who lived the highlight or heartbreak moments with Coach.

Barnes Hauptfuhrer

FEB. 28, 1969 — PRINCETON VS. COLUMBIA

Princeton 60-Columbia 59
Compiled by the 1969 Undefeated Ivy League Champion
Princeton Basketball Team

The Princeton-Columbia game on Feb. 28, 1969, was a crucial, early turning point in the career of Coach Pete Carril. The Coach VBK-Bill Bradley-era had established Princeton as a national basketball power. VBK's 1966-67 team had won the Ivy League, won a first-round NCAA tournament game, and finished fifth in the national rankings. When VBK left to become coach of the Los Angeles Lakers, Pete Carril, with only one year of college coaching experience, became the Princeton coach. With a strong core remaining (John Haarlow, Joe Heiser, and Chris Thomforde), and two top level recruits joining the team (John Hummer and Geoff Petrie), expectations were sky high for the 1967-68 team with huge pressure on its new coach.

However, in 1967-68, Columbia ended Princeton's domination of the Ivy League. Columbia won the prestigious ECAC Christmas Tournament at Madison Square Garden and, after an early loss at Cornell, proceeded to scorch its way through the Ivy League. It beat Princeton at Columbia and when Princeton returned the favor at home, wound up tied with Princeton for the league title. Columbia then crushed Princeton in the one-game playoff and was off to the NCAA Tournament. It beat LaSalle in the first round and only an overtime loss to Davidson kept it from the Elite Eight. Columbia finished seventh in the final national rankings. Having lost only its center Dave Newmark, Columbia was the overwhelming favorite to dominate the Ivy League again in 1968-69.

In 1968-69, Princeton played the second toughest schedule in the nation, facing five teams in the top 10 and seven in the top 20. There were a number of tough losses. In Coach's words, the team was "born out of indignity and adversity." It only found its stride with the start of the Ivy schedule. There were a couple of close wins against an emerging Penn team, the second being the inaugural game at Jadwin Gym. Columbia, meanwhile, was racing through its early schedule, beating a Purdue team that would later play in the national title game and losing only to Santa Clara, which was ranked in the top five for the entire year. Columbia arrived at Princeton on Feb. 7 with a record of 14-1 and ranked 14th in the nation.

Hummer, Petrie, and Thomforde had been nursing a grudge since the playoff loss the previous year. Princeton played probably its best game of the year that night, routing Columbia 68-49 in the first of the two regular-season games between the two teams. Columbia was so shell-shocked that it lost to Penn the next night, giving it two losses in the Ivy League.

During February both teams won their remaining Ivy contests. Columbia was 18-3 before the second game even though its disastrous weekend had knocked it out of the national rankings. Columbia was still in the Ivy race if it could beat us on its home court and we lost our final game at Cornell. Failing that, the Lions still wanted revenge for being embarrassed earlier at Princeton.

The Columbia gym was a bandbox, poorly lit, with Grecian columns at the four corners of the court. Seating was limited, so there were only a handful of Princeton fans. The Columbia fans were not welcoming and seemed to be sitting just inches from the court. During warmups they serenaded Jim McMillian, their best player and a future NBA star, by singing *Jimmy Mack*, the popular song by Martha and the Vandellas.

The game was intense! We were a bit sloppy early on, committing 13 turnovers in the first half and falling behind by nine points. But the team fought back. Bill Sickler managed our offense and played great defense. Petrie shot well and led all scorers with 27 points, 17 in the second half to give us a lead. At one point, when he was double-teamed on the baseline, he faked, turned and then rose up above his two defenders to hit a commanding jump shot. Hummer played outstanding defense, holding McMillian to just 11 points, while driving to the basket on offense and scoring 18 himself. Ed Stanczak, who replaced the ineligible Tom Chestnut, neutralized Columbia's captain, Roger Walaszek. Thomforde was a presence under the basket along with Hummer, rebounding and blocking shots. George Starke was the Columbia center. He would later go on to become an NFL offensive tackle for the then-Washington Redskins. He was more than formidable, but not much of a scoring threat, so Thomforde could sag into the middle of the lane and clog up any attempted drives by the Columbia players.

With about 4:30 left in the game, Columbia's star guard Heyward Dotson stole the ball and turned to go in for a Columbia score. Thomforde chased him down and blocked his layup. The ball ricocheted to McMillian, who was also racing down court. McMillian pulled up to shoot a jump shot only to have his shot blocked by Hummer. The Tigers would not let up!

Columbia turned up the defensive pressure. Princeton led only 56-55 with 30 seconds to go. Columbia decided to foul Sickler because he was a sophomore. It was deemed a non-intentional foul, meaning that it would be a one-and-one situation. The first foul shot bounced around the rim before dropping in. The second went cleanly through, giving Princeton a three-point lead. Columbia immediately brought the ball down and scored, reducing the lead again to a single point, but now only 19 seconds remained. Larry Gordon of Columbia intentionally fouled Sickler, who sank two more free throws to push the lead back to three. Columbia hit a jump shot as time ran out, but it was too little too late. Princeton had won!

Joyous celebration took place on the court! Hoisted upon the shoulders of his teammates, Thomforde cut down the net! A group of disgruntled Columbia students attacked him as he did so, but teammates Scott Early and Dom Michel defended him from their onslaught. Celebration continued in the locker room with shouts and embraces. Bill Bradley, who had come to watch the game and cheer us on, came into the locker room to congratulate us all. Coach Carril was as happy as we had ever seen him, as it seemed a weight had been lifted from his shoulders. After the game, Columbia coach Jack Rohan told *New York Times* reporter Gordon S. White, Jr., "a good game…both teams clawed at each other…"

Lou Carnesecca, the Hall of Fame coach of St. John's, who was scouting a potential NCAA tournament opponent, said, "Princeton is a real championship team. They took every bit of pressure Columbia gave them and held on to win. That's a good team!"

With that win, Princeton won the Ivy League championship, fully avenging its loss the previous year and re-establishing its dominance. The following night, Princeton went on to defeat Cornell in Ithaca to become the first team to go undefeated in the Ivy League! This was the first of many more championship teams created in the Carril image—movement on offense, tough defense, a spirit of determination to win, fashioned by hard work.

There was one funny incident immediately following the game. Coach Carril remembered this up to his very last conversation with Thomforde, on his 92nd birthday, July 10, 2022. Thomforde's mother often came to games to cheer on the whole team. She had bought a silk scarf with an orange and black tiger-skin pattern. While the team was celebrating on the floor after the game, one of the Columbia fans, irate at the celebration, ran up to Mrs. Thomforde, tore the scarf out of her hands and tried to run away. Without hesitation, Mrs. Thomforde ran after her, sprinting across the floor through the crowd, grabbed the Columbia student by the arm, and retrieved her scarf. Coach Carril often commented on Thomforde's mother's grit and determination with a big smile on his face—and a cigar in his hand!

DEC. 29, 1969 - FINAL OF THE BRUIN CLASSIC

UCLA 76-Princeton 75
Bill Sickler with help from teammates

Today, with a different NCAA champion crowned every year, it is hard to fathom the dominance of the UCLA basketball program from the mid-1960s to the mid-1970s. Over a 12-year period, UCLA won 10 national championships. They won small, with no starting player over 6'5." They won big, with Lew Alcindor and Bill Walton. During the period when they won seven straight national titles, they lost a total of five games—*five games in seven years!*

We were scheduled to play in the Bruin Classic, a four-team tournament set for Dec. 27th and 29th. Our players, home for a brief Christmas break, left from airports near their individual home locations on Dec. 26. Most came from the Northeast or Midwest and had to take off through a bad winter storm, leaving a cauldron of wind, sleet, and turbulence and arriving in an L.A. of sun, warmth, and clear skies seemed like arriving in heaven.

We played Indiana in the first game and beat the Hoosiers in a close back-and-forth contest, 82-76. When UCLA beat Georgia Tech 121-90 our reward was to play the Bruins in the final.

UCLA had won the previous three NCAA titles and would go on to win the next four. While they had lost Alcindor to graduation, all the members of their current starting five would be drafted into the NBA, four of them in the first round. In their previous four games against Division 1 teams the Bruins had, on average, *scored*

120 points per game and won by 45 points! They liked to fast break and had run their previous opponents off the court.

Coach knew we could not run with UCLA. Our only chance was to slow the Bruins down and play half-court basketball. The day before the game, he told us not to try for offensive rebounds but to aggressively run back on defense once UCLA had the ball. The defensive match-ups were interesting. John Hummer had to guard Sidney Wicks, the Bruins' dominant offensive threat. Bob Ryder would guard Curtis Rowe. Reggie Bird would guard Henry Bibby and I would guard John Vallely. So far, not too bad. But this meant that Geoff Petrie, at 6'4", would have to guard Steve Patterson, UCLA's 6'10" center. Patterson most often posted up high at the elbow where he would not be too dangerous offensively. But Geoff wanted to know what he should do if Patterson wanted to come down to the low post. Without skipping a beat, Coach looked at Geoff and said, "Geoff, if he tries to slide down low, just give him a crack across the neck." We all looked at each other and wondered what that meant. I am not sure Coach had any idea what that meant either.

As we were watching the consolation game between Indiana and Georgia Tech, Gerry Couzens and Al Dufty, two of our sophomore teammates, spied Sidney Wicks standing near one of the entrances and decided to go down and get his autograph (talk about an unorthodox way of trying to intimidate your opponent!). When we got to the locker room, someone asked Al if he had been successful in his quest. Al and Gerry said yes, but warned John Hummer that Sidney had incredibly bad breath.

During warm-ups, UCLA had this dance routine that they had copied from the Harlem Globetrotters. They stood in a circle near half-court while the loudspeaker played *Sweet Georgia Brown*. Each player in turn would spin the ball on his fingers or perform some other trick before passing to his teammate. I am not sure our layup line at the other end of the floor was intimidating them.

Once the game started, the autograph-seeking and dance routines were over, and it was time to play. We implemented our strategy as outlined by Coach. We shut down their fast break by aggressively running back on defense. Reggie stole the ball from Henry Bibby a couple of times, and after the 6'7" Curtis Rowe set a blind, hard pick on Reggie with a forearm in the back, Reggie followed him into the UCLA timeout huddle, yelling, "You want part of me?" This set a certain tone and rendered the UCLA offense more tentative.

When we were on offense, we took our time to get a good shot. There was some ball and player movement, but the key was to get the ball to either Geoff or Johnny and let them work against the man guarding them. In the time I played with Geoff and Johnny, I saw each of them have great games. But I rarely saw them each have a great game in the same game. That was the case this night. They were the two best players on the court, better than anyone on the UCLA side. Their offensive play and Coach's defensive strategy, kept us in the game.

Just before halftime, with us ahead by three points, we had a couple of breakdowns on defense. UCLA ran a couple of fast breaks and scored to take the lead at halftime. You could feel the burden lift off their players, coaches, and fans as they ran into the locker room. Finally, the spell had been broken. They were back to UCLA basketball and would run these Ivy League nobodies off the court in the second-half.

In retrospect, our late breakdown might have been a blessing. Maybe UCLA did not make the adjustments they should have made, content to believe that they had the game won. They never sent Patterson to the low post to see if we would implement the notorious "crack across the neck" defense.

The second-half continued much as the first. We shut down their fast break, forced them to play half-court and got the ball to Geoff and Johnny. We got back in front, but never by more than a couple of points.

The UCLA players were frustrated—Bibby and Vallely were

complaining to the referees about our tight defense. The UCLA fans were restless. They had rarely, if ever, seen their team struggle like this. When we were on offense, they began to clap in unison with each dribble to protest that the pace was too slow. This was annoying, but it did not affect us. However, some of their other antics were less benign.

Midway through the second-half, Johnny was shooting a free throw. As he completed his follow-through, something small and hard struck him in the face. Some UCLA fan had taken it upon himself to dangerously fling a projectile at Johnny to disrupt his concentration. If this had struck him in the eye it could have caused serious injury. The referees either did not see it or chose not to see it.

With less than a minute to go in the game, we had a three-point lead and the ball. Unfortunately, we turned the ball over twice in succession, and UCLA scored both times to go ahead by one point with about 25 seconds to go. In our timeout, Coach put in a play with Geoff as our first option and Johnny as our second. At this point in the game, Geoff was exhausted. As documented in several player chapters, he had had a serious back injury and had only come back to play just prior to this trip. Given his out-of-shape condition, his play in the tournament and this particular game was astounding.

We inbounded the ball and worked it to Geoff. He made a move toward the right elbow and launched a shot toward the rim. It did not go in, but Johnny was there to put back the rebound. We led by a single point. UCLA got the ball to half-court and called a timeout with eight seconds left.

There was no finesse to how they won the game. They inbounded the ball and got it to Sidney Wicks on the left side. Sidney took a couple of dribbles toward the left baseline and launched a jump shot over Johnny Hummer's outstretched hand. It went cleanly through the hoop and UCLA won, 76-75.

In the aftermath, Sidney Wicks, followed by Curtis Rowe, broke away from their team's celebration to run over to our bench and, each in succession, grabbed Geoff and Johnny by both wrists and congratulated them on the games they played. This rare, spontaneous display of sportsmanship indicated how fortunate they felt to have won.

1969-70 was a difficult season for us. We had conflict issues and staggered to a third-place finish in the Ivy League—a huge disappointment. It is disheartening and embarrassing to say that a loss was the high point of our season, but maybe it was. It is never appropriate to make excuses when you lose. But there are certain truths to that game that are undeniable. For large segments of the contest, we outplayed UCLA. We had the two best players on the floor. We had a coach who outmaneuvered the man who is considered to be the greatest college coach of all time. And we put one helluva scare into the best team in the nation on its home floor.

DEC. 6, 1971 PRINCETON VS. NORTH CAROLINA

Princeton 89 – UNC 73
John Berger with an assist from Jim Sullivan

The 1971-72 season started with a lot of optimism. With Ted Manakas and Brian Taylor, a junior who would become an All-American, we had one of the best backcourts in the country. We had the electrifying senior, Reggie Bird, who could and did steal the ball from anyone. Our captain was solid Al Dufty, and we had three promising sophomores—6'10" Andy Rimol and forwards John Berger and John Sadlosca.

In a preseason game, we blew out the Italian Olympic team and then, in our season opener, we destroyed heavily favored Rutgers 99-68 in front of a sellout crowd at Jadwin.

The next home game on our schedule was against second-ranked North Carolina, which would go on to win the Atlantic Coast Conference and make it to the NCAA Final Four. UNC was loaded with talent. The Tar Heels were led by future NBA Hall of Famers Bob McAdoo and Bobby Jones. The rest of the team—George Karl, Dennis Wuycik, Steve Previs, and their sixth man, Billy Chamberlain (who had been the NIT MVP the previous season) —would all be high-round NBA or ABA draft picks.

With two days to prepare for the game, Coach Carril was firing on all cylinders. The slightest mistake in practice became an existential crisis. Here was a great coach who wanted to compete and win at the highest level and was determined not to be embarrassed by the Tar Heels. To add to the overall challenge was the 6'10" McAdoo, with whom Brian Taylor had played in the Pan Am Games the previous summer. When Coach asked Brian how fast McAdoo was, Brian replied, "As fast as me."

Coach Carril also relied on the scouting of Artie Hyland, our freshman coach. Thanks to Artie, we were more than prepared to beat UNC's vaunted full-court press, and prepared defensively.

On game day, the atmosphere in Jadwin Gym was electric. There was a sell-out crowd, and ticket-scalpers were busy. The student body was there en masse.

The game started with UNC's Dennis Wuycik making two three-point plays the old way: before the three-point shot. The score remained close with Princeton having a two-point lead at halftime. At the 12- minute mark of the second half, we had a one-point lead, and thanks to Reggie Bird's three quick steals, we went on a 16-4 run that sealed the game. Andy Rimol was the star of the game while going head-to-head with McAdoo. Two years later, McAdoo's NBA Buffalo Braves would draft Andy at McAdoo's insistence. Bob said that Andy was the strongest player he had ever faced. The game ended with Rimol scoring 23 points, Manakas 21, Taylor 16, Dufty and Berger eight each, and Bird three. An unsung hero of the game was Sadlosca, who came off the bench and had 10 points in the second half.

With the final score 89-73, the roar of the crowd was deafening, and all was good in Tigertown.

DEC. 15, 1972 PRINCETON VS. FLORIDA STATE

Princeton 61–FSU 59
John Berger

We entered the 1972-73 season having lost All-American Brian Taylor to the ABA, and captain Al Dufty and defensive stalwart Reggie Bird to graduation. With less team speed than the year before, this team would play at a slower tempo.

The year started ominously with losses against Penn State and Villanova. The third game of the year produced a victory over Rutgers. Post-game, Coach told the media that our new offense was "ugly basketball." He added, "I don't like to teach it, and I try not to watch it. But we have to use it to win games this year. We can't play a run-and-shoot game. If we do, we will get murdered on the boards. I think Bobby Knight could coach this team better than I can."

Brushing this commentary aside, the team added signature wins versus Davidson and Virginia before heading to Huntington, W.Va. to play in Marshall's holiday tournament. We were matched against then-second-in-the-nation Florida State in the opener. FSU was coming off a season in which they lost in the NCAA Finals to Bill Walton-led UCLA, 81-76. FSU had four returning stars—6'10" Reggie Royals, 7' Lawrence McCrae, 6'4" sharpshooter Ron King and 5'7" point guard (mini-me) Otto Petty. Needless to say—on paper we were seriously overmatched. True to his coaching philosophy, when facing a heavy favorite, Coach Carril went to his "ugly basketball" strategy. And as often happened when a high-scoring, freewheeling team met the disciplined Tigers, frustration and mistakes crept in. At halftime, we were down by four. Andy Rimol was more than holding his own against FSU's big front court. Jimmy Sullivan was having a memorable game and would be named to the all-tournament team. When Coach was told Jimmy had made the team, he replied, "So did the guy he was guarding." The star of the game was senior Ted Manakas. He had a great career at Princeton, and this game ranks among his finest moments. Princeton won the game 61-59, with Ted scoring 27 points and making two free throws with two seconds left to clinch the victory.

MARCH 1975 – THE NIT CHAMPIONSHIP

Barnes Hauptfuhrer

Certainly, winning the NIT championship (and winning the last 13 games of that 1974-75 season) was a highlight for all of us. We entered the tournament confident that we could compete with any team.

Having said this, preparation for the opener against Holy Cross was not so good. Coach told us that Holy Cross had a lethal full-court press. To prepare, he had us try to break the full-court press of our freshman team with one twist—he allowed the freshmen to have six players on the court. Trust me… it mattered.

The scrimmage was held in Dillon Gym rather than Jadwin. After about 45 minutes of varsity turnover after turnover, and Coach screaming "what the hell is going on here," Coach mercifully halted practice. It was ugly. I do not think Coach felt we were prepared. He had merely seen enough.

Holy Cross was led by freshmen Chris Potter and Michael Vicens. At Princeton, freshmen were ineligible to play varsity. During our ill-fated scrimmage against our freshmen, Coach installed a press-breaking technique involving our out-of-bounds player throwing a pass to another out-of-bounds player who then inbounded the ball. It worked! Starters Armond, Mickey, and Timmy, coupled with sixth man Peter Molloy, totally destroyed the Holy Cross press, getting layups and open jump shots, ultimately resulting in a 21-point win (84-63). The game was also marked by huge contributions from our bench, which collectively scored 32 points. Mark Hartley (16 points) and Brian O'Neill (12 points) led the way.

Next up: The South Carolina Gamecocks, a team that had beaten us by 17 points (65-48) on its home court in the December Carolina Classic. One thing about that December game: Armond felt we had been cheated by the refs. Message to all: never, ever make Armond feel like his team was cheated. In any event, Armond (arguably the most unselfish superstar in Princeton history) decided that he would teach the Gamecocks a lesson. And did he ever.

Early in the game, Armond passed the ball to me on the wing but came right over to get it back from me. I had two thoughts: one, I had never seen him do this before; and two, this game is about to get really interesting.

Before discussing Armond's exploits, a few words about this South Carolina team. It was loaded.

1. Center Tom Boswell (a future first-round pick of the Celtics)
2. Forward Alex English (a second-round NBA pick who went on to play 15 years in the NBA, average 21.5 points per game and make eight NBA All-Star teams)
3. Guard Mike Dunleavy (a star from NYC, who led the team in scoring and went on to play and coach in the NBA)
4. Forward Nate Davis (an incredible leaper, reminiscent of David Thompson of North Carolina State)
5. Guard Jack Gilloon (a flashy, Pete Maravich-style player (also from NYC), who ultimately ranked second in career assists at South Carolina)

Basically, this game can best be described as "Armond buried them all." It did not matter who South Carolina sent out to guard Armond that night. Armond scored 18 in the first half. We led by 18 (42-24) and went on to win by 19 (86-67). On this night, Armond

Hill laid down the law. Maybe it was because Armond felt we were previously cheated in South Carolina, maybe it was a NYC thing. After all, this was Madison Square Garden, and the return of the highly-touted New York City guards, Dunleavy and Gilloon, had to be dealt with. Armond knew he was much better than both of them. That night everyone who watched the game understood that Armond was the best guard in the building—by far.

Beyond Armond, we all chipped in that night, but two performances stand out. First, Tim van Blommesteyn: Timmy was always fast. Maybe not Brian Taylor fast, but very fast. Coming off the bench, he led the team in scoring that night with 24 points. Second, seldom-used, 6'11" sophomore Lonnie Ramati gave us an unexpected lift. Our starting center that year, Jim Flores, was not able to play in the NIT due to a late-season broken jaw. In theory, we entered the NIT vulnerable to a big, physical team like South Carolina. Lonnie was the X factor that helped us defend against South Carolina's imposing frontline. That frontline scored 20 points fewer than its season average. A few extra rebounds, a couple of blocked shots, a charge—these things mattered to our success that night. Coach made sure that we understood this.

We had to face a daunting Oregon team in the NIT semifinal. This group was led by the Adonis-like shooting guard Ronnie Lee and rugged forward Greg Ballard. Both were high NBA draft picks. In addition, Oregon head coach Dick Harter was an ex-Penn coach. He knew our offensive schemes, and he knew our defensive schemes. We had faced Oregon a year before in Kansas' Jayhawk Classic. We lost that game. If we were going to win this one, it was going to be a 40-minute grind, and that is exactly what it was, ending with a 58-57 win for us.

Everyone on the team showed guts that night. Late in the game we were down 57-56. Armond was fouled and sank two clutch free throws with perfect swishes. With less than 30 seconds to go, we had the lead and the ball. Oregon fouled reserve Ramati. As he had done against South Carolina, Lonnie had given the team solid minutes this night, but I think it is fair to say, he was not ready for the one-on-one that he faced. His foul shot came up two feet short. Oregon ball.

Lee was the guy for Oregon. Our smaller sixth-man, 5'10" Peter Molloy, had the cover after a switch. There was a chest bump. Adonis got knocked off balance and had to throw up a Hail Mary. Ballgame to Princeton.

I will never forget walking off that court. I was so happy. Waiting to come on the court were the New York Knicks. Passing by Knick and former Princeton star Bill Bradley, I saw a big smile on his face. The moment was quite pleasing.

For me, the outcome of our NIT final against Providence was assured before we took the court. There was no way we could lose that game. Thankfully, co-captains Hill and Steuerer understood we still had to play the game. Their leadership, coupled with stellar performances by van Blommesteyn and Molloy, ruled the day. Mickey, Timmy, and Peter made 21 of 28 shots from the field and collectively scored 54 points. Armond focused on defense in this game, shutting down Providence star Joey Hassett. Princeton wins it all, 80-69.

The 1975 championship was Coach Carril's only post-season title. Despite the nonexistence of long-distance three-point field goals, we scored 80 or more points in three of the four NIT games. We out-assisted and out-rebounded each of our four opponents. Although there are no statistics available for turnovers, I suspect we had fewer than our opponents. Similarly, I suspect we retrieved more loose balls and picked up more charges, but this too is just my guess. Any way you cut it, it was truly a team triumph that shocked many (albeit not us).

The next day I was back on campus, which was largely empty due to spring break. As I walked across campus, I thought about the campus-wide celebration that would have occurred if Duke (where

I considered playing) had won the NIT. Initially, I suppose I was a bit sad—a raucous crowd would have been fun. I thought the NIT championship was a pretty big deal, but no one was around. No one seemed to care. I paused to reflect on the moment and then remembered Coach's teachings about the importance of humility. It was time to move on.

MARCH 13, 1976 — NCAA TOURNAMENT

Rutgers 54-Princeton 53
Barnes Hauptfuhrer

When discussing the parameters of this book, John Berger told me, "Just put in the stories about great wins and skip the losses." As tempting as this suggestion was, I resisted. This book had to be the real deal. Coach lived it all. He had so many highs and so many lows across 29 years at Princeton. I felt that we needed to try to capture as many of these as we could.

So, below is the story of our team's loss to Rutgers in the 1976 NCAA tournament. At the outset, it is important to understand a few things about the NCAA Tournament that year.

1. The field comprised just 32 teams (not today's 64-plus team field).
2. The regionals involved teams from designated geographic regions, so our East Regional included all the East Coast powerhouses (including the ACC tournament winner).
3. There was no seeding, so regrettably, despite our being a top 15 team most of the year, our first round opponent was second-in-the-nation Rutgers.
4. All teams in the tournament, except us, were allowed to play freshmen.

It is also important to understand how loaded the 1976 Rutgers team was from a physical talent perspective. The Scarlet Knights had five players who got drafted by the NBA and played in the NBA

(Eddie Jordan, Phil Sellers, Michael Dabney, Hollis Copeland, and James Bailey). Sixth man Abdel Anderson was also a talented player. Rutgers was undefeated going into the NCAAs (28-0). They averaged 93.3 points per game, and their coach, Tom Young, was solid.

On Feb. 2 that year, we played Rutgers in Jadwin Gym. We lost 75-62. A couple of things about that game. As I recall, it was a close game until Armond got his fourth foul early in the second-half. Shortly thereafter, I picked up my fourth foul. We had talented replacements, but this was not our day. Approaching the NCAAs in March, that earlier loss was not intimidating. We knew Rutgers was good and we knew we had to play our best to win. But we felt we could win.

The 1974-75 Princeton team was good, but the 1975-76 team was better. Certainly, the latter team had less speed (due to the graduation of Tim van Blommesteyn). Certainly, it had injury issues. Mickey Steuerer had battled a severely strained wrist all year. This limited his playing time and stats. Talented sophomore Frank Sowinski had to sit out several games prior to the Rutgers game due to a severe leg contusion. Ever the compassionate one, Coach would constantly get on Frank by saying, "What good are you hurt?" These words became a lifetime joke between Frank and me.

But the 1976 team also marked the return of Bobby Slaughter, who had taken a voluntary leave of absence from the University the prior year, and he made us defensively better. Sowinski brought guts, smarts, and shooting skills to the squad. Sophomore Bill Omeltchenko and senior Peter Molloy capably filled Mickey's reduced playing time. We were confident we could beat Rutgers.

The game itself was a low-scoring grind. Neither team could grab a double-digit lead, but, as I recall, Armond fouled out with about five minutes left in the game. I believe we were down by five or seven points. With Armond gone, and Mickey ailing on the bench, I knew we were in serious trouble. But our reserve backcourt, Peter and Omo, stepped up big time. With under two minutes to play, there was a pass to Frank Sowinski in the corner. Shot, swish. Princeton now down by three. With under a minute to go, Peter gave me a perfect pass at the top of the key. With Coach's voice in the background saying, "Take it," I swished the shot. Princeton now down by one.

Rutgers was panicking. You could see it in their faces. Suddenly, Omo cleanly stole the ball from Dabney. The ball got poked into my hands with Omo open for a layup, but the whistle blew. Foul on Omo. Total bulls##t, but it is what it is, so you deal with it.

Dabney missed the front end of his one-and-one. Somehow, 5'10" Peter Molloy got the loose ball. Time for a final play. Coach called no time out. He believed he had the smarter team on the court. He trusted us to figure it out. We got fouled with one second to play. We faced a one-and-one to go to the Sweet 16...

All seven of us who played that day stepped up to the foul line. Each of us put our right hands under the ball in the correct position. The seams were lined up correctly. Our collective shot was true—dead middle. One problem, the shot was a half-inch too long. Game over, season over, college careers over for Armond Hill, Mickey Steuerer, Peter Molloy, and me. A very tough moment.

Since that moment, there have been plenty of "what if" reflections by many. I suppose that 1976 was probably Coach's best chance to get to the Final Four, as Rutgers advanced there by cruising over UConn by 15 points and VMI by 24 points. But "what ifs" are bulls##t. We lost, period.

Perhaps we knew it then, but we certainly know it now (46 years later)—the four of us are Brothers. We ran the Pete Carril gauntlet together, we experienced the high of the NIT championship together, we experienced the crushing defeat to Rutgers together. Life has taken us all in different directions, but we remain united by the thankfulness we feel toward Coach Carril. For several years, we visited Coach knowing that his personal game clock was winding down. Sure, these visits demonstrated our feelings about Coach, but they were also statements about what we learned from Coach. He taught us that commitment to team over self was the law. Honesty and accountability were the law. Personal humility was the law. Expressing our thankfulness was important to all of us.

As I thought about taking on the challenge of editing a book collecting many different individual memories from 26 to 55 years ago, I sensed that there was (and is) a larger brotherhood of Princeton basketball players out there. The chapters in this book collectively tell a story. There is a larger brotherhood out there; we are family. It may be spread across the continent and be disconnected by the fact that many never met the players before or after them—but the Princeton basketball family is an important component of the untold story of Peter J. Carril.

JAN. 3, 1977 – PRINCETON VS. NOTRE DAME

Princeton 76–Notre Dame 62
Several Members of the 1977 Team

On that date in January, Notre Dame came to Jadwin ranked eighth in the nation after having been ranked second the week before. They had an outstanding coach, Digger Phelps, as well as many talented players, including Duck Williams, Toby Knight, Dave Batton, and Billy Paterno.

Princeton was a relatively young team with captain Bob Slaughter the lone senior on the squad, a group of solid juniors returning from the prior year's Ivy League championship team (Frank Sowinski, Billy (Omo) Omeltchenko, Rich Rizzuto, Bob Kleinert, Rich Starsia, and Doug Snyder), and the talented high school All-American sophomore Bob Roma. Both Paterno and Roma were heavily recruited by Notre Dame while at Christian Brothers Academy in Lincroft, N.J. But while Paterno went to Notre Dame, Roma chose Princeton over the Irish.

The Tigers were beginning to mesh as a squad at the start of 1977. Coach Carril had put together a challenging early schedule, which led to losses to Maryland and Rutgers, victories against St. Joseph's and Villanova, and a Tiger win in the Kodak Classic in Rochester, N.Y., against Ohio State and St. Bonaventure to end the calendar year. It was the first holiday tournament won by a Princeton team since 1965. The team was beginning to execute Coach's main strategies and philosophies: play solid defense, be patient on offense, and handle full-court pressure.

However, the odds against beating Notre Dame were high. There were prognostications that if Princeton played well, defended as a team, and worked hard—and Notre Dame played poorly—the Tigers could be competitive at the end of the game. Interestingly, the game would be played on the 200th anniversary of the Battle of Princeton, where the British were defeated by an undermanned Colonial army. It was now the Irish that were marching into Princeton to face another seemingly undermanned unit.

Over the holiday break, practices leading up to the Notre Dame game were loose but very focused. Unfortunately, starting guard Doug Snyder's sprained ankle would keep him out of the lineup. Coach would need to develop and fine-tune another perfect game plan against a "superior opponent." For instance, he added a wrinkle to his strategy on how to break Notre Dame's full-court press. Tim Olah was a sophomore guard. He had excellent speed, solid ball-handling skills, and was developing into the role of press-breaker. Although Coach stressed diagonal passes to beat a press, he felt that Olah was fast (and small) enough to dribble past the taller Irish players to break the press on occasion. That piece was added into the playbook. Ultimately, Coach stressed that success would come only through relentless defense and patience in running offensive schemes that would allow us to beat them backdoor and find the open man. But we had to hit our open shots because second shots would be limited by Notre Dame's superior size. However, we were confident enough not to be intimidated by the Notre Dame mystique.

Notre Dame arrived to a record crowd at Jadwin, where nearly 8,000 people were in the stands, the majority of whom likely had come to see the Irish. Notre Dame came out on the court led by immaculately dressed coach Digger Phelps. For pregame layups, Notre Dame wore three different layers of brand-new gold and green warmups that looked like beach wear. The crowd rushed to the Notre Dame side of the court, sometimes three-deep, to get a close-up look at their uniforms, especially when a layer was removed. Our side of the court was empty. Coach, dressed in his customary short-sleeve shirt, narrow tie, and rolled-up program in hand, scowled at us if we even dared to look over to the Notre Dame side of the court. However, Coach Carril's pre-game interview, pessimistic as expected, was also cryptically optimistic when he said, "There is a lot of magic in the Notre Dame name. There is some real magic in the Princeton name, too."

The game started as a back-and-forth affair with Notre Dame taking an early lead on 8-for-11 shooting from the outside, but Princeton was not backing off or folding under the pressure and kept fighting back to tie it at 19-19. The Irish pressed, but the backcourt of Omo, Rizzuto, and Olah were handling it, keeping the offense patiently in gear, finding the open man, and playing tough. The Tigers took the lead at 25-23 mainly as a result of their outstanding defense, which forced 17 first-half turnovers and held Notre Dame to 2-for-14 shooting to close out the half. The momentum was clearly turning in Princeton's favor. Jadwin shook when Omeltchenko stole the ball and scored just as the halftime buzzer went off. Princeton went into the locker room on a 22-6 run and with a 35-25 lead. Slaughter, Roma, and Sowinski had scored 31 of the Tigers' 35 points. Sowinski took five shots and a handful of free throws and did not miss one of them. The Irish clearly had to regroup or they would be run out of Princeton, like the British 200 years before.

In the second-half, it became a Princeton clinic as the Tigers handled Notre Dame's press, patiently worked Carril's offense to near perfection, and continued to hit open jump shots. The lead ebbed and flowed between 19 and 13 points, before Notre Dame cut it to 12. However, some key baskets by Slaughter, Roma, and Bob Kleinert from his favorite spot in the corner sealed the 76-62 victory. As the final buzzer sounded, the fans stormed the court in celebration. In the end, Slaughter led the way with 19 points, Sowinski had 18 "perfect" points—he shot six-for-six from the field and six-for-six from the free throw line—and Bob Roma had 17 points. Billy Paterno led the Irish with 15 points, so in the end it seems that Roma got both the best of the Irish and his high school teammate. That night, Princeton's nation-leading defense forced 26 turnovers and held the Irish to 39% shooting from the floor. The Tigers shot 54%.

Princeton basketball always found a way to be competitive. Princeton teams always were prepared. Princeton players always gave their best. There was probably no better example of this than when Princeton faced off against Notre Dame in this game. It was truly a team effort: We all did our jobs and executed Coach's strategy to near-perfection. Later, when Coach Carril reflected on the 1976-77 season, he mentioned that our team did not realize just how good we were. That game gave us the confidence to play our best basketball in the Ivy League and win the championship for the second year in a row.

Just as the British found Princeton to be a tough place to be on January 3, 1777, the Irish and their fans went away with little sympathy from the natives. (Except rumor has it that Bob Kleinert's father did send sympathy cards to all the Notre Dame fans in their hometown of Franklin Lakes, N.J., who thought the Irish would win by a substantial margin.)

MARCH 17, 1989 — PRINCETON VS. GEORGETOWN

Georgetown 50- Princeton 49
Jerry Doyle

The 1988-89 hoops season was a slog. The previous year had featured a senior-laden team that had mastered the art of beautiful basketball. But for a few incredibly unlucky bounces and breaks at the end of the year, that team by all rights should have represented the Ivy League on the national stage that was the NCAA tournament. Instead, a poser Cornell team somehow won the league title. The Big Red lost by 40 to Arizona in the first round of the tournament in a game that was not as close as the score indicated. The seniors from the 1988 Princeton squad had the unfortunate distinction of being the first of Coach's recruiting classes to go four years without winning a league title. The dark cloud that seemed to hover over the 1988 squad followed the Tigers into the following year.

Right from the start, things were not easy. The team was composed entirely of freshmen and sophomores, with the exception of senior heartthrob Bobby Scrabis and junior enigma Matt Lapin. Scrabis was everything that the rest of the team was not—accomplished, well-known, and attractive to the opposite sex. As the senior captain and leader, he must have felt very lonely. Lapin was the only other upperclassman. Congenial and self-deprecating, he was on the opposite end of the intensity scale from Bobby. He could go months without getting a rebound or folks knowing he was on the team, yet he was an absolutely indispensable player. Inexplicably, he led the entire country in three-point shooting percentage his senior year without any of his teammates realizing it. Rounding out the team were 13 freshmen and sophomores. What these players lacked in precision or skill, they more than made up for with their inexperience. Their collective defining characteristic was that they were knuckleheads, but at least they were an extremely close group of knuckleheads.

Needless to say, Coach had his work cut out for him, and he knew it. Ever the perfectionist, his indomitable will was tested mightily by the 1989 team. Members of the previous squad had spoiled the coaches with its precision cutting and deft passing, while the 1989 team had forwards who often whizzed passes into the bleachers and guards who ran in directions unencumbered by the offensive sets. One guard personally drove Coach to rip open five sweatshirts over the course of the season. The players became accustomed to a fairly predictable pattern. Coach's eyes would bulge with astonishment after witnessing some insult to basketball order and precision. He would start with a series of curse words and then slowly mix in other odd words and phrases that by themselves would not make much sense, but coupled with their volcanic presentation somehow intensified the situation. His hands would slowly rise to his sweatshirt collar, which he would grip so tightly that his knuckles would burn white through the skin as they started shaking. The words morphed into pained grunts and primal noises. Then, in a truly awesome display of strength and anger, Coach would rip open his sweatshirt from top to bottom in one explosive motion that would have made the Hulk blush. For the rest of the practice Coach's impressively matted torso would add an exclamation point to his unworldly stamina and energy. Practices were long, practices were hard, and practices were not for the faint of heart.

At least there was Kit, who was the team's sophomore center. Kit was the glue. Besides being an amazingly effective player, Kit had a great sense of humor and kept everyone sane. He had been so effective so early in his career that, by the time he was a sophomore, he was considered a veteran. Because Kit was so reliable and there were always so many other pressing concerns for the coaches to focus on, he rarely (never) received any harsh words from the coaches. This allowed him to hone his craft in those two areas in which he was truly remarkable: a quirky post game that relied less on his sneaky athleticism and more on his amazingly intuitive feel for the game, and attempting to make his teammates laugh while they were being dressed down by Coach. Kit liked to position himself casually behind Coach and directly in the line of sight of whichever teammate was being "instructed." Through a series of eyebrow raises and perplexed expressions, Kit would react in real time to whatever insulting malaprops were being hurled towards the hapless player. Teammates quickly learned to avoid Kit's gaze at all costs and that the best course of action was to stare at the floor until Coach finished saying his piece.

Throughout the year Coach kept up the intensity, and the team slowly got better. At no point during the year did the team appear to be "a team of destiny," as the Ivy League was neck-and-neck and the title came down to the final weekend. Princeton had to beat Harvard at Harvard to secure a berth in the NCAA tournament. In a game that was tight the entire way, Princeton pulled out a victory in the last minute. Boston native Matt Henshon fittingly played a key role in the victory. When the final buzzer sounded, spontaneous joy erupted as the entire team formed a dogpile at center court. This was long before the team had any meaningful number of fans or any hint of a national following. It was just 15 guys playing for each other and being wildly happy. As fun as the immediate postgame celebration was, it was trumped by an epic bus ride back to Princeton. The coaches and players bonded in a very special way. Instead of sitting in the front seat as was the tradition, the coaches made their way to the back of the bus and joined the players. Beverages were shared and full-throated singing ensued. Nobody was thinking about the NCAA tournament. The goal of winning an Ivy League championship had been accomplished, and the sense of relief and joy was palpable. It was a very happy time for everyone.

A couple of days later, the players gathered in a dorm room to watch the CBS Selection Show to see whom they would play in the first round. As fate would have it, the Selection Show was scheduled to begin after the Big East final, in which No. 1-seed Georgetown completely dismantled Syracuse. As we watched the game, we kept our expectations modest; the consensus was that we wanted to fly on a plane to some place warm, and we wanted to play any team except Georgetown. The Selection Show was like a punch in the gut. The very first pairing had Georgetown playing Princeton in Providence, R.I. So not only were we likely to be humiliated, we also had to drive five hours in a smelly bus for the privilege. This was long before national cameras were strategically set up in staged settings to watch players mug for the fans and jump all over each other when the selections were announced. If a secret camera had been rolling that day, it would have captured a bunch of stunned players discussing how best to feign injury so as to avoid the trip and go on spring break. From that point forward there was a lot of gallows humor leading up to the game. The team was keenly aware that there had been a national discussion related to rescinding the Ivy League's automatic berth in the NCAA tournament, which gained credence after Cornell had been steamrolled the year before. Playing Georgetown seemed to us to be a bit of a set-up, intended to drive home the point that the league could not compete at the highest levels. Unfortunately, we were not sure there was a lot we could do to disabuse folks of this notion.

Practices started right away, and they were intense. Coach was a master at getting his teams ready, but we could tell that he was nervous. As best they could, the coaches attempted to recreate the buzzsaw that was waiting for us in Providence. There was one practical problem, however. There really was no way to mimic the talent and athleticism the Tigers were about to face given that all of the

Georgetown players were better than all of the Princeton players. The starters attempted to run the offense against seven defenders, with very predictable results. This was not a confidence builder. The coaches asked 6'7" freshman Jimmy Lane to play the role of Alonzo Mourning, who led the country in blocked shots and was likely the most dominant force in college basketball. Jimmy was game, but even the most imaginative of players had trouble buying into the transformation. The following day the coaches may have overcorrected a bit, as they had assistant coach Jan van Breda Kolff, who at 6'10" was essentially the same size as Mourning, patrol the lane with a broom that extended well above the top of the backboard. This led to some truly farcical shots, as the team would have to somehow navigate a defense with two extra players and then launch a shot 20 feet or so into the air. It is not clear whether a single basket was scored in the practices leading up to the game.

Coach's intensity had made the team incredibly close and the gallows humor kept everyone loose. The locker room was still a very fun place to be. At one point one of the younger players felt emboldened and declared that if they all had to go to the trouble of missing spring break and driving all the way to Providence, they might as well go ahead and try to beat Georgetown. There was an awkward pause, and then everyone burst out laughing. Much locker room discussion focused on the fate of freshman power forward Matt Eastwick. Easty was the team's best dunker, and Coach had instructed him to "send a message" to Mourning by dunking on him early in the game. This led to all sorts of conjecture as to what would actually happen to Eastwick if he were to try such a thing. Half the team thought that Mourning would pin the ball to the glass, and the other half thought that Mourning would pin the entirety of Easty's body to the glass. In the latter scenario, conversations devolved into the specifics of exactly how Easty would need to be extracted from the glass and how long the game would be delayed while he was scraped off.

Given that the team had no reason to believe it would ever be on national television again, someone had the incredibly bad idea to encourage everyone to get crew cuts. The concept was to tap into the karma and mystique of the underdog in the movie *Hoosiers*. With long, flowing blond hair, Bobby Scrabis had much more image credibility to lose than the rest of the players and wisely opted out. Kit chose a hybrid approach, shaving the top of his head but keeping the curls around his neck. If it is not a look he regrets while looking back, it should be. The crew cuts made things difficult for the game announcers, who consistently had trouble telling the players apart during the broadcast.

The game was held on St. Patrick's Day, and Notre Dame was the second game of the doubleheader. Some of the fans may have been over-served. While there were not many Princeton fans at the start of the game, by the middle of the first-half the entire place was rocking and *loud*. The game is a bit of a blur, but everything started clicking. Coach had prepared us for everything without our even realizing it. Bobby Scrabis stepped up and put consistent pressure on the Georgetown defense, streaking towards the basket with wild abandon. Kit heroically battled a frontline that towered above him and more than held his own. Freshman point guard George Leftwich had the awesome responsibility of handling the vaunted Georgetown pressure, and he was unflappable. Matt Lapin started grabbing key rebounds like Charles Barkley and also made some huge shots. Key contributions were made by three-point shooting marksman Troy Hottenstein as well as Matt Eastwick. By the time halftime arrived, Princeton was inexplicably up eight. The team ran into the locker room, and no one knew how to act—players were bouncing off the walls. Everyone was shouting at once. The coaches finally managed to calm everyone down for a few minutes and stressed the importance of staying disciplined going into the second half.

The advice was good but not heeded, and within a few short

minutes the lead had evaporated. This was a script that had been witnessed many times over the years, with an undermanned team putting up a fight for a while and then folding like a cheap tent. The stage seemed to be set for a similar outcome, but something strange happened that night. After being pinned back on its heels the first few minutes of the second-half, Princeton recovered and began trading blows with the best team in the country. Every time Georgetown scored, Princeton had an answer and the lead volleyed back and forth for the duration of the game. It was white-knuckle basketball at its most extreme, with every possession eliciting a spontaneous burst of energy from the increasingly delirious crowd. Princeton actually scored the final bucket of the game, taking a 49-48 lead. Georgetown countered when Alonzo Mourning, who was a notoriously bad free-throw shooter, hit both ends of a pressure-packed one-and-one. Princeton had the ball down one point and would have one possession to pull off the greatest upset in NCAA tournament history. Coach called upon team captain and best player Bobby Scrabis to come off a ball screen set by Kit to take the final shot. The play was snuffed out by the uber-athletic Mourning, who managed to get a hand on the shot. There was a scramble for the ball, and Princeton had one last chance off an inbounds play. Kit smartly sealed off Mourning and would have had an easy layup to win the game, but for some reason the ref held the ball forever and Matt Lapin did not get a chance to make the pass he so desperately wanted to try. Kit still managed to get a shot up and there may have been some contact, but no foul was called. The game was over.

None of the Princeton players had any clue that the game would take on a life of its own. Back then only a small fraction of first-round games were on television. The plan was to show the first few minutes of the Georgetown-Princeton game and then switch to a more competitive game, but for obvious reasons the switch was never made. It was the highest-rated college basketball game in

ESPN's history, and it demonstrated to CBS executives the allure and potential of televising all the games of March Madness. The game also had the nice byproduct of showing the country what the Princeton hoops community already knew: that Coach Pete Carril could coach the heck out of a basketball game.

MARCH 14, 1996 – PRINCETON VERSUS UCLA

Princeton 43-UCLA 41
Sydney Johnson, Chris Doyal, Mitch Henderson,
Steve Goodrich, Gabe Lewullis and Brian Earl

For the guys on our 1995-96 team, any talk about the UCLA game has to start with acknowledging the game that helped us get there. In an Ivy League overtime playoff game at Lehigh, in front of a packed crowd split equally between Princeton and Penn fans, we finally got the monkey off our backs and knocked off the Quakers. Penn will always be our bitter rivals, so a win against those guys to get to the NCAA Tournament could not have been any sweeter.

Coach's retirement announcement in the locker room immediately after that game was jarring and emotional but also fleetingly so. You have heard the story by now of what Coach wrote on the board in the locker room ("I'm retiring. I'm very happy"), but after that he never mentioned those words around us again. For that brief time, our Coach finally exhaled. Twenty-nine seasons of being absolutely relentless, exacting, demanding, brilliant, insightful, innovative, and at times, ruthless. He put all of those Hall of Fame traits aside for one moment and shared a bit of himself—maybe all of himself—with a group of guys who years later carry the honor of being the last college basketball team that the legendary Pete Carril ever coached. "I'm retiring. I'm very happy." And then, Coach quickly returned to form.

The next time the coaching staff and players were back in Jadwin Gym together, it was all about how to beat UCLA. Coach made it clear what he wanted. With our team, Coach delivered mandates when he spoke and few of us dared to put an interpretive spin on anything he instructed us to do on the court. What can you offer a genius at work except your willing compliance?

And so he instructed us: Don't even think about running with these guys (relentless, demanding, and exacting). On every shot, all five guys run back on defense. No one run in for offensive rebounds (brilliant, insightful, innovative). Take care of the ball, and do not do anything stupid (ruthless).

Were we flawless in executing the game plan? Yes and no. Early on, we got sucked into an open-court game with UCLA, and dug ourselves a 7-0 hole. Maybe we were a little slow at controlling the tempo; we usually had Earl starting alongside us to help out, but Coach had decided to change the lineup and start Brian on the bench. Other player missteps followed, culminating in an intentional foul at half-court with UCLA being awarded two free throws and the ball with the game tied 41-41 and 1:02 left on the clock. None of us would lie and deny that this mistake looked like it was going to cost us the game. But UCLA missed both free throws, momentum swung fully our way, and Steve and Gabe eventually connected for the now legendary center-forward backdoor play. And the rest is history.

There are a lot more quirks, runs, and uniqueness to that game (Reggie Miller, anyone?) that we could discuss, but that is for the fans. What may embody the UCLA game for our team could be summed up in mentioning Chris Doyal. Chris Doyal—a highly-touted senior forward from Texas—was adored by the guys on the team but would not qualify as Coach's favorite player. Coach turned up the heat on Doyal on every occasion throughout the season, and that is the way it was for some of the rest of us at times. We all had a choice about how to respond (see earlier reference to "genius"). I do not think it is too much to say that our 1995-96 team thrived behind how bravely Doyal responded during his senior campaign. Doyal stopped caring how Coach said things and just started doing. So, of course, it was Doyal who disobeyed Coach's pregame instructions and chased down a pair of key offensive rebounds to help us secure the game. In the end, Coach was right about Doyal, he was right about UCLA, and he was right about us. But, above all else, Coach challenged us to think and have the courage to take calculated risks as Doyal did.

We beat UCLA because we had a genius as our head coach leading the way. We beat UCLA because we rarely could ever achieve the on-court perfection that Coach sought, but Coach's tireless, enlightening, and unforgiving march towards that goal made our team great on that night. We beat UCLA because from day one of preseason practice to that magical night in March 1996, Chris Doyal and every member of our team summoned enough of the qualities that Coach demanded to get us across the finish line.

Coach in Sacramento looking befuddled

Coach enjoying the show and offering advice (or humor)

Life is good in Sacramento

Part of Geoff's family

Whether You Think You Can
Or You Can't
You're Probably Right

If you think you are beaten, you are;
If you think that you dare not,
you don't;
If you'd like to win, but you think
you can't,
It's almost certain you won't.

If you think you'll lose, you've lost;
For out in the world you'll find
Success begins with a fellow's will.
It's all in the state of mind.

If you think you are outclassed, you are;
You've got to think high to rise;
You've got to be sure of yourself before
You can ever win a prize.

Life's battles don't always go
To the stronger or faster man;
But sooner or later the man who wins
Is the man who thinks he can.

This poem was a favorite of my high school coach, Joseph Preletz, who coached football and basketball at Liberty High School, in Bethlehem, Pa. Every player who played football or basketball for him read this every day on the way to the field or court. - **Pete Carril**

ACKNOWLEDGMENTS

As the idea guy behind this book, my goals were simple—honor Coach, unite the Princeton basketball family, and pay it forward (i.e., do something that might, on the margin, contribute to the future success of the Princeton basketball program).

I have many people to thank for their contributions to this book.

First and foremost, I want to thank my wife Cammie for her patience with me as I dedicated hours, days, weeks, and months to developing this book. Her encouragement of my work will always be much appreciated.

Second, I want to thank Coach's daughter, Lisa Carril, for the understanding, support, and encouragement she provided to me along this journey. Her photos, contacts, memories, comments and can-do attitude contributed mightily.

Third, I want to thank my longtime assistant Kathleen Buck for coming out of retirement to do so much typing, editing, organizing, etc., etc. No one like her. I particularly appreciate her quick work enabling Coach to see a first draft of *Coach* and her patience in turning so many edits to this book.

Fourth, I want to thank my friend and Princeton alum Ned Kelly '75, who was the first real editor of this book. He read the book in its rawest form and transformed it into one that all authors could be proud of. I am so appreciative of his time and talent.

Fifth, I cannot express my gratitude enough to two Princeton grads who went on to become *Sports Illustrated* legends—Peter

Carry '64 and Alexander Wolff '80. The fact that these two legends took time to read an earlier draft of this book was beyond flattering. But they did so much more than this; they both added big-time value. Alex provided good counsel and helpful contacts as the book progressed. He discovered the long-lost Marvin Bressler essay from the catacombs. He permitted me to include the wonderful article that he wrote after Coach died, and he provided helpful edits. He was also kind enough to provide a back-of-the-book quote. Peter read a late draft and provided page-by-page improvements to the text. He also drew my attention to the connections between Sports Illustrated, Princeton and Princeton basketball, including calling my attention to the 1978 article by Kent Hannon. I was blown away by each of their individual contributions.

Sixth, I must thank Sean Gregory, another Princeton alum '98 and accomplished writer/editor for *TIME Magazine*. His advice during the development of this book was helpful.

Seventh, I thank my friend Jay Bilas for many things, including his wonderful book *Toughness*, which got me thinking about writing; his always brilliant commentary about college basketball; and his back-of-the-book quote.

Eighth, my thanks are owed to legendary sportswriter, author and commentator John Feinstein for allowing me to reprint his nice article about Coach in chapter 36 and for contributing his own back-of-the-book quote. I am also indebted to Bill Raftery for his willingness to provide a quote for the back cover of the book. Both men fully understand the nuances of playing and coaching basketball. In addition, it was most kind of Raff to attend the September 30, 2022 celebration of Coach's life in Jadwin Gym. Given that Raff once raided Coach's hangout (i.e., Andy's Tavern) after his Seton Hall team beat Princeton, I suppose such respect was owed!

Ninth, I want to thank three authors of Princeton basketball-related books—John McPhee '53, who wrote *A Sense of Where You*

Are; Dan White, who wrote *Play to Win*, and teamed up with Coach on *The Smart Take from the Strong*; and Paul Hutter '76, who wrote *The Golden Years of Ivy League Basketball (1964-1979)*. John's book motivated me (and many others) to come to Princeton and try to follow in Bill Bradley's legendary footsteps. Dan's books profiled Princeton's 1974-75 team (and related NIT championship) and provided a nice overview of Coach's basketball philosophy. Paul's book honored the old guard of Princeton basketball and motivated me to develop this book.

Tenth, I want to thank local writers from Pennsylvania and New Jersey, Brad Wilson (of Lehigh Valley Live) and Matt Drapkin (of *The Daily Princetonian*), for also allowing me to reprint their nice articles about Coach in Chapter 36. In addition, I want to thank Jerry Price and Elliott Carr of Princeton for providing me hundreds of Coach Carril photos to sift through and include in this book.

Eleventh, I want to thank multiple Princeton friends who added value here and there to this book. Former roommate Jeff French and longtime friend Bill Walton must be mentioned. Bill's attention to detail—off the charts!

Twelfth, I want to thank all Princeton players, managers, coaches, and former athletic director Gary Walters for their contributions to this book and, more broadly, to the Princeton basketball program. My interaction with all was a unique privilege.

Coach was never intended to be a history of the Princeton basketball program. Rather, it is a collection of player memories of times with Coach Carril that span the full 29 years of Coach's tenure at Princeton. Having said this, now that I have interacted with so many former players over the past year, I think I have a pretty good handle on the history of Princeton basketball (at least the time period beginning shortly before Coach joined Princeton through a couple of years after Coach retired). With this in mind, I share a few personal reflections about how I see that history below.

I cannot intelligently comment on any aspect of the history of Princeton basketball before Bill Bradley's three varsity years (1962-65) so my comments necessarily begin with the Bradley years.

Any casual observer understands that Bill Bradley put Princeton basketball on the map. With his 1964-65 team going to the Final Four after beating highly-ranked Providence 109-69, and Bradley being selected as Final Four MVP after scoring 58 points in Princeton's 118-82 consolation game win over Wichita State, no other conclusion is possible. Moreover, given Bradley's commitment to academics, basketball, and public service (as reflected by his Rhodes Scholarship, his 10-year NBA career with the Knicks (1967-77), and his 18-year career in the US Senate (1979-97), Bradley's overall contributions to Princeton have no equal.

But this is not a book about Bill Bradley. It is a book about legendary coach Peter J. Carril, who became Princeton's basketball coach two years after Bradley graduated.

Before commenting on the early years of Coach Carril's tenure at Princeton, a few comments about his predecessor, Butch van Breda Kolff (VBK), and his magnificent 1966-67 team are in order. As Bill Sickler points out in his chapter, VBK was a "large personality who had big, bold charisma." He also had a tremendous winning record at Princeton; he was a great recruiter. It is quite possible that his 1966-67 team was the best Princeton basketball team of all time. After all, that team went 25-3, finished the season ranked fifth in the nation and lost in overtime in the Elite Eight to UNC (in part due to injuries) after beating UNC in Chapel Hill earlier that season. Accordingly, this book would not be complete without paying tribute to the stars of that team—Chris Thomforde, Joe Heiser, John Haarlow, Ed Hummer, Gary Walters, Dave Lawyer, Robby Brown, and Larry Lucchino. Men, you are not forgotten. In particular for me, while Nitro Joe (Joe Heiser) has sadly died, I want to thank him for schooling me in a scrimmage one summer night before I became a varsity player for Princeton. Nitro Joe taught me the meaning of the "pursuit of excellence" and "class."

Next we come to a player who bridged VBK and Coach Carril—the incomparable Chris Thomforde. Excuse me, I meant to say, INCOMPARABLE. I am not going to focus on Chris' basketball excellence since any astute observer understands that Chris ranks among the top six Princeton basketball players ever. Rather, my focus on Chris relates to his unwavering dedication to ministry, his lifelong service to G-d, and his 55-year friendship with, respect for, and love of Coach Carril. His tireless fielding of emails related to this book and his kind outreach to Peter Carry, will never be forgotten by me. I will stop here. He was, and is, a one-of-a-kind human being.

Then there is Geoff Petrie. Geoff became the most accomplished Princeton basketball player of the Coach Carril era—NBA Co-Rookie of the year (with Dave Cowens) after averaging 24.8 points a game in 1970-71; the second guard in NBA history (alongside Oscar Robertson) to score 2,000 points in his rookie season; two-time NBA All-Star selection; NBA One-on-One champion in 1973; and his jersey retired by the Portland Trailblazers. All this by a guy who had a terrible back at Princeton hampering his senior season and that of the 1969-70 team. Ridiculous. But like Chris, Geoff's true colors shined even more brightly after his playing days. Specifically, as the Sacramento Kings' president of basketball operations, Geoff's hiring of Pete Carril as a Kings' assistant coach enabled him to guide Sacramento to within a whisker of winning the 2002 NBA championship (and resulted in Geoff being named NBA Executive of the Year twice). Importantly, Geoff's hiring of Coach also gave Coach a second life after Princeton. On behalf of many of Coach's Princeton players, I humbly say thank you to Geoff for his kindness to Coach. Geoff made him a part of his family and gave Coach so much personal happiness. His contributions to this book were beyond belief, and I thank him for them. Another one-of-a-kind human being.

Next there is Johnny Hummer. O.K., let's get real—Johnny was, and still is, his own unique animal. He follows the beat of a different drummer. Who else would write about winking at a cheerleader 52 years after doing it? Now, on a more serious note, John should be remembered for three things: one, he was a great player (one of five Princeton basketball players with a long NBA tenure); two, John is a smart guy (who had significant success in the venture capital world through his Hummer Winblad Venture Partners firm); and three, John, like his Princeton running mate Petrie, loved Coach Carril. I will never forget a phone call with John the day that Coach passed. The crack in his voice was palpable. You cannot fake such things.

Then there are two less-famous "old guard" names—Bill Sickler and Reggie Bird (Note: "old guard" is defined by me as anyone as old as or older than I am!). These were the two names that Coach constantly thrust in the faces of my 1974-76 teammates and me while emphasizing their consistent effort, toughness and defense. It seemed as if Bill Sickler's name was in front of us weekly; he was kind of a poster child for what Coach wanted us to be. As for Reggie, when two professional greats like Petrie and Taylor tell you that Reggie Bird was perhaps the best defensive player they ever played against, pro or college, you immediately understand that Reggie's on-ball defense and related defensive tenacity was the best in Princeton basketball history. When you read of the surreal Princeton game against UCLA in 1969 and visualize 6'1" sophomore guard Reggie Bird walking into a UCLA time-out huddle to challenge rugged 6'7" forward Curtis Rowe, you feel the inherent toughness of this great player from Boston. But for a freak injury after his senior season, this lesser known name (to some) may have become another Princetonian with a long-running NBA career; after all, he was a fourth round draft pick of the Atlanta Hawks—the 55th pick in the nation—in 1972. A highlight for me as I developed this book was simply catching up with Reggie for an hour by phone.

There are many other old guard star players who could be mentioned here (e.g., Ted Manakas, Andy Rimol, Tim van Blommesteyn, and Mickey Steuerer), but I will include just three more. Two obvious names are Brian Taylor and Armond Hill. There was never a jet like Brian. There is no doubt in my mind that his speed terrified UNC in Princeton's big 1972 upset win over the Tar Heels. There is no doubt that his athleticism terrified every team that Princeton played in his era. Brian was simply an unbelievable athlete. As for Armond, what can I say? Armond was Princeton's ultimate unselfish superstar. My teammates and I are all very aware of our good fortune to have played with him. But Armond was so much more than unselfish—he epitomized grace. He was loved by Coach, by his teammates and by everyone across campus. After his playing days were over, he had a long, successful run as an assistant coach in the NBA. When he became a Boston Celtics assistant and the Celtics won the 2008 NBA championship, I was so happy for him. If anyone deserved an NBA ring, it was Armond Hill.

A not-so-obvious old guard player who deserves comment is Jimmy Sullivan. In part, I list him because of his fine play at Princeton epitomized by the 1973 night that he shut down Barry Parkhill and Princeton beat Virginia in Jadwin. Talk about living in someone's jock strap—Jimmy must have channeled his inner Reggie Bird that night. But the real reason I mention Jimmy (as he will certainly appreciate) is his wife Katie who, as Jimmy's chapter captures so well, bonded uniquely with Coach. The two Sullivans stood by Coach for five decades and brought him much happiness. Jimmy's relationship started as a player-coach relationship but it evolved into a familial relationship (just as Chris Thomforde's and Geoff Petrie's had). Personally, I think this speaks volumes about both player and coach.

Now, the younger guard (those after my 1976 graduation) may claim the above narrative reflects excessive deference to the old guard. Maybe so, but there are two important reasons for going into the detail above.

First, as Paul Hutter described so well in his book, the 1967-76 teams were mostly Goliaths (i.e., regularly ranked in the top 20 nationally). They typically played a more up-tempo brand of basketball and their schedules typically included many top 20 opponents. Over the next 20 years, Princeton had many good teams and many good players, but over time (with the exception of the outstanding 1996-98 teams and perhaps a few others), Princeton became better known as a David or a Goliath Killer. This is because Princeton was never able to land another long-term NBA caliber talent after Armond Hill. In general, the 1977-96 teams typically played a slower-tempo game and, after 1985, when three-point shots were allowed, emphasized such bonus shots. In addition, these teams' schedules typically included fewer top 20 opponents.

Second, as editor of this book, talking with players across Coach's 29-year Princeton tenure, it became increasingly obvious to me that the love and respect that many Princeton players from 1967-76 collectively showed for Coach was special. This was apparent in so many ways and it was incredibly powerful. This is not to say that there were not many younger guard players who also had incredibly close relationships with Coach (e.g., Howie Levy comes to mind). The difference is merely the length of these relationships.

The younger guard who played for Coach includes many enormously successful teams. The younger guard also includes many individually talented players such as Bobby Slaughter, Frank Sowinski, Bill Omeltchenko, Bob Roma, Steve Mills, Randy Melville, Craig Robinson, Billy Ryan, Kevin Mullin, Howie Levy, Bobby Scrabis, Kit Mueller, Sean Jackson, Chris Mooney, Rick Hielscher and the entire 1996 group of starters.

Focusing on Coach's final 1996 Princeton team, it should be noted that many of the key players on that team were underclassmen in

1996. Accordingly, they continued to play at Princeton in 1996-97 and 1997-98 under Coach Bill Carmody and achieved wonderful records in those years (24-4 and 27-2), and finished the 1997-98 season ranked eighth in the nation. While it can be argued that Coach Carril laid the foundation for this success, just as VBK had arguably laid the foundation for Coach Carril's early success, both the players and Coach Carmody deserve much praise. They played beautiful team ball.

My interaction with the players on Coach's final Princeton team (including current Princeton coach Mitch Henderson) during the development of this book produced various emotions and insights for me. While each player's relationship with Coach was undoubtedly different, I would say that some, or even all, of the stars of this balanced group of players were ready for 66-year-old Coach Carril to retire and ready for much-respected, longtime assistant Bill Carmody to replace him. I would also say that Princeton athletic director Gary Walters was supportive of a transition in 1996. Given Coach's "spider-sense" awareness to any and all issues that might impact team performance, I wonder if those feelings contributed to his end-of-season retirement decision. Whether my personal opinion on this issue is right or wrong does not really matter. What I know is this—Princeton lost an incredible teacher when Coach retired.

To be clear, my remarks above are not meant as a criticism of anyone. They are merely my way of completing an authentic record of Coach's life at Princeton. Perhaps Coach had become too old and crusty in 1996. Perhaps Coach's style was not right for the time. And perhaps Coach was overly critical of his 1996 players. Alternatively, perhaps some of the players were less tolerant of Coach's style than those who preceded them. If so, was it a function of the team's youth? Maybe other factors were involved. Who knows? It is what it is.

It should not be lost on anyone that Coach turned down multiple offers to coach elsewhere during his 29 years at Princeton. For some reason, he decided to stay at Princeton and stay with "his boys." Imagine that—loyalty to Princeton, to the basketball program and to his players mattered to Coach.

Coach's record at Princeton was 514 wins and 261 losses. His teams won or shared 13 Ivy League championships, advanced to 11 NCAA tournaments, and his 1975 team won the then-prestigious NIT Tournament. In the 22 years since Carmody's departure from Princeton in 2000, the Princeton men's basketball record has been 357 wins and 258 losses (with six Ivy League titles and four NCAA appearances). Good—but not great.

As Mitch Henderson begins his 12th year as head coach of Princeton basketball, I am hopeful that the program is embarked on an upswing with the team having gone 23-7 during the 2021-22 season. Mitch retains the competitive fire of his playing days and is very much his own man. Certainly, I wish him well. It is never easy to replace a legend, even when one takes the position some 15 years after the legend retired.

One final comment and a query.

Comment: I believe basketball mirrors life—plenty of highs and lows, ups and downs, wins and losses. Coach certainly experienced his fair share of each. His style and his words sparked feelings across the spectrum, from love to hatred. He certainly was not perfect, but when it comes to basketball, he was "right" most of the time. Was he right 86%, 87%, or 88% of the time (as Coach apparently pondered with his 1995-96 team, per Steve Goodrich's chapter)? Who knows? All I know is, no matter how you cut it, Coach Carril had a heckuva run at Princeton—a great basketball coach (of course), a great teacher (certainly), and a developer of many young men for life after Princeton (without question).

Query: Across the entire history of Princeton University, how many teachers (in academics or athletics) have commanded the respect (and in certain instances the love) of their students for 26 to

55 years after they taught their final Princeton class? I can still see Marvin Bressler smoking his pipe pondering the question—what were the ingredients for that secret sauce of Pete Carril?

Barnes Hauptfuhrer

Marvin Bressler
Princeton Professor (1963-93)
Chair of the Sociology Department for 20 years

ABOUT THE EDITOR

Barnes Hauptfuhrer '76

To be clear, the idea guy of this book would not rank himself among the top 50 players in Princeton basketball history. Given my molasses-like foot speed and a best case vertical leap of three inches, such a conclusion seems reasonable. However, I do realize that I am one of the "three-car-garage" guys who challenged Coach's assumptions about such types. More importantly, I am the stubborn and opinionated SOB who was determined to get this book done in 2022. Simply stated, I felt it was time to unite the Princeton basketball family of players who ran Coach Carril's gauntlet. Coincidentally, it also enabled me to include the photos of me above attacking the enemy—in this instance, John Engles of Penn in the storied Palestra. After all, I feel compelled to end this book by saying, "F##k Penn," something that all Princeton players can readily identify with. Coach injected a competitive DNA in all of us. Trust me, his injection lasted a lifetime. It needed no booster shot.

A 1974 graduate of Princeton, I have been devoted to the University and broadly engaged with its academic and athletic missions. I am fortunate to have had many special and valued Princeton experiences, including rowing on the undefeated Henley-winning lightweight crew of 1973. Now, some 50 years and a business career later, few lessons have been as valuable as those learned through athletics. I understand how important these experiences can be to the development of young men's and young women's core values and I believe in the positive impact that athletics can have on future Princetonians. Pete Carril uniquely appreciated this and, as this book highlights, his players benefited from his leadership, values and life lessons. I never played for Coach Carril, but I admired his authenticity, character, quest for excellence and perfection, and accomplishments. Given my basketball-noteworthy name, I will never forget how Coach Carril scorched me when we first met: "Bill Walton, huh? Princeton has a Bill Walton, and it's you. Just my luck." A frontal assault just like the ones he sometimes launched on his players, but with humor as well.

—Bill Walton
Managing Member, Rockpoint Group

Made in the USA
Coppell, TX
12 June 2023